the **100** best
volunteer vacations
to enrich your life

OTHER BOOKS BY PAM GROUT

The 100 Best Worldwide Vacations to Enrich Your Life

The 100 Best Vacations to Enrich Your Life

Recycle This Book:
And 72 1/2 Even Better Ways to Save "Yo Momma" Earth

Art and Soul:
156 Ways to Free Your Creative Spirit

Living Big:
Embrace Your Passion and Leap into an Extraordinary Life

Kansas Curiosities:
Quirky Characters, Roadside Oddities & Other Offbeat Stuff

Colorado Curiosities:
Quirky Characters, Roadside Oddities & Other Offbeat Stuff

Girlfriend Getaways:
You Go, Girl! and I'll Go, Too

You Know You're in Kansas When: 101 Quintessential Places, People,
Events, Customs, Lingo, and Eats of the Sunflower State

Jumpstart Your Metabolism: How to Lose Weight
by Changing the Way You Breathe

God Doesn't Have Bad Hair Days

the **100** best volunteer vacations to enrich your life

PAM GROUT

NATIONAL GEOGRAPHIC

WASHINGTON, D.C.

Published by the National Geographic Society
1145 17th Street, N.W., Washington, DC 20036-4688

ISBN: 978-1-4262-0459-3

Founded in 1888, the National Geographic Society is one of the largest nonprofit scientific and educational organizations in the world. It reaches more than 285 million people worldwide each month through its official journal, NATIONAL GEOGRAPHIC, and its four other magazines; the National Geographic Channel; television documentaries; radio programs; films; books; videos and DVDs; maps; and interactive media. National Geographic has funded more than 8,000 scientific research projects and supports an education program combating geographic illiteracy.

For more information, please call 1-800-NGS LINE (647-5463) or write to the following address: National Geographic Society, 1145 17th Street N.W.,Washington, D.C. 20036-4688 U.S.A.

Visit us online at: www.nationalgeographic.com.

Interior design by Sanaa Akkach and Linda Johansson; series design by Melissa Farris.

Printed in the U.S.A.

contents

This book is for everyone who believes
a better world is possible and can feel a better,
more loving, more peaceful world rising up.

introduction

This is the moment when we must come together to save this planet.
—Barack Obama, then-candidate for President of the United States,
in Berlin, July 2008

Call it the Al Gore Factor, the Katrina Effect, or simply the impulse to have an authentic experience not listed in a typical brochure, but more and more people are combining volunteering with traveling. And it's not just high-profile celebrities like George Clooney, Angelina Jolie, and Hilary Swank—who went to Palampur, India, to teach at an orphanage after her 2006 divorce—who are abandoning their bubble of luxury to lend assistance to folks in developing countries.

According to a 2008 survey by the University of California, San Diego, 40 percent of Americans would like to volunteer while on vacation, and another 13 percent are ready to devote an entire year to hopping on a plane and providing goodwill.

The reasons for wanting to volunteer vary. Some do it to gain experience, to add some heft to the old resumé. Others want to test themselves or to act out a fantasy. Still others are tired of waiting for their government to act. They want to stand up and be counted. Now.

But the thing all volunteer vacations share? They shed light. They give us a more realistic picture of the world. Suffice it to say, the nightly news does not provide an accurate lens through which to view our planet. Most news reports are one reporter's opinion, a sliver of life that one cameraman stumbled onto and captured in one four-minute time slot.

Even people who travel—people who have ticked off, say, the Taj Mahal and the Arc de Triomphe on their life lists—don't always have a realistic vantage point. Fancy hotel chains have set up mini-Americas all over the world. You can go to Costa Rica and check into the San José Marriott without ever realizing that the kids in the village down the road play soccer with plastic bags they tied together. You can follow the bellman into your suite at the Four Seasons Hotel Mumbai without it occurring to you that his six kids could eat for a long time on what you'll be paying for room service.

With the vacations in this book, you'll leave that plastic state of mind behind. You'll see a country for what it really is, neither a sound bite or a statistic of those who died in the last tragedy. You'll get to know real people. You'll work beside them, share their struggles, learn what it feels like to live in a village where no men are over 50, and experience what it's like to be invisible to outsiders.

Pillow menus are fun and all, but they don't hold a candle to meeting people like Termana, Indrah, and Bu Mayan, who are putting together a Balinese literary journal. Hotel perks like carsitters and personal fireworks shows sound impressive, but pale in comparison to the satisfaction received from singing "Itsy Bitsy Spider" to Gwani, a five-year-old Nigerian who just lost her mother to AIDS.

Which brings us back to that light we promised to shed. If you decide to take a volunteer vacation, you can let go of nearly all your preconceived notions, suppositions, and assumptions. This idea that you, noble person that you are, are volunteering in order to swoop in and save the so-called poor unfortunates? Kiss it good-bye.

Ask any seasoned volunteer. People in developing countries have a depth of joy, a richness to which those of us consumed with material things are often blind. The question persists: Who ends up getting helped the most when you travel to help others?

In fact, if you really want to save the day, your best bet is to show up, shut your mouth, and listen to and learn from the people you meet on your journey. Find out the truth behind the sound bites and then go home and spread the word. Effective volunteers often end up making a bigger difference back home than they did in their short time spent volunteering.

This book is divided into six regions of the planet. That way, you can pick a place that has always enticed you and find a dam with a hole in it that needs your finger. Rest assured, there's not a country among the world's 194 nations that couldn't use some kind of help.

By choosing a volunteer vacation by destination, you'll get to travel to the country of your dreams, the one that's been on your radar since second grade or since the president of the PTA came back from there and started passing out pictures that made you jealous. You'll be able to immerse yourself in that wild dream country in a way not possible on the average tour bus. Instead of spending time with Bill Smith from one state over, you'll spend time with the very people that inhabit your longed-for country. Through volunteering, you'll get a unique insight into their culture, their beliefs, and, yes, their dreams.

So if you want to know what's really going on in the world, this book could be a potent starting gate. Put your toes on the line and listen up.

—Pam Grout

north america
& the caribbean

We are the ones we've been waiting for.
— Hopi expression

They say that charity begins at home and in this chapter you'll find 16 ways to make a difference right outside your own doorstep, or at least a few hours away from it by car, plane, or train.

Whether you want to monitor climate change, revolutionize our crumbling medical system, or excavate a *Stegosaurus,* there's an organization right here in this hemisphere that needs you. Your ideas, your passion, your sweat, and your toil will be welcomed.

You can deliver food and supplies to Haiti, providing a beacon of hope in a place that sorely needs one. You can help preserve a colonial-era fort in the Caribbean, offering a bulwark against the sands of time.

As President-elect Barack Obama said in his election night victory speech in Chicago's Grant Park, "So let us summon a new spirit of patriotism, of responsibility, where each of us resolves to pitch in and work harder and look after not only ourselves but each other."

excavate stone tools & other ancient artifacts

CORTEZ, COLORADO

> Every archaeologist knows in his heart why he digs. He digs … that the dead may live again, that what is past may not be forever lost, that something may be salvaged from the wrack of ages, that the past may color the present and give heart to the future.
> —T. Geoffrey Bibby, English archaeologist

1 Get out your trowel and whisk broom. On the campus of the Crow Canyon Archaeological Center, a 170-acre paradise outside Cortez, Colorado, students live in Navajo hogans, spend all their time outdoors, and consider themselves dressed up if they happen to be wearing a pair of clean jeans. That's because the students at this unique facility set in a canyon between the 13,000-foot peaks of the La Plata Mountains are learning about archaeology not by reading about it, but by getting down into the dirt and actually digging. This unique school dedicated to exploring the ancestral Puebloan culture of the Mesa Verde region has always had the same mission: Get people interested in an ancient culture by letting them see it for themselves, letting them experience the thrill you can only get from, for example, uncovering a 1,400-year-old pot.

When it was started in 1983, Crow Canyon amounted to a couple of pie-in-the-sky archaeologists, living in tepees and state-surplus trailers, trying to convince anyone who would listen to them that preserving ancient cultures is important. They were obviously pretty convincing, because in the ensuing quarter century, their initial humble idea has morphed into a nationally recognized research center with classrooms, a lab, and student housing.

"Crow Canyon was founded to make archaeology more public—to enable nonarchaeologists to learn about and participate in archaeological research," research associate Bill

COVER-UP IN CORTEZ

The story of when Willard met Rachel includes both murder and intrigue, with a dollop of the one that got away. And if mystery writers hear about it, they might come calling to tell the tale.

Thankfully, though, the massive cover-up happening in Cortez, Colorado, is only a rug—the world's largest Two Grey Hills rug. Because of their fine quality and their intricate workmanship, most of the Navajo weavings known as Two Grey Hills are used as wall hangings. Finding a 5-by-7-foot Two Grey Hills would be a rare enough occurrence, but the one in Cortez at the Notah Dineh Trading Company measures a jaw-dropping 12 feet by 18 feet. That represents a whole lot of knots, and a whole lot of finely carded wool. It took more than three years to weave, and the trader who commissioned Diné artist Rachel Curley, who came from a long line of weavers, to weave the unusual rug was murdered before it was completed.

Two Grey Hills rugs, bordered rugs that use wools in black, brown, gray, tan, and white, are considered the gold standard of Navajo rugs. Because their weave is fine and extremely complicated, these rugs are not something that the average weaver can produce. A rug with a weft count—that's the number of threads running across and woven into the warp threads of the textile—of 50 per inch is considered a fine rug. If a rug has a weft count of 80 or more, then it qualifies as a tapestry. Two Grey Hills rugs, with weft counts of 120 or more, far surpass even that high standard.

Willard Leighton, who was called Chis Chilly (curly hair) by the Diné or Navajo, contracted Rachel Curley to weave the unique rug in question in 1957. Before she could finish making it, however, Leighton was murdered. In 1960, Curley finally completed the rug. Bob Leighton, Willard's brother, hoped to keep the rug, but couldn't afford to do so. Instead, he took it with him on a trading trip. In Montana, he persuaded a rancher that he should furnish his new house not with Persian rugs, but with Navajo rugs. Deal done, Leighton reluctantly parted with Rachel Curley's masterpiece.

Bob Leighton always hoped that he would see the rug again. Thirty-one years later, Bob's friend Mark Winter contacted him about a rare masterpiece rug that he'd found in Santa Barbara. The rug was too large for the room for which the owner had purchased it. Sure enough, it was the rug that Willard Leighton had commissioned.

After touring the country in an exhibit of Navajo weavings, the rug is finally resting in the Leighton family's Notah Dineh Trading Post in Cortez. The trading post also houses the largest collection of Navajo rugs in the Four Corners area. *Notah Dineh Trading Post, 345 West Main Street, Cortez, CO 81321, 800-444-2024, www.notahdineh.com.*

Lipe explains. "The whole field has benefited. Crow Canyon has educated thousands of students and adults about what can be learned from archaeology, the difference between 'pothunting' and real archaeology, and the importance of protecting sites."

Every year, hundreds of students of all ages and nationalities work alongside archaeologists, anthropologists, and folks like Lipe to excavate thousands of artifacts, an average of 75,000 per year. They recently excavated Goodman Point Pueblo, an ancient Pueblo village that was inhabited during the late 1200s and has been protected by the federal government since 1889. The site had a large community kiva, as well as a hundred smaller kivas, plazas, towers, and a wall around it. The first phase was completed in 2007, which included excavating the community's kiva, plaza, and towers. Now, archaeologists, anthropologists, and eager volunteers have started Phase II, Goodman Point Community Testing, which involves test excavations at 15 smaller sites around the large village, including habitation sites, ancient roadways, and possible agricultural fields.

AWARD-WINNING AND GLOBE-TROTTING

In Tulsa, Oklahoma, on October 23, 2008, the National Trust for Historic Preservation presented the Crow Canyon Archaeological Center with a National Preservation Honor Award. Ricky Lightfoot, Crow Canyon president and CEO, accepted the award, saying, "I believe the award recognizes that the archaeological sites here in the Four Corners region are nationally significant and are part of our national treasure and our national cultural heritage. It also recognizes Crow Canyon's mission and its work in promoting the preservation of archaeological sites."

Richard Moe, president of the National Trust, said, "Crow Canyon's dedicated staff and volunteers work in a remote corner of America—but their efforts to preserve and showcase the richness of our past reach around the globe. Its commitment to collaboration with American Indian tribes has demonstrated pioneering leadership and ensured that all of the Center's programs honor the cultural perspectives and insights of the first Americans."

In fact, Crow Canyon's programs extend far beyond the Four Corners, as the center also sponsors what it calls archaeology adventures in other parts of the Southwest, as well as China, Mexico, and Turkey. In 2007, nearly 5,000 students and adults participated in Crow Canyon educational and travel programs both at the center's campus and remotely through partnerships.

It's not a project for wimps. On each of the six "Adult Research Weeks," as Crow Canyon calls them, volunteers hike to the Goodman Point site at the Hovenweep National Monument, lift buckets of dirt, kneel on the ground, and work at an elevation of 6,700 feet.

They learn basic excavation techniques and spend time in the lab washing and cataloging pottery and stone tools. Volunteers also attend a wide variety of lectures and take tours of Mesa Verde National Park and Sand Canyon Pueblo, a site excavated by Crow Canyon in previous years.

In addition to its work in the Four Corners area, Crow Canyon also offers educational trips that spotlight Pueblo cultures in Arizona, New Mexico, and Colorado, and international trips that visit such sites as French caves and the Nile Delta. The educational trips, led by archaeologists and including visits to museums and ancient cliff dwellings, backcountry hikes, and excavations, range from $1,695 to $2,720 for domestic trips. International trips range from $5,100 to $8,795.

If you're not quite ready to get your hands dirty, but still are interested in learning more about the center's work, you can sign up for one of the five lectures in the winter Distinguished Lecturers series, which is cosponsored by the center and Friends of Crow Canyon. Wine and appetizers are followed by presentations on a wide range of relevant topics, which vary depending on the speaker. The series raises money for the Four Corners Youth Scholarship Fund, which helps underwrite the participation of more than 900 local students in Crow Canyon programs every year.

Research program tuition ranges from $1,050 to $1,400. Rates vary depending on age, experience, and membership in Crow Canyon. Membership fees are $50 for an adult or $85 for a family. The three-week high school field school is $3,950 for donors and $4,075 for nondonors. Tuition includes all lodging (shared accommodations), meals, fees, and permits, as well as in-program transportation once you arrive in Cortez.

HOW TO GET IN TOUCH

Crow Canyon Archaeological Center, 23390 Road K, Cortez, CO 81321, 800-422-8975 or 970-565-8975, www.crowcanyon.org.

unlock the prehistoric past

MALTA, MONTANA

Fossil hunting is by far the most fascinating of all sports.
—George Gaylord Simpson,
paleontologist at New York's American Museum of Natural History

2   There are no school uniforms and no tests, and you'll use your muscles as much as your brain, but if you want to gain knowledge, there's probably no school as rich as the Judith River Dinosaur Institute in Malta, Montana. Your teachers will be Leonardo, Roberta, Giffen, Ralph, Elvis, and a few other 77- to 150-million-year-old creatures that have a lot to teach not only you but all of mankind.

Nate Murphy, the khaki-clad paleontologist and curator who serves as the dinosaurs' agent and mouthpiece, organizes five-day field research trips three to four times each year. Sponsored by the Phillips County Museum and the Judith River Dinosaur Institute, which sprang up after the inventory of dinosaurs grew beyond the walls of the county museum, these trips are hot, rugged excavations. Basically, you'll be lifting stones, chipping at rock, and piecing together mysteries from millions of years ago. You'll learn all the stuff you could probably find in an encyclopedia,

TAKE A RIDE ON THE DINOSAUR TRAIL

Montana may be the only state with its own dinosaur trail. There are 13 stops on this unique trail, which has its own map, prehistoric passport, and website (www.mtdinotrail.org). Joining Malta's Phillips County Museum and the Judith River Dinosaur Field Station, where you can watch Murphy and his cronies prepare dinosaur fossils, the trail includes stops in the Museum of the Rockies, a Smithsonian affiliate that's headed by paleontologist Jack Horner, a consultant on *Jurassic Park;* and the Fort Peck Field Station of Paleontology, which is run by the University of Montana and serves as a state fossil repository.

all the facts and data that paleontologists know so far, but the most exciting part about these dinosaur digs is that you'll also likely learn things that nobody else knows yet.

One of the most exciting examples took place in 2000, when a team member on the last day of a five-day dig noticed the exposed midsection of a *Brachylophosaurus* tail. Finding a new dinosaur specimen would have been thrilling enough, but this one had 90 percent of its fossilized soft tissue intact, giving paleontologists all sorts of new information about this 35-foot-long duck-billed herbivore's diet, range of movement, and methods of locomotion. Keep in mind that paleontologists normally piece together entire life histories from something as minuscule as a 2-inch tooth. Famous dinosaur researcher Robert Bakker reportedly fell to his knees when he first saw the find, tears in his eyes. "It was," he said, "like seeing the 'Pietà.'"

The new two-ton find was named Leonardo because of graffiti scrawled onto a nearby rock: "Leonard Webb loves Geneva Jordan 1916." *Newsweek* ran a cover story and the body of knowledge exploded, not just for the Judith River scientists but for every paleontologist, evolutionary biologist, and, for that matter, layperson interested in prehistoric creatures.

"Paleontology is not an exact science," Murphy observes. "All we have are bones, and from there we develop theories about what the animals looked like, how they moved, and what they ate. A specimen like Leonardo will take a lot of guesswork out and really tell us if Steven Spielberg's getting it right."

Murphy likes to say he's not running a "paleo dude ranch" and that the work on his expeditions is tiring and hot, but anyone who has ever taken his expeditions (including a group of regulars who call themselves the "paleochicks") claim they're loads of fun, including late night sing-alongs of such campfire classics as "Dead Skunk in the Middle of the Road."

The fee for Judith River's five-day expeditions is $1,695, which includes meals, beverages, and all excavation tools. Your accommodations are the tent and sleeping bag that you're required to bring. Three expeditions are offered in June and July to individuals 14 years and older, in groups of 16 diggers. In 2009 JRDI is hosting three excavations at the Little Snowy Mountain site near Billings; volunteers (16 per team) will be digging up a *Stegosaurus* graveyard.

HOW TO GET IN TOUCH

Judith River Dinosaur Institute, P.O. Box 429, Malta, MT 59538, 406-654-2323, www.montanadinosaurdigs.com.

excavate george washington's whiskey distillery

MOUNT VERNON, VIRGINIA

It takes very special qualities to devote one's life to problems with no attainable solutions and to poking around in dead people's garbage: Words like "nosy," "masochistic," and "completely batty" spring to mind.
—Paul Bahn, archaeologist and author of *Bluff Your Way into Archaeology*

3 It's an old joke: George Washington slept here. Some of the claims may be true. Others not so much. But if you want to poke around in a place where there's no doubting the nocturnal allegations of our first president, consider joining Mount Vernon's archaeological volunteer program.

If it weren't for volunteers, much of the 500-acre site (in the 18th century, Mount Vernon comprised 8,000 acres) would still be a mystery. Since 1987, when a permanent archaeology program was established on the estate, volunteers (with the help of their professional mentors) have uncovered everything from tobacco pipes and wig curlers to forks made from animal bones.

All of this was accomplished without help from your tax dollars. Mount Vernon receives no funding from the U.S. government. Instead, the "First Home" is maintained by the Mount Vernon Ladies' Association, the oldest historic preservation organization in the United States.

The association was founded in 1853 by Ann Pamela Cunningham, a South Carolina woman disabled after falling from a horse. Cunningham's mother, while taking a tour down the Potomac River, was shocked to see Mount Vernon's peeling paint, overgrown weeds, and columns so rotten that the famous portico was propped up with a sailing ship's former mast. She wrote a letter to her daughter describing the unacceptable condition of the first President's home, exhorting her to do something.

The governments of both the United States and Virginia had already turned down the offer to purchase Mount Vernon, and there was even some talk of demolishing the home. Cunningham decided that if the men of the country (at that time, women didn't even have the right to vote) wouldn't renovate the historic site, the women would. Within five years, her women's group raised $200,000 and bought the mansion, the outbuildings, and 200 acres. An 1858 photo on their website shows the dilapidated state of the famous home when they took over.

And take over they did. Using donations, private grants, admission fees to the grounds (more than a million people show up every year), and volunteer help, this savvy outfit has restored 20 structures and 50 acres of gardens as they existed in 1799 (the year Washington died), the tombs of George and Martha, Washington's greenhouse, and a collection of artifacts dug up by staff archaeologists, interns, and volunteers. In late 2006, a state-of-the-art orientation center, museum, and education center opened with much fanfare. The museum boasts 25 galleries filled with fascinating multimedia exhibits, including a lab that shows how three forensically correct figures of Washington displayed in the galleries were created.

The Archaeology Department at Mount Vernon has a wide range of volunteer opportunities involving both field and laboratory work. Needless to say, excavations vary from year to year. For instance, volunteers processed and wrote reports on artifacts dug up from Washington's distillery. At the end of the 1700s, it was the country's largest whiskey distillery, using five stills and a boiler to produce 11,000 gallons of whiskey a year. The rebuilt distillery was completed in the spring of 2008, 210 years after Washington began distilling corn and rye whiskey. Costumed distillers operate it every day from April through October; samples are available at special events, and bottled whiskey also is sold. Washington's distillery is considered the gateway to the American Whiskey Trail (www.discus.org/trail).

DIG IT!

The archaeological excavation at Mount Vernon is one of more than 250 fieldwork projects listed in the bulletin put out each year by the Archaeological Institute of America. If you want to volunteer for an archaeological excavation, the *Archaeological Fieldwork Opportunities Bulletin* is the best place to start. It lists hundreds of excavations, from a Stone Age site in South Africa to a site on Easter Island in Chile. Each listing provides an in-depth description, including accommodations, price, and contact information. The yearly volume can be accessed on the institute's website (www.archaeological.org); a paperback version is also available each year from Oxbox/David Brown Books, 800-791-9354.

ONE-DOLLAR PORTRAIT

Anyone who has ever seen a dollar bill knows what our first President looked like. Or do they? When the Mount Vernon Ladies' Association wanted exact likenesses of good old George for the new education center, they turned to a forensic anthropologist to figure out how the great general might have looked at ages 19, when he was a frontier surveyor; 45, when he served as commander-in-chief of the Continental Army; and 57, when he was sworn in as President.

Although anthropologist Jeffrey H. Schwartz wasn't allowed to dig up Washington's bones, the easiest way to tackle such a task, he was able to reconstruct the first leader by examining his false teeth (on display at the museum—they were made of human teeth, ivory, and ox bone), a mask of Washington created by a French sculptor, letters, diaries, and old clothes. Turns out the familiar Gilbert Stuart portrait of Washington, called the "Athenaeum" portrait, the likeness of which was used on the one-dollar note, is not exactly accurate. Washington had a pockmark on his left cheek from the smallpox that afflicted him at 19. He also had taut lips from holding in dentures, and, as he grew older, a chin slightly longer on one side than the other caused by bone loss associated with tooth loss.

Volunteers have also excavated Mount Vernon's laundry room, gristmill, gardens, a dung repository, and many other sites on the property. The Archaeology Lab exhibits finds from the Slave Quarters, the Blacksmith Shop, the Upper Garden, and the South Grove Midden. Recovered artifacts provide clues about the daily life of not only Washington's family, who owned the property from 1726 until the Mount Vernon Ladies' Association took it over in 1853, but also the slaves, craftspeople, and laborers who lived and worked on the plantation.

There is no fee to volunteer. Although the Archaeology Lab doesn't provide housing for its volunteers, there are many nearby hotels. Volunteers can work at excavation projects any Monday through Friday and will be given 50 percent off meals at the Mount Vernon Inn, the on-site restaurant serving typical colonial fare.

HOW TO GET IN TOUCH

Mount Vernon Ladies' Association, 3200 Mount Vernon Memorial Highway, Mount Vernon, VA 22121, 703-799-6314, www.mountvernon.org.

blaze a new trail or be a wilderness camp chef

NEW MEXICO, COLORADO, WYOMING, IDAHO, MONTANA

A desk is a dangerous place from which to watch the world.
—John Le Carré, author of espionage novels

4 Most volunteer vacations charge participants for the chance to do grunt work without pay. Not the Continental Divide Trail Alliance (CDTA), which runs two- to seven-day trips for absolutely nothing. So what's the catch? CDTA is a bit behind schedule in building this trail (it was originally slated to be complete by 2008, the trail's 30th anniversary) and needs all the help it can get.

The Continental Divide Trail stretches from Canada to Mexico. It crosses five states, three national parks (including Yellowstone), 20 wilderness areas, and five very distinct ecosystems. Measuring 3,100 miles in length, it's the longest of all trails in the U.S. trail system. It has been dubbed "the king of trails" and "the backbone of America." It's also received a few other choice epithets bestowed by would-be thru-hikers who are forced to bail out before finishing. Given its seriously rough terrain, only a couple dozen hikers are able to traverse it from end to end each year.

To give you some perspective, roughly 800 people—out of the 4,000 who try— succeed in thru-hiking the Appalachian Trail in an average year. Yet those daunting

THE BIG LEAGUE OF HIKING

Hiking the Continental Divide Trail is not for the weak of heart. It's remote and wild, posing numerous hazards. Watch out for everything from grizzly bears and charging moose to fickle weather complete with lightning strikes. On large stretches of the trail, you'll be above timberline. One hiker joked that his friends argued about who would get dibs on his gear once his body was found—if his body was found.

odds shouldn't keep you from at tackling one gorgeous segment or another, such as the Bridger Wilderness section in Wyoming or Baker Gulch in Rocky Mountain National Park.

So what's the problem? The Continental Divide Trail isn't finished yet. Congress, while acknowledging that the trail is worthy of preserving, didn't allocate enough funds to complete it. Nearly a third of the proposed route has yet to be built. People who do attempt to thru-hike it end up following paved roads or sometimes getting lost in the woods.

To remedy such Hansel-and-Gretel mishaps, the Continental Divide Trail Alliance (CDTA), a nonprofit organization formed in 1995, is attempting to stitch together existing segments with new trails through federal lands, state lands, and private ranch lands. But since the CDTA depends on private donations and volunteer labor, they need your help to do so.

Every summer, the CDTA hosts around 50 volunteer trail-building projects divided among the five states. While a few of the projects take place near easily accessible car camping locations, most of the work is done in the backcountry, where you can't just skip over to the convenience store for a hot coffee. If you volunteer with CDTA, you'll be sleeping in a tent, eating food cooked on a camp stove, and hiking each day just to get to your work site. Suffice it to say, there's no cell phone reception.

So what do more than 9,500 volunteers (the number who have chipped in since 1996) eat after a hard day of raking underbrush, moving rocks, digging roots and constructing bridges? Chicken tikka masala, ratatouille, lamb bruchettes, thai spring rolls, lemon pancakes, crème brûlée, and other gourmet delights, all of which can be cooked on a one-burner camping stove or with a blowtorch.

Each team has a volunteer camp chef and sous chef. So if you prefer to wield a spatula instead of a shovel, this could be your gig. Crew chefs plan the menus, shop, and make sure all the troops are satiated when they return to their tents each evening. Don't worry if you're not a whiz with a dutch oven. CDTA hosts yearly training for backcountry chefs, where you'll learn everything from how to make chocolate cake in a hollowed-out orange to how to fry eggs in a paper bag. You'll also have access to CDTA's *Crew Chef Cookbook* and a wide range of backcountry cooking gear.

As for your kitchen? Most of the trail is above 8,000 feet in elevation. You'll see vistas the average person sees only on postcards. And since CDTA volunteers range from investment bankers to rodeo bull riders to highway crew workers, the after-dinner chats can get mighty interesting. Roxanne McKay, a cardiothoracic surgeon in her 60s who has volunteered on the trail for two years in a row, said the post-dinner fireside chats ranged from "previous trail projects, the Vietnam War, and Peace Corps experiences in Uzbekistan to opinions on stock investments and the latest camping gear."

Best of all, you get the chance to make history, to open a trail that accesses the wildest and most remote parts of our country. You'll get a glimpse of the West as it was when Lewis and Clark traversed its wild tracts. Volunteer opportunities are plentiful. If you choose one of the many organized projects (they range from building a new trail on Berthoud Pass in Colorado to replacing a bridge in Bridger Wilderness in Wyoming), you can sign up to be a crew leader, a crew chef, or just one of the gofers that rakes up underbrush, clears out rocks and roots, and helps inventory the trail.

Or maybe you'd rather sign up for CDTA's Explorer Program, which invites volunteers to scout the backcountry for new routes. In other words, you'll literally explore virgin territory. Heather Gordon, for example, recently blazed a new 15-mile segment between Big Spring and Antelope Spring in the Cibola National Forest of New Mexico. Before her work, hikers on the trail were forced to take a forestry road they shared with diesel-belching logging trucks.

The only cost to volunteer on one of the CDTA projects is a $19 fee, but participation is free for members. If you prefer, you can submit a membership fee of $31 (a penny for each mile of the trail). CDTA membership for a family is $50, and it allows all members of a household to volunteer for free.

HOW TO GET IN TOUCH
Continental Divide Trail Alliance, P.O. Box 628, Pine, CO 80470, 888-909-2382 or 303-838-3760, www.cdtrail.org.

create costumes for a historic outdoor theater

DANVILLE, KENTUCKY

I never used a blueprint. I would just put up a board and start nailing.
—Eben C. Henson, founder of the Pioneer Playhouse

5 For volunteers with stars in their eyes, here's a place where you can spend your summer being part of one of the country's oldest summer stock theaters. In 1951, there were only two states with official performing arts commissions: New York and Kentucky. In fact, the Kentucky Arts Council led the country in progressive arts planning, thanks to a funky outdoor theater in the unlikely town of Danville (pop. 15,477).

It all started in 1950 when Col. Eben C. Henson, a Danville native who had briefly studied acting in New York, decided to turn a 200-acre cornfield into the Pioneer Playhouse. Lacking sufficient funds to build even so much as a stage, Henson talked a state mental hospital into hiring him to produce plays while he scrounged up used and abandoned materials for his theater. Often joking that he was the country's first recycler, Henson traded a fifth of whiskey for the century-old main timber beams, scavenged lights from an ice-cream parlor, and somehow managed to incorporate a couple of World War II army barracks into the playhouse. He even hired prisoners from the local county jail to help him lay the first foundations.

His tenaciousness paid off. In the 1950s and 1960s, Pioneer Playhouse became known as the King of Summer Stocks. Although Henson passed away in 2004, the Pioneer Playhouse is going strong nearly six decades after its founding.

Every summer from early June to mid-August, Pioneer Playhouse stages five plays in ten weeks—and indeed they're still scrounging. The theater depends entirely on volunteers to make costumes, hang posters, usher, assist backstage, and basically do everything that needs doing to make sure the five-play season goes off without a hitch.

In 1969, when he was only 15, John Travolta appeared at Pioneer Playhouse in *The Ephraim McDowell Story*, an original play about a 19th-century Kentucky surgeon. Other actors who honed their skills at Pioneer include Lee Majors, Bo Hopkins, and Jim Varney. The real star at Pioneer Playhouse, though, was Colonel Henson, the string-tie wearing charmer who staged more than 300 plays. Other accomplishments from his wide-ranging and storied career include working as an alligator wrestler in Silver Springs, Florida; acting in dozens of movies, notably *Raintree County, April Love,* and *The Treasure of Matacumbe;* and performing in plays with Tony Curtis, Bea Arthur, and Harry Belafonte while studying drama in New York. In 2003, PBS aired a documentary about Henson and his world-famous Pioneer Playhouse.

Every April, Henson's daughter Holly, a stand-up comedian in Minneapolis and the current artistic director, goes to New York to audition actors for the summer season (they're the only ones who get paid). As Holly is quick to point out, "It's not for everyone. We're definitely off the beaten path. I always say we're looking for the anti-divas of the theater world."

Volunteers come in from around the country (one volunteer has been driving here from Nevada for nearly a decade), and they either camp at the campground on the 200-acre Pioneer Playhouse site or land a spot in one of the theater's rustic rooms. In return for four or five hours of help per day from Thursday through Saturday, they get three meals a day (except Sunday, when the cook gets a day off) and free tickets to all five performances. An outdoor preshow dinner of fried chicken, barbecue brisket, corn pudding, green beans, and other southern delights is served.

Besides the campground, the Pioneer Playhouse theater complex includes a drama school, a museum, a re-creation of an 18th-century Kentucky village, and a box office that was once the train station in MGM's Civil War epic *Raintree County.*

There is no charge to volunteer at the Pioneer Playhouse.

HOW TO GET IN TOUCH

Pioneer Playhouse, 840 Stanford Road, Danville, KY 40422, 859-236-2747, www.pioneerplayhouse.com.

protect loggerhead sea turtles

WASSAW NATIONAL WILDLIFE RESERVE, GEORGIA

> For most of the wild things on Earth, the future
> must depend upon the conscience of mankind.
> —Archie Carr, scientist and author who almost single-handedly
> turned the tide on the extinction of sea turtles

6 The dinosaurs didn't make it. But giant sea turtles, which have survived for 175 million years, still have a fighting chance, even though they're endangered. The days when hunters nearly killed them off are mostly in the past, but today high-rise condominiums are taking over their nesting grounds and the mammoth sea turtles are laying eggs on shaky ground.

Since 1978, *Caretta caretta*—better known as the loggerhead turtle—which nests largely in the southeastern United States, has been on the threatened species list. Their numbers have been in steep decline since humans began vacationing on their nesting grounds. The good news is that, even before the Federal Endangered Species Act added the loggerheads to the list, the Caretta Research Project on Wassaw Island, one of Georgia's many barrier islands, has been tagging them and doing their best to protect the vulnerable creatures.

And that's where you come in. Between May and September, the research facility invites volunteers to Wassaw Island to help scientists patrol the beach. Each week, six volunteers come to tag and measure female turtles as they emerge from the sea to lay their eggs, move the nests if they're too close to the tide line, and protect them from raccoons, feral hogs, and other predators. Volunteers even cheer on

ADOPT A TURTLE

If you can't make it to Wassaw Island, consider adopting a loggerhead sea turtle, nest, or hatchling. During the summer, you can even log onto the Caretta Research Project website and track your adopted turtle's nesting activity. For your $25 adoption fee, you'll receive a list of adoptees and an adoption form, a semiannual newsletter, and a Caretta Research Project bumper sticker.

LOGGERHEAD STATS

- While hatchlings are a mere 2 inches in length, adults can be up to 3 feet long and weigh as much as 350 pounds.
- Only 1 in 1,000 hatchlings survives to adulthood.
- Females, which lay as many as ten clutches at a time, lay eggs only every two or three years.
- The average loggerhead lives 50 to 75 years.
- The loggerhead's name comes from the turtle's unusually large head.
- Even though loggerheads don't reach maturity for 20 or 25 years, they some-how remember where they were born and return to the same place two decades later to lay their eggs.
- Loggerhead turtles migrate more than 8,000 miles—alone, without other tur-tles guiding the way. The journey, which takes them across the Atlantic past the Azores, takes five to ten years to complete.
- Although their streamlined bodies and flippers are perfect for the ocean, they are nearsighted and defenseless on land.
- When loggerhead hatchlings break out of their shells at night, they instinc-tively crawl toward the brightest light on the horizon. On an undeveloped beach, that's the moon's reflection off the surf. However, on a developed beach, the brightest light can be a light from a nearby disco.
- An estimated 14,000 females nest in the southeastern United States each year.

the tiny 2-inch hatchlings when they finally peck their way out of their shells 60 days after mom deposits her eggs in the sand.

Working in cooperation with the U.S. Fish and Wildlife Service, the Savannah Science Museum, and the Wassaw Island Trust, the Caretta Research Project has been around since 1972. It's one of the longest running marine turtle tracking projects in the United States. And while scientists are slow to take credit, there is striking evidence suggesting the project has been successful. The number of loggerhead clutches on Wassaw has gone from 50 or 60 in the mid-1980s to more than 100 in recent years.

Wassaw Island is a 10,053-acre national wild-life refuge with rolling dunes, live oaks, vast salt marshes, and a 6-mile-long beach where the female loggerheads sneak in each summer to lay nests of 120 eggs the size of Ping-Pong balls.

CANNONBALLS AND TURTLE EGGS

During the Civil War, Wassaw was occupied at different times by both Confederate and Union soldiers. Blowing sands once revealed the complete skeleton of a soldier, along with a .56-caliber bullet and a button from the uniform of the First Georgia Regiment. Cannonballs have been found along the full length of the island's northern end.

Well before the war, though, in the early 1800s, the island was owned by Anthony Odingsell, a black planter who listed 11 slaves among his possessions. In 1866, the island was purchased by George Parsons, a wealthy entrepreneur, who built the existing housing compound as a hideaway for his family and friends. In October 1969, after 103 years of Parsons family ownership, the island was sold to the Nature Conservancy for one million dollars. The Conservancy, in turn, deeded the land to the U.S. Department of the Interior to be managed as a wildlife refuge. For this transaction, though, the cost was the princely sum of one dollar.

In 1898, during the Spanish-American War, the U.S. Army Corps of Engineers supervised the construction of Fort Morgan on Wassaw Island's north end. Though portions of the fort, which was built by civilians, survive today, it is threatened due to erosion.

Getting there requires a 45-minute boat ride from Landings Harbor Marina on Skidaway Island.

Volunteers stay in a rustic cabin (no air-conditioning or indoor showers). Because turtles lay their eggs at night—it's safer that way—turtle patrol usually begins around nightfall and lasts until roughly 5 a.m. Daytime is when you'll sleep and have free time to explore, hike the island's many dirt roads, swim in the pool, and go bird-watching. Not only does Wassaw support rookeries for egrets and herons, but a variety of wading birds also show up each summer.

Volunteers pay $750 per week. This includes transportation to and from Skidaway Island, a cabin bunk, and all meals.

HOW TO GET IN TOUCH

Caretta Research Project, P.O. Box 9841, Savannah, GA 31412, 912-447-8655, www.carettaresearchproject.org.

help transform health care

The best medical thing we can do for patients is help them develop grand friendship skills and find meaning in their lives.
—Dr. Patch Adams, founder of Gesundheit!

7 The fact that comedian Robin Williams was chosen to play Patch Adams in the eponymous 1998 movie about his life should be your first clue that Dr. Adams is not your average M.D. and that the Gesundheit! Institute that he started in rural West Virginia is not your run-of-the-mill hospital. Situated amid beautiful mountains, hardwood forests, and at least three waterfalls, Gesundheit! is a holistic hospital and health-care community based on the radical notion that medicine should actually be fun and free.

Whether you saw the movie or not, it's probably obvious by now that a volunteer vacation to Patch's 317-acre institute promises to be unorthodox and extraordinary. Although the "silly hospital" that Patch envisioned is still on the drawing board, there's an active community of artists, dreamers, healers, and clowns interested in changing the medical paradigm. They're living at the institute, preparing the land, and building the community that will sustain the hospital once it is built. Volunteers of all stripes are welcome.

A significant component of the Gesundheit! experience is education. Programs are based on Patch's vision for world peace, social justice, and the recognition that the health of the individual cannot be separated from the health of the

WACKY HOSPITAL

The 40-room Gesundheit! Hospital will be completely free, with no malpractice insurance and no third-party insurance. If you think that's wacky, you ought to get a load of the architectural blueprints. A giant ear sticks off one end of the building and giant feet mark the entrance. Below the main hospital floor, there's a waterway that allows people to travel from one end to the other via paddleboat. Beautiful murals cover the walls, toys line the floors, and secret doorways and slides add mystique and amusement.

For 35 years, Patch Adams has been involved in what he calls "clown healing work." He and a posse of clowns have visited hospitals on every continent, and often go to places where few dare to venture, for what he calls "humanitarian clowning." Since 1984, he has taken clowns to Russia each year for two weeks of clowning in hospitals, orphanages, prisons, and nursing homes. The clowns now go on six to eight overseas missions per year. For instance:

- In 2006, Patch and 45 clowns and 8 builders constructed a seven-room clinic in Perquin, El Salvador.
- Patch and 22 clowns from six continents took 10 tons of aid into war-torn Afghanistan.
- Patch took clowns into both Bosnia and the Kosovo refugee camps.
- His merry band has brought joy to Romanian AIDS orphanages.
- Patch took a team of 17 clowns to Cuba.
- Patch and his clowning pals have visited African refugee camps.
- In 2006, Patch took clowns to tsunami relief camps in Sri Lanka.

community. The idea is that volunteers should learn about Gesundheit!'s utopian ideas so they can return to their homes and spread the vision.

While living at the Gesundheit! Institute, volunteers might prepare fresh whole foods for the three dozen or so attendees of the institute's annual School for Designing a Society or build a deck on the back of the barn or collect buckets of sugar maple sap. For their community service projects, they might don red noses for clowning at the Pocahontas Care Center in Marlinton or pick up trash along U.S. 219 between Locust Creek Road and Hillsboro.

Every year, the institute hosts work camps, visitor weekends (where volunteers work for a day or two) as well as an increasing number of educational offerings. For example, medical students come each year to learn about medicinal herbs, health-care clowning, and other topics pertinent to Patch's vision of integrating medicine with fun, art, and friendship.

Patch's big, crazy dream began in 1971 when he and a couple of other doctors opened a free hospital located in Arlington, Virginia. It was a six-bedroom house where Patch and 20 adults (including two other docs) lived and practiced medicine. Their "zany hospital" was open 24/7, for all manner of medical problems. They saw 500 to 1,000 people each month, including many who took up residence. Patch called the pilot project "ecstatic, fascinating, and stimulating." After nine years of no donations and being refused for some 1,400 foundation grants, the project was finally disbanded. Dr. Adams, of course, persevered, making, as he describes it, a deal with "the devil"— to cooperate with the movie and get some publicity for his project.

Volunteers are needed at the Gesundheit! Institute from April through October with a minimum commitment of one month. In exchange for 35 hours of work per week, Gesundheit! provides room and board. Some of the positions include gardeners, cooks, builders, and housekeepers. If you can't spare a month, consider the Visitor Weekend Program or a short-term work camp, which could involve such service work as organic gardening, shitake mushroom gathering, composting toilet building, or even answering phones. All three options are—you guessed it— completely free.

HOW TO GET IN TOUCH
Gesundheit! Institute, P.O. Box 268, Hillsboro, WV 24946, 304-653-4338, www.patchadams.org.

help run a booming tourist town

MEDORA, NORTH DAKOTA

We are, each of us, angels with only one wing; and we can only fly by embracing one another.
—Luciano de Crescenzo, Italian writer and actor

8 To hear Teddy Roosevelt tell it, Medora, a ranching town in western North Dakota, was the "romance of his life." In fact, he used to say that if it wasn't for his experience in North Dakota, he'd have never been elected President. Roosevelt first showed up in the North Dakota badlands for a buffalo hunt in 1883, when he was a young New York politician. He liked the area so much that he eventually bought two ranches, the Maltese Cross, just south of Medora, and Elkhorn, 35 miles north.

Medora today is still a mystical place where people come because, like Roosevelt said, it has the power to change your life. In the winter, the little community has barely a hundred people, mostly folks who ranch or manage the Theodore Roosevelt National Park or the government business of being the Billings County seat. But in the summer, when folks are out of school or off work, they flock from all over the country to Medora in droves. Something like 300,000 show up during any given summer.

Needless to say, that's far too big a crowd for the permanent residents to be able to feed and house and sell souvenirs to all of them. So, in 1998, the Theodore Roosevelt Medora Foundation, a nonprofit organization that promotes the area, came up with the brilliant scheme of bringing in volunteers who could serve the locally famous pitchfork fondue (steaks speared on nickel-plated pitchforks and cooked over a campfire in a cauldron of boiling oil); usher at the Burning Hills Amphitheater, a 2,900-seat theater that since 1958 has been presenting the high-energy Medora Musical; staff the Harold Schafer Heritage Center; clear tables at the Chuckwagon Buffet; and greet tourists at the information center. Preseason volunteers get the town ready for its summer close-up.

The volunteer season runs from mid-May to mid-September and is divided into three segments. If you come in mid-May, you'll be in charge of painting, planting flowers, and sprucing up the little town with its wooden sidewalks, split-rail fences, barn-board buildings, and wooden benches. This perfectly coiffed town could easily double as Disneyland's Frontierland. Those volunteer stints run for five days. If you time your visit right, you'll be able to catch the Cowboy Poetry Gathering on Memorial Day weekend.

Starting in June, when the musical kicks off, volunteers come for eight-day "terms" to do everything from answering questions at the Medora Doll House—an antique doll museum housed in the old home of the Marquis de Mores, the guy who founded Medora back in 1883—to passing out programs at the Old Town Hall Theater for the one-man show on the life of Roosevelt, aptly entitled *Bully*. Around August 15, after the college kids have all returned to school, volunteers even take over such end-of-season duties as catering, running the Bully Pulpit Golf Course, and managing the retail establishments.

In return for roughly six hours of work a day, the foundation provides volunteers with a room at the Spirit of Work Lodge and a name badge (complete with photo) that allows them to eat free at the Maltese Burger, Chuckwagon's all-you-can eat buffet, or the Badlands Pizza Parlor.

When the staff of the Theodore Roosevelt Medora Foundation launched the volunteer program in 1998, they received 44 applications for the 16 positions. Today, more than 400 volunteers show up each year, 22 per week from early June through the first of September.

There is no charge to volunteer, but you do have to get your dibs in early. As of press time, more than 800 people had already signed on to the volunteer list for the 2009 season.

HOW TO GET IN TOUCH

Theodore Roosevelt Medora Foundation, P.O. Box 198, 301 Fifth Street, Medora, ND 58645, 800-633-6721 or 701-623-4444, www.medora.com.

ANOTHER THOUGHTFUL COMMITTED CITIZEN:
KIANA SEARS

To Kiana Sears, a manager with the Arizona Corporation Commission, volunteering is something that comes naturally, like brushing her teeth or hugging her daughters. "I grew up in New Orleans and my mom was always volunteering for something or another. Many a Saturday when I was a young child, we'd gather up our extra clothes and take them to the homeless shelter. If we had extra food, we'd take it to the neighbors. It was just something we did," Sears says.

"Volunteering is my life's purpose. It's what inspires me, what keeps me connected with my heart," she explains. After years of volunteering locally with her daughters' Girl Scout troops and with the Fresh Start Women's Resource Center, her oldest daughter, who was invited to go to Australia on a People to People International (PTPI) exchange program, dragged her to a meeting.

"I knew immediately that this was what I wanted to do, if not with my whole life, at least my spare time. I knew from personal experience that being introduced to different cultures changes a person and I knew I wanted to support People to People in any way I could. We live in a global economy and other countries might just as well be next door neighbors. My spirit was aching to be nurtured by that human connection," she says.

Sears now often uses her vacation to volunteer for People to People International, a nonprofit started in 1956 by President Dwight D. Eisenhower. "The idea behind Eisenhower's agency was to develop friendships with different nations. He figured that if people got to know each other, it would increase peace in the world," Sears says.

Last summer, she led a delegation of teens from six countries at a Future Business Leaders Summit in New York. During the ten-day summit, the teens, strangers before meeting in America, came up with a business plan to create and market a disaster relief kit—rations, candles, water, and other necessities that would sustain a family of four for two weeks. Setting aside any differences, they worked together to come up with the kit that could be used by FEMA and other disaster relief agencies around the world.

For Sears, volunteering with a delegation of international teens was a way to stay connected to other cultures and appreciate the world's diversity. She says, "Even though I've never been to Ireland, I feel I have a connection there now, because one of the boys on my team was from Belfast."

That deep connection is what drives her. "People get so busy and so stuck in their routines that they don't stop to help each other," Sears says. Yet volunteering counters that lost connection. "It fills my spirit up. It connects me back to my humanity. . . . Other people are always the best reflection of how much we have. I always get back so much more than I ever give."

serve as a lighthouse keeper

WISCONSIN, MICHIGAN, RHODE ISLAND, AND WASHINGTON

We cannot hold a torch to light another's path
without brightening our own.
—Ben Sweetland, author, motivational speaker, and psychologist

9 Let there be lighthouses. And volunteers to keep them. Imagine living on a windswept island, listening to the waves crash against the shore as gulls wheel overhead. You're tending the lights, performing heroic rescues, and … okay, so that's not the exact job description, but lighthouses throughout the country use volunteers to keep the home fires burning. Here are just five:

Devil's Island, Sand Island, and Michigan Island: The Apostle Islands National Lakeshore, a scenic archipelago of 22 islands around the northern tip of Wisconsin's Bayfield Peninsula, uses volunteers to staff three of its six lighthouses: Devil's Island, Sand Island, and Michigan Island. As keeper, you'll greet the public, give tours (you'll get lots of exercise walking up and down the lighthouse stairs), mow lawns, serve as an emergency contact, and occasionally perform light maintenance work. Three weeks is the minimum stay at these lighthouses, and you'll be required to take all your food and supplies with you. Applications for these popular positions are accepted year-round, and selections for the upcoming season are made by March 31. There is no charge.

Apostle Islands National Lakeshore, 415 Washington Avenue, Bayfield, WI 54814, 715-779-3397, www.nps.gov/apis/supportyourpark.

Grand Traverse Lighthouse: With 3,000 miles of coastline, Michigan has more lighthouses (130) than any other state except Alaska. From April through December, the Grand Traverse Lighthouse—located in Leelanau State Park—accepts volunteers who live in the former assistant's quarters, greet visitors, provide history lessons, and help out in the gift shop. Volunteers pay $440 for two weeks, $220 for one week.

Grand Traverse Lighthouse Museum, P.O. Box 43, 15500 North Lighthouse Point Road, Northport, MI 49670, 231-386-7195, www.grandtraverselighthouse.com.

The New Dungeness Light Station: Located at the tip of the nearly 5-mile-long Dungeness Spit in Sequim, Washington, this lighthouse has been in continuous operation guiding ships through the Strait of Juan de Fuca since its completion in 1857. In 1994, all the duties of the lighthouse keeper were taken over by volunteer members of the New Dungeness Light Station Association, who serve in one-week shifts. Volunteers stay in the three-bedroom Keeper's Quarters and give tours of the lighthouse (74 steps), mow the lawn, and perform general maintainance. Volunteer keepers pay $315 ($165 per child) to join and must attend orientation.

The New Dungeness Light Station, P.O. Box 1283, Sequim, WA 98382, 360-683-6638, www.newdungenesslighthouse.com.

Old Mission Point Lighthouse: This lighthouse, which was decommissioned in 1933, is located halfway between the North Pole and the Equator on the 45th parallel. You'll be expected to pitch in with light maintenance work, staff the gift shop, and act as an informal guide to field visitors' questions (not to worry, there's an orientation). The $600 per person fee covers a month's stay in private quarters that include a bedroom, a fully equipped kitchen, a living room, and office space. In your free time, you can explore the 18-mile-long peninsula's beaches, vineyards, hiking and cycling trails, and sites like a furnished log cabin and an 1850s general store.

Old Mission Point Lighthouse, Old Mission, MI 49673, 231-386-7195.

Rose Island Lighthouse: Rose Island, an 18-acre island in Narragansett Bay, across from Newport, Rhode Island,

---

BETCHA DIDN'T KNOW

- The first lighthouse in the United States was built in Boston in 1716.

- The country's tallest lighthouse, at 191 feet, is at Cape Hatteras, North Carolina.

- The Statue of Liberty was the first lighthouse to use electricity.

- The United States Lighthouse Society has compiled extensive lighthouse data and publishes a magazine dedicated to lighthouses, *The Keeper's Log.*

has been used as a fort by the U.S. Infantry and as a torpedo station by the U.S. Navy. The island's Victorian-looking lighthouse, built in 1870, was refurbished in 1984 by the Rose Island Lighthouse Foundation and now uses volunteers to work as lighthouse keepers. You'll be responsible for tidying up the lighthouse, greeting visitors (who come over on the Jamestown Ferry in the summer), and collecting money from the landing fee boxes and the gift shop. After listening to the marine weather forecast each morning, you'll make your rounds, starting by raising the flag (you'll lower it at sunset) and checking on the wind-powered electric system and rain water collection system. A two-hour orientation precedes your weeklong (Sunday to Sunday) post. Prices run $700 to $2,300 depending on the time of year, with summer being more expensive than winter. Be sure to call ahead—the volunteering is by invitaiton only.

Rose Island Lighthouse Foundation, P.O. Box 1419, Newport, RI 02840, 401-847-4242, www.roseislandlighthouse.org.

excavate a piece of american history

U.S. NATIONAL FORESTS

The true meaning of life is to plant trees,
under whose shade you do not expect to sit.
—Nelson Henderson, Manitoba pioneer farmer and family man

10 Perhaps the first volunteer for the U.S. Forest Service was Smokey Bear who has been around since 1944 reminding us in one campaign or another that only we can prevent . . . well, you know the rest of the line.

Forty-four years after Smokey became a well-known national figure, the U.S. Forest Service started a volunteer program that even humans can participate in. Called Passport in Time (PIT), this nationwide program uses volunteers to help professional archaeologists and historians survey, excavate and restore historic and archaeological sites within national forest land. And unlike other programs in the same vein (Earthwatch, for example), participation in PIT programs is completely free.

PIT projects, listed on the website, vary from year to year. Maybe you'll restore an old gold miner's cabin in the mountains of Colorado or record gravestone data from historical cemeteries in Vermont. Maybe you'll gather oral histories, restore art, or catalog artifacts. Whatever your job (and you can apply for any project that interests you), you'll be working to rescue an important page in America's history books.

Over the years, Pitheads, as longtime volunteers call themselves, have done  everything from excavate ancient tools in Mississippi to survey an old military road in Oregon to stabilize cliff dwellings in New Mexico. As of 2007, the Bureau of Land Management began working with Passport in Time, so now there are even more protected lands where Pitheads can contribute.

But watch out. It can become an obsession. Some PIT volunteers have contributed more than 500 hours. There's an honor roll that keeps track.

Projects range from two days to several weeks, but the average project lasts five days. Accommodations range from backcountry camping to campgrounds with RV hookups to Forest Service cabins or watch towers. Either way, you'll be well looked after by the Forest Service archaeologists and historians who'll be your hosts. After applying, you'll receive an actual Passport in Time passport on which to log hours.

HOW TO GET IN TOUCH
Passport in Time Clearinghouse, P.O. Box 15728, Rio Rancho, NM 87174, 800-281-9176 or 505-896-0934, www.passportintime.com.

SMOKEY DOESN'T HAVE A MIDDLE NAME

Smokey's full name is Smokey Bear, though he's often mistakenly called Smokey the Bear. The problem started in 1952 when a couple of songwriters, Steve Nelson and Jack Rollins, penning an ode to the popular firefighter, added a "the" to maintain the song's rhythm. Unfortunately, the song, "Smokey the Bear," become a hit and people have been confused about Smokey's name ever since. Here are few other facts about our nation's fire bear:

- Smokey was preceded as the Forest Service talking head by Bambi. Soon after the popular movie made its debut on August 13, 1942, Walt Disney gave the Forest Service permission to use Bambi and company in their fire prevention public service campaigns, but only for one year.
- August 9 is Smokey's birthday. It's the anniversary of his first poster that came out a year after Bambi retired.
- Smokey was a popular radio show guest during the 1950s. He also shows up often in comic strips and cartoons; recent appearances include *The Far Side, The Simpsons,* and *South Park.*
- Smokey made guest appearances on TV and radio ads with such celebrities as Ray Charles, Bing Crosby, B. B. King, Art Linkletter, Roy Rogers, and Dinah Shore.
- A school district in Hill City, South Dakota, uses Smokey Bear as its mascot, an honor they received after students volunteered to battle a devastating fire in the nearby Black Hills.
- Poet Gary Snyder wrote a Buddhist chant called the "Smokey the Bear Sutra" that depicts Smokey as the reincarnation of the Great Sun Buddha.
- There's a U.S. federal law protecting Smokey's name and image. The Smokey Bear Act of 1952 takes Smokey out of the public domain and mandates that all of his royalties go for education on forest fire prevention.

transform a village in jamaica's blue mountains

RURAL JAMAICA

I could not, at any age, be content to take my place
by the fireside and simply look on.
—Eleanor Roosevelt, former U.S. First Lady and social activist

11 Bob Marley, the Jamaican musician who almost single-handedly introduced the world to reggae, probably said it best: "We should all come together and create music and love, but is too much poverty…. The most intelligent people are the poorest people. Yes, the thief them rich, pure robbers and thieves, rich! The intelligent and innocent are poor, are crumbled and get brutalized daily."

And while tourists who visit Jamaica see gorgeous coastline, fancy all-inclusive resorts, and people living the high life, there's another side to this former British colony. In fact, the farther you travel into the interior, the worse conditions get—washed-out roads, crumbling homes, communities that are lucky to have one phone.

Global Volunteers (GV) works with four communities in Jamaica's misty Blue Mountains, exactly where they started when they launched their ground-breaking nonprofit organization in 1984. GV was one of the first organizations to send do-gooders on volunteer projects; *USA Today* called it "the granddaddy of the volunteer vacation movement."

The genesis for GV occurred four years earlier on a honeymoon. In January 1980, Michele Gran and Bud Philbrook were planning a barefoot honeymoon cruise in the Caribbean. "It was the era of the Vietnamese boat people," Philbrook recalls. "[Michele] didn't want to play while people were on the same water, fighting for their lives."

So they compromised; they spent five days at Disney World, Philbrook's childhood dream, and spent five days in rural Conacaste, Guatemala, helping villagers obtain funds for a much-needed irrigation project. After the local newspaper wrote a story about their unusual honeymoon, people started hounding them for info: How can we do the same thing? In 1984, Bud and Michele established Global Volunteers to provide people with an opportunity to make a difference in the lives of others around the globe. Bud led the first two volunteer service programs that year, to Woburn Lawn, Jamaica, a sister village of Conacaste.

Since then, Global Volunteers has hooked up volunteers with hundreds of projects, from building schools in Ghana to caring for orphans in Romania to teaching English to children in China. Volunteers have done everything from tracking the kakerori in the Cook Islands, and constructing and repairing buildings in Tanzania to landscaping public spaces in Costa Rica.

GOOD TO THE LAST DROP

Rising as a backdrop to Kingston, Jamaica, the lush, rugged Blue Mountains are home to more than 500 flowering plants, 65 species of orchids, and a curious tree named *Chusquea abietifolia* that flowers, simultaneously, only once every 33 years. The next bloom is in 2017, in case you're wondering.

The Blue Mountains also grow what many believe is the world's best coffee. One of the believers was author Ian Fleming. James Bond, his alter ego, of course, wouldn't let anything but the very best—Smirnoff vodka, Brut blanc de blanc champagne, and Blue Mountain coffee—cross his spying lips. The Queen of England also drinks Blue Mountain coffee. Here are five other facts you may not know about this exclusive brew:

- The average price of Jamaican Blue Mountain coffee beans is an astonishing $55 per pound.
- Jamaican Blue Mountain coffee beans sell for as much as $80 a pound in Tokyo, where a single cup has been known to fetch $25.
- The Japanese purchase more than 90 percent of the Blue Mountain beans produced each year.
- Blue Mountain coffee beans provide the flavor base for Tia Maria, a coffee liqueur which is made in Jamaica.
- Around 1723, King Louis XV of France sent three coffee plants to the French colony of Martinique. Two of those coffee plants perished before landfall. However, either the third plant itself or some of its progeny were given to Sir Nicholas Lawes, the former Governor of Jamaica. By the early 1800s, the island boasted more than 600 coffee plantations.

In Jamaica over the years, GV volunteers have painted classrooms, built school chairs and desks, installed water systems, expanded a community center, improved local church facilities, constructed footbridges, and cleared brush from an old coffee plantation. They've even performed well-baby exams and offered health-care services to home-bound senior citizens. The four Jamaican communities with whom GV has been working with for 25 years let the team manager know beforehand what projects are most needed in any given year.

Which brings up an excellent and essential point about volunteer vacations. A good volunteer organization works under the tutelage of those they serve. Their purpose is not to come up with projects they think are needed. How are they to know, sitting at their American desks, looking through their American lenses at what a rural community in the wilds of Jamaica might need? Global Volunteers, like all good volunteer organizations, constantly critiques and assesses the impact they're having.

A two-week program, including lodging with a host family and all meals, runs $1,995.

HOW TO GET IN TOUCH

Global Volunteers, 375 East Little Canada Road, St. Paul, MN 55117, 800-487-1074 or 651-407-6100, www.globalvolunteers.org.

CARIBBEAN VOLUNTEER EXPEDITIONS
preserve a caribbean treasure

ISLANDS ACROSS THE CARIBBEAN

Twenty years from now you will be more disappointed by the things you didn't do than by the ones you did. So throw off the bowlines. Sail away from the safe harbor. Catch the trade winds in your sails.
—Author unknown

12 Anne Hersh, the architect who started Caribbean Volunteer Expeditions (CVE), calls the work of her nonprofit "preservation in paradise." She started the agency in 1990 after her own volunteer stint documenting a slave village and cemetery in the U.S. Virgin Islands. She recognized right away the importance of preserving the Caribbean's rich heritage and the lack of resources dedicated to doing so.

Even though universities offer degrees in historic preservation, money for historic preservation is scarce. Imagine the need in tiny countries like St. Kitts or Nevis that didn't even achieve independence from Britain until 1983. And because Caribbean islands too often are the first to be hit by the battering rams of summer and fall hurricanes, time is of the essence.

CVE recruits volunteers for six to ten trips each year. Working with the island's national trusts, museums, national park services, and local historic societies, volunteers work to preserve everything from colonial-era forts to historic gardens to pre-Columbian archaeological sites.

"Some people in the islands have overlooked the great history their ancestors left for them. The fact that

CHRISTOPHER COLUMBUS, BLACKBEARD, AND YOU

San Salvador, one of 700 islands in the Bahamas, is where the famous explorer first made landfall in 1492. CVE volunteers are mapping the ruins of a plantation on this easternmost Bahamian island that was also a popular haunt for the infamous pirate Blackbeard. Working with archaeologist John Winter, volunteers haven't unearthed any pirate booty yet, but they have found ancient artifacts from native Indians, as well as Spanish and other European colonists.

our volunteers think it's important enough to fly to the islands and spend their vacations documenting and preserving these invaluable sites and genealogical records creates a sense of national pride," Hersh says.

Projects vary by island, but some of the most popular ones are cemetery inventory and archaeology projects. Working alongside preservationists, architects, and historians, you'll piece together ruins and walls, survey old buildings, computerize archives, and take inventories of weathered grave stones. Or you could sign on for some light construction, such as the wattle-and-daub house CVE volunteers built in St. Eustatius, a tiny 8-square-mile island in the West Indies.

CVE has projects throughout the Caribbean, including the Virgin Islands, Puerto Rico, Bahamas, Trinidad and Tobago, Jamaica, St. Lucia, Barbados, St. Vincent, Grenada, Nevis, and St. Kitts. Since 1997, CVE has also offered programs for those 55 and older that are booked through Elderhostel (www.elderhostel.org). Families can be accommodated on some projects; contact CVE to inquire.

Volunteers usually knock off after five hours of work to swim, hike, or visit other historic sites on the island. The trips are often planned to coincide with island festivals, complete with parades, music, and local food.

CVE programs typically run seven days, Sunday to Sunday, usually between November and March when Caribbean weather is on its best behavior. Costs range from $800 to $1,500, depending on the location, and include lodging—usually at a beachside resort—and some meals.

HOW TO GET IN TOUCH

Caribbean Volunteer Expeditions, P.O. Box 388, Corning, NY 14830, 607-962-7846, www.cvexp.org.

monitor
climate change

ARCTIC CIRCLE, MANITOBA, CANADA

*Climate change poses clear, catastrophic threats. We may not agree
on the extent, but we certainly can't afford the risk of inaction.*
*—Rupert Murdoch, chairman and CEO of global
media conglomerate News Corp.*

13 Skeptics! Be gone! The 2007 report of the UN-established Intergovernmental Panel on Climate Change (IPCC), a panel that reeled in the Nobel Prize that year, put to rest any remaining skepticism on whether climate change was real. But we still don't know how fast the time bomb is ticking.

That's what scientists at the Churchill Northern Studies Center (CNSC), a research facility at the edge of the Arctic in Manitoba, Canada, are trying to figure out. What exactly happens as the Earth warms up? What are the consequences? How much time do we have?

So far, we know this: As the world warms, permafrost thaws. While that might not sound terribly threatening, permafrost contains a massive amount of carbon. When it melts, as it's starting to do with increasing speed, carbon dioxide and methane—the biggest greenhouse gas culprits—are released into the atmosphere, creating a vicious cycle of even more thawing.

This remote and rugged outpost is on the coast and within the Hudson Bay Lowlands, situated at the mouth of the Churchill River. Because many different biomes can be found in the vicinity, including forest, forest-tundra, tundra, wetland/peatland, estuarine, and marine, it's particularly susceptible to warming temperatures and the changes that they cause. And since at least 20 percent of the world's carbon is locked in these Arctic wetlands, it serves as the proverbial canary in the mine shaft. The best case scenario is a

THE BEAR TRUTH

Churchill, located in Manitoba, Canada, is the self-proclaimed "polar bear capital of the world." The town's 800 residents appreciate the throngs of tourists that are drawn here to see the 1,600-pound animals that migrate through the area each October and November. Yet in the interest of safety, they've been forced to instigate a 24-hour Polar Bear Alert program to address those hungry bears that inadvertently lumber into town.

The first tack taken to keep the tiny town free of polar bears is to meet intruding bears with earsplitting "cracker shells." Polar bears who make more than one foray into town are tranquillized and take the paddy wagon to polar bear jail, a holding tank near the airport that can house up to 30 bears. The inmates are then kept hydrated with snow until they can either be helicoptered away from the area or let out to cross the frozen bay. Giving the captive bears food is a strict no-no, a lesson learned after past inmates returned to tried to break *into* the jail.

The polar bear, or *Ursus maritimus,* mainly eats seals, but they have been known to attack humans. They have a keen sense of smell and can move quickly. Chief among the guidance from leaflets handed out to tourists and the knowledge of polar bear authorities:

- Do not run.
- Do not play dead.
- Do not try to outswim a polar bear.
- Do not make direct eye contact, which is a sign of aggression.
- Do not dress up like a seal (okay, that one's a tongue-in-cheek reference to Halloween, which occurs during polar bear season, complete with bear patrol).

dramatic alteration of this region alone. In the worst case scenario, climate change will catastrophically affect all life on the planet.

Scientists have been conducting climate change research in this dramatic environment since the 1970s. But there's only so much a couple scientists with 365 days can do. In 2000, as the climate change issue heated up along with temperatures, the number of research sites in the area rose from four to eleven. In short, volunteers allow them to accelerate their timely, desperately needed research.

If you volunteer for this project, you'll stay at the research center and use ground-penetrating radar, microclimate data loggers, and soil coring to calculate organic carbon content. You'll also live-trap small mammals, evaluate growth rings of trees and shrubs, and monitor plant development. If you go in the winter, you'll travel by *qamutik,* sled in Inuit, to classify ice crystals, measure snowpack, and record temperatures.

Churchill, located in the largest mountain wilderness in North America, is a sparsely populated outpost on the shores of Hudson Bay. There's no road, so you either have to fly in or take a 36-hour train ride from Winnipeg. The CNSC, where you'll stay, is one of the world's premier research facilities and a former rocket testing site.

Activities include beluga whale-watching (some 57,000, the world's largest population, surface every summer), tundra buggy touring, and plenty of opportunities to see polar bears (pop. 1,200), golden eagle, moose, elk, and caribou. It's also the best spot on the planet for viewing the northern lights. Choose one of the winter trips and you can even build and sleep in an igloo, comfortable down to minus 40 degrees Fahrenheit.

Eleven-day trips cost $2,950 and include shared lodging at the research center and three meals per day. Trips of the same length with similar activities for 16- and 17-year-olds are $3,350.

HOW TO GET IN TOUCH

Earthwatch, 3 Clock Tower Place, Suite 100, Box 75, Maynard, MA 01754, 800-776-0188 or 978-461-0081, www.earthwatch.org.

join a dirt cheap work camp

CANADA AND BEYOND

We're all waiting for the government, someone or something,
to save the planet for us. And it's not going to happen
unless we do something about it.
—Marcelo da Luz, inventor of a solar car who recruited
CADIP volunteers to help him set a world distance record

14 Not all of CADIP's work camps are as unique and adventurous as the 2008 Power of One project that recruited volunteers to drive the support vehicle for Marcelo da Luz's record-breaking, 10,000-mile journey in a solar car.

The former Brazilian flight attendant who built the futuristic vehicle calls it the Power of One (Xof1, for short) to show people that sustainable energy and clean technology is possible and to inspire them to come up with their own ideas for saving the planet.

Most of CADIP's work camps stay in one place and use teams of between ten and twenty international volunteers, unlike the Xof1 project that only needed two volunteers to support da Luz's historic journey from Buffalo, New York, to Inuvik, Northern Territories.

The idea for volunteer work camps originated in 1920 near Verdun, France. Former military personnel from France and Germany came together to build homes on the same battlefield where some 700,000 soldiers lost their lives in one of the longest and bloodiest battles of World War I. This gesture of reconciliation caught on quickly: Today there are hundreds of volunteer work camps in nearly every country on the planet.

CADIP projects extend around the world from building hiking trails in a historic herring village in remote Djúpavik, Iceland, to playing with kids at a children's center in Jerusalem. The Canadian projects range from downtown Vancouver—near museums, art galleries, trendy shopping, and Stanley Park—to Great Bear Rainforest overlooking the Pacific.

MORE POWERFUL THAN A TOASTER

Marcelo da Luz was minding his own business, watching the 1987 World Solar Challenge from his home in São Paulo, Brazil, when suddenly it became impossible to sit there and do nothing about the imploding energy crisis.

"I saw those cars and what they were doing and I got so inspired. . . . so I decided I had to build a solar car," says the former Air Canada flight attendant. Even though he had no experience, nothing even close to an engineering background, he pulled together a half million dollars and a team of friends and experts to build the Power of One, a car that runs entirely on the energy of the sun. Other facts about this car:

- It looks like a spaceship and, in fact, is so unusual-looking that da Luz was stopped by the police a half dozen times on his record-setting journey from Buffalo to Inuvik.
- The Xof1, as it's nicknamed, runs on less energy than a toaster.
- The car's average speed is about 30 miles an hour. Yet with abundant sunshine, it can reach a maximum speed of 75 miles an hour and accelerate from zero to 50 miles an hour in six seconds.
- It has three wheels.
- The Xof1 was chosen to represent the car of the future in the Centennial Anniversary of the 1908 Great Race. Though the race was postponed due to a recall of permits by China, it's rescheduled for April 25, 2009.
- The interior temperature of the car can reach 93 degrees Fahrenheit.

As da Luz is quick to point out, the car is not ready for mass production, but he hopes it will inspire others to imagine and dream about what is possible. He eagerly shares all information he has compiled about the car's solar technology with anyone interested. As he says, "Individuals alone cannot change the world, but can inspire others to come together to make change happen."

Volunteer tasks vary from project to project. Volunteers who accompanied da Luz on his record-breaking journey set up the solar arrays that charged the car's batteries, took photos, carried spare tires, and interacted with the media. Volunteers at the work camp in the Great Bear Rainforest are rebuilding a ceremonial big house for the Heiltsuk First Nations while volunteers on the Vancouver detail garden with senior citizens.

Volunteers work six hours a day, five days a week, so there's plenty of time for extracurricular activities and bonding with your fellow workers off-site. Work camp sponsors (that is, members of the community who have requested CADIP's help) often plan activities for the visitors. The Djúpavik work camp, for example, takes its volunteers kayaking in the fjords and swimming in a famous geothermally heated pool in Krossnes.

As one CADIP volunteer, Rowan, said, "Work camps are a brilliant idea. You get to really experience the culture of the country you are in and there are many young people who are willing to do voluntary work for good causes. It's great being part of an international group of volunteers as well. It makes for a good time when you're not at work."

There's nothing fancy about CADIP's accommodations. You'll share a school or a cabin, or maybe even a tent, with members of your team. While food is provided, you will split cooking duties and other household chores. But it's hard to quibble with the price: $340 Canadian (U.S.$290) for a two- to three-week volunteer vacation that includes lodging and meals.

HOW TO GET IN TOUCH
Canadian Alliance for Development Initiatives and Projects (CADIP), 907–950 Drake Street, Vancouver, British Columbia V6Z 2B9, Canada, 604-628-7400, www.cadip.org.

AIRLINE AMBASSADORS INTERNATIONAL

deliver food
and supplies to haiti

HAITI

Things must change here.
—Pope John Paul II, after a visit to Haiti in 1983

15 This is not a gig for the faint of heart or the weak of will. Plagued for decades by poverty, corruption, military coups, dictatorships, and foreign military intervention, Haiti is a place that foreigners scramble to leave . . . not to visit. It's the poorest country in the Western Hemisphere, with 45 percent illiteracy and 70 percent unemployment. Those lucky enough to find jobs make an average $150 per year. Some homes here are so small that family members take turns sleeping.

It's easy to shrug and think, "Well, it's a good thing the UN sent a 9,000-member peacekeeping force, because I'm not getting involved."

That sentiment, the sentiment that most of us have, isn't good enough for Airline Ambassadors International (AAI), a nonprofit that personally carries supplies and assistance to children in 52 needy countries. Since 1992, when flight attendant Nancy Rivard started the group of flight attendants who use their pass privileges to do good, AAI has sent $50 million worth of aid to help people in more than 50 countries.

One beneficiary of Rivard's good works? The children of Haiti, where AAI has organized regular humanitarian missions. Unlike other development and relief organizations that beg for monetary donations, but shun hands-on help, AAI believes everyday Joes can make a difference. And you don't have to be a flight attendant or have any specialized skills. AAI operates on the assumption that all of us have the ability— and the responsibility—to make communities whole again. And even when the State Department issues travel warnings, as they did after Haiti's 2008 violent demonstrations, AAI continues to send volunteers with vital supplies into the country.

They can't just turn their backs on the children in Haiti (75 percent of the country's population of eight million) who endure illiteracy, malnutrition, and

THAT'S KING GHOST, TO YOU

The people of Haiti believe the ghost of mad King Henri Cristophe still prowls the Citadelle Laferrière, the massive fortress he built atop a 3,000-foot mountain called Bonnet à l'Évêque. As Haiti's most revered national symbol (and probably best candidate for drawing tourists), this engineering marvel is featured on postage stamps and currency. Harry Belafonte even wrote a song about it.

From the beginning the Citadelle, the largest fortress in the Western Hemisphere, was shrouded in mystery and intrigue. Christophe, a former slave who led the rebellion against France, started building the fortress soon after Haiti became the world's first free black nation.

It took 20,000 men 15 years to build the structure, and more than 10,000 of them lost their lives during construction. It has 15-foot-wide walls and 365 cannon, each of which took three months to move from the coast to the fortress. As for Cristophe himself? Eight years after he declared himself the first king of Haiti, he shot himself through the heart with a silver bullet.

---

child slavery. Ten percent of them don't make it to four years old. As if all these problems weren't enough, Haiti's children, like the rest of the island's population, bore the devastating effects of Hurricane Gustav (August 26, 2008), tropical storm Hanna (September 1, 2008), and Hurricane Ike (September 7, 2008). When the back-to-back storms hit they killed hundreds of people and further reduced food supplies at a time when some people here had already been reduced to eating mud cookies due to high prices and shortages. In December 2008, AAI delivered one million dollars in aid, stuffed into every overhead bin and cargo area of an A-300 American Airlines lent the group.

Dr. Luc Pierre, a minister working with AAI, leads volunteers to Haiti two or three times a year. Volunteers take food, drinking water, and books. He also plans to use volunteers to rebuild a school demolished by the hurricanes of 2008.

Recent volunteer trips to Haiti have cost $1,000, including lodging and meals. Yet Pierre, the organizer, is so desperate for help that he's willing to negotiate.

HOW TO GET IN TOUCH

Airline Ambassadors International, 418 California Avenue, P.O. Box 459, Moss Beach, CA 94038, 866-264-3586, www.airlineamb.org. Rev. Dr. Luc R. Pierre can be reached at 917-969-1084 or lpierre2001@yahoo.com.

assist with free health clinics

If you think you're too small to have an impact,
try going to bed with a mosquito.
—Anita Roddick, activist and founder of the Body Shop

16 Until 1974, Milt Camp was a flight instructor and engineer for Hewlett-Packard. Then one of his students, a doctor who felt a little edgy about tackling the dirt runways in rural Mexico, talked him into coming along on a one-time medical mission. He needed moral support, he told Camp.

Providing that moral support changed Camp's life forever. He was so moved by the villagers treated by the doctor and their dire need for medical care that he returned to Hewlett-Packard, put up posters, and began raising money and gathering supplies for a second trip.

That trip was followed by another and soon Camp, who quickly became certified as a medical and dental technician, launched Los Médicos Voladores (LMV–The Flying Doctors), a group of volunteer pilots and doctors who regularly fly into remote areas of Mexico and Central America to set up weekend medical clinics. And it's not just doctors, dentists, pilots, and translators who are needed. The improvised clinics that are set up in schools, churches, and, once, in the village mayor's back bedroom, also use what LMV calls general volunteers.

Each LMV team has a doctor or nurse, a translator, and a pilot. When there's space on a trip, general volunteers are invited along to help with everything from equipment sterilization to keeping records to writing reports.

Your job could be anything from shining a flashlight into dental patients' mouths to renting a taxi and driving around with loudspeakers to inform villagers that the docs have arrived. Needless to say, it doesn't take long for lines to start forming.

Unlike Cancun, Acapulco, and other Mexican resort towns, where you're just as likely to run into American tourists as you are Mexican citizens, the LMV trips will take you to remote villages rarely seen by most Americans. Take Huasabas, for example, a tiny 17th-century town of 900 in the Bavispe Valley. Its airstrip, a dirt patch outside of town that also serves as a playground and racetrack, is used only for emergencies. And sometimes LMV pilots have to fly into the town down the road. Or Isla Cedros, an island that's inaccessible except by small plane or boat. Or Villa Hidalgo, a small village in the Mexican Sierra Madre that is a remote ranching community.

Although days are busy, with lines of patients stretching down dusty streets, volunteers usually find time to fish, watch whales, see cave paintings, and sample tequila.

Weekend trips to northern Mexico are scheduled the first weekend of each month. Your team will split the jet fuel—$350 for the Mexico trips. Lodging, usually arranged by LMV, will either be in family's homes or in a small hotel. Average price for a four-day mission, including accommodations, some food, medical supplies, and your share of fuel is around $1,000.

HOW TO GET IN TOUCH

Los Médicos Voladores, P.O. Box 5172, Fair Oaks, CA 95628, 800-585-4568, www.flyingdocs.org.

SEEKING REAL MEXICAN FOOD

Many folks in the United States tend to think of larded refried beans and mounds of processed cheese when you bring up Mexican food. That is a shame, since the real cuisine of Mexico sings with fresh ingredients and complex flavors.

Strides toward culinary understanding have been made, however, by such ambassadors as Diana Kennedy and Rick Bayless. Kennedy was born in the United Kingdom but lived in Mexico from 1957 to 1966 with her husband, *New York Times* correspondent Paul Kennedy. The Kennedys moved to New York, where Paul died in 1967. Legendary *Times* food editor Craig Claiborne then urged Kennedy to teach Mexican cooking, so she spent a few years traveling and doing research. *The Cuisines of Mexico,* her first of seven cookbooks, was published in 1972. She became a fierce advocate of classical Mexican cuisine.

Rick Bayless lived in Mexico from 1980 to 1986 with his wife Deann and penned the classic *Authentic Mexican: Regional Cooking From the Heart of Mexico* in 1987. That same year, they opened Chicago's Frontera Grill; its upscale sister restaurant, Tobolobampo, followed in 1989. More recently, Bayless wrote *Mexico: One Plate at a Time* and is hosting the PBS series of the same name.

CHAPTER

2

central & south america

We cannot live only for ourselves.
A thousand fibers connect us with our fellow men.
—Herman Melville, author of *Moby-Dick*

Latin America is wilder than its North American cousin, with the world's largest rain forest and a rainbow of indigenous cultures and ruins—both well known and yet to be discovered—of ancient civilizations.

Unfortunately, the economic gap between the haves and the have-nots is wide in this developing realm, where makeshift shacks and slums sit next to skyscrapers and luxury apartments. The region's extraordinary biodiversity is under constant threat as its wild places are impacted by its burgeoning economy. Needless to say, Latin America has lots of endangered animals and cultures that could use your help.

In this chapter, look for opportunities to track jaguars, collect butterflies, work in a soup kitchen, harvest coffee, help at-risk preschoolers, and fight AIDS.

Can one person really make a difference? The truth is that most of the problems addressed by volunteers here are complex and caused by years of social and political upheaval. Your stint as a volunteer is perhaps best served by devoting yourself to learning about the myriad forces that keep people impoverished and focusing on the unbridled development that wreaks havoc on habitats. Enhancing your appreciation of other cultures and other landscapes will hopefully inspire a lifelong commitment to creating the just and equitable world that we all really want.

give hope to at-risk preschoolers

CARTAGENA DE INDIAS, COLOMBIA

> The key to ending poverty is to create a global network
> of connections that reach from impoverished communities
> to the very centers of world power and wealth and back again.
> —Jeffrey Sachs, author of *The End of Poverty* and director
> of the Earth Institute at Columbia University

17 Tourists flock to Cartagena, Colombia, for its quaint plazas, cobblestone streets, colonial churches, and art museums. But just beyond the thick-walled colonial city that UNESCO designated a World Heritage site in 1984 are tens of thousands of children who live in poverty.

Ambassadors for Children (AFC), an Indianapolis nonprofit that sends volunteers to serve children around the world, recently added Cartagena, Colombia, to its arsenal of good works. AFC founder Sally Brown noticed that, like many overseas tourist destinations, this Caribbean treasure was divided into two worlds—a bustling city of four-star hotels for the wealthy on one side and makeshift, flimsily constructed homes for many of the local families on the other. Brown and her team quickly stepped in to help, sending volunteers to work in two preschools and at a children's hospital.

More than 20,000 people live in La Cienega de la Virgen, a Cartagena barrio with no running water, let alone an infrastructure that can provide a good education. Mabel Penas, a social worker who started a school in this area with money from her own pocket, relies on the good hearts of volunteers to help her feed and educate a hundred children who attend Sueños de Libertad (Dreams of Freedom). For some of the students, the two meals they are fed at school each day represent the bulk of their diet.

As a volunteer with AFC, you'll distribute shoes and school supplies at Sueños de Libertad, teach English, plant trees, and update the library by building new shelves or painting the walls. At Villa Gloria, the other preschool where AFC sends volunteers, you'll teach English, help build a playground, and help stabilize this beachside school that suffers continuous problems with standing water during the rainy season. You might work on building or fixing fences or even constructing an addition to the school.

At Casa del Niño, the children's hospital, you'll interact with the young patients, dress up in costume to entertain them, and possibly paint murals or landscape the garden. Representatives from the Fundación Cartagena Global will introduce you to children suffering from cystic fibrosis, and their medical team. In the United States, people with cystic fibrosis live on average to be more than 35 years old, but in Cartagena, the life expectancy for a cystic fibrosis patient is 14 to 16 years. Then, you will take some patients on an outing to the botanical garden.

AFC plans a full itinerary on this weeklong volunteer trip, equally balanced between working with children and partaking of Cartagena's rich bounty.

Founded in 1533 by Spanish conquistadores as a port to ship gold, Cartagena is a historical treasure on the Caribbean coast of Colombia. Sir Francis Drake

MUD IN YOUR EYE

They call it the Volcano of Youth. Colombians who make the trip to soak in Volcán del Totumo, a volcano that spews warm mud, not hot lava, fill bottles with the ooze to take home. They swear by its medicinal properties.

Located between Cartagena and Barranquilla, this spewing cone of mineral mud is formed by decaying plant material and stands about six stories high. While there, most people opt for simply floating around in the thick muck that looks an awful lot like melted chocolate, and perhaps having a massage. Locals provide bodywork and will also take pictures for you, among other services. Then you descend to rinse off the mud in the lake below (with the enthusiastic help of local women known as *bañadoras*, or bathers).

There's a small fee to float in the soothing mud of Volcán del Totumo. An exfoliation scrub, massage, or other bodywork while you're bobbing along is well worth an additional small fee, paid as a tip, or *la propina*. In fact, all the helpers at the volcano work for tips, but a tour from Cartagena—including ample tipping and sometimes lunch—costs about $30 to $40. A tiny price to pay for muddy bliss!

looted the city in 1586, stripping it of ten million pesos, a giant emerald, and the bells from the cathedral. Shortly thereafter, construction began on a fort, massive walls, and ramparts 50 feet thick. Today, those 10 miles of walls—plus flower-filled balconies, courtyards, and the type of aristocratic residence that author Gabriel García Márquez, a part-time Cartagena resident, writes about—make this a popular stop for cruise ships. And because the city is situated right along the Equator, the temperature is a perfect 85 to 95 degrees year-round.

You'll visit the San Felipe Fortress, the historic Central District, the Gold Museum, and the major cathedrals. You can also soak in a volcanic mud bath (see sidebar p. 59) and take dancing and cooking lessons. A one-hour boat ride will take you to the Rosary and San Bernardo islands, a group of about 30 islands that Colombia's government declared a marine national park in 1977. The Parque Nacional Corales del Rosario y de San Bernardo includes an environmental trail and an *ocenario,* or open-water aquarium, with dolphins, sharks, turtles, and a host of other reef creatures.

This AFC volunteer trip runs $1,200 for double accommodation at Hotel Costa del Sol, a four-star hotel on Cartagena Bay, and 14 meals.

HOW TO GET IN TOUCH

Ambassadors for Children, 40 Virginia Avenue, Indianapolis, IN 46204, 866-388-3468 or 317-536-0250, www.ambassadorsforchildren.org.

help *campesinos* harvest coffee beans

NICARAGUA

> I pity the man who wants a coat so cheap that the man or woman
> who produces the cloth will starve in the process.
> —Benjamin Harrison, 23rd President of the United States

18 Coffee is the world's second most valuable traded commodity (petroleum is first), with 25 million farmers and coffee workers in more than 50 countries around the world.

And even though the United States consumes one-fifth of the 12 billion pounds of coffee produced each year, few Americans realize that the people who grow their precious morning wake-me-up often toil in what some observers have described as "sweatshops in the fields." What's even worse, amid a volatile market, many small coffee farmers receive less for their coffee than it costs to produce. Some years, farmers (*campesinos*) are forced into debt, which makes it impossible for them to break out of an endless cycle of poverty and also makes it difficult for them to provide adequate food for their families.

Global Exchange is a San Francisco-based nonprofit that organizes socially and politically conscious tours, which they call Reality Tours, to more than 30 countries in Latin America, Africa, Asia, and the Middle East. Every December, it sends coffee pickers to Nicaragua to work at a fair-trade coffee cooperative, La Central de Cooperativas Cafetaleras del Norte (CECOCAFEN). Volunteers live with a family and work alongside the farmers to harvest the coffee, as well as learn about the global issues involved in coffee and fair trade.

Fair-trade practices give small farmers a seat at the bargaining table. It keeps them from being exploited by global corporations that sometimes insist they take the price offered for their coffee beans, even when it is clearly inadequate pay for their labor and their product. Instead, fair-trade importers offer small-scale farmers a minimum price per pound and provide them with credit and technical assistance.

ONLINE COFFEE SHOP

Okay, so you're not quite ready to travel to Nicaragua to pick coffee beans, but you are willing to put your money where your heart is. Global Exchange operates three brick-and-mortar stores (one each in San Francisco and Berkeley, California, and one in Portland, Oregon) and an online store that sell fair-trade products from 40 countries around the world.

The online store, which celebrated its tenth anniversary in 2008, offers such products as:

- mother-of-pearl boxes from Egypt
- crocheted necklaces from Argentina
- baby slippers made by Thailand's Lisu tribe
- finger puppets from a Peruvian village on the shores of Lake Titicaca
- baskets woven by Zulu artisans
- sweatshop-free sneakers from Pakistan
- leatherbound journals from India
- laptop bags made by survivors of genocidal rape in Rwanda.

As for their fair-trade coffee shop, they sell a wide variety of coffees from companies such as Cloudforest, Dean's Beans, Equal Exchange, Global Giving, and Peace Coffee. They also sell Thanksgiving Coffee Company's Gorilla Coffee, which supports both farmer-owned cooperatives in Rwanda and the Dian Fossey Gorilla Fund.

Check out all the goods at www.globalexchangestore.org.

According to Global Exchange, "To become fair trade certified, an importer must meet stringent international criteria; paying a minimum price per pound of $1.26, providing much needed credit to farmers, and providing technical assistance such as help transitioning to organic farming. Fair trade for coffee farmers means community development, health, education, and environmental stewardship."

One of the most troubling issues facing millions of coffee farmers is the recent precipitous drop in global coffee prices. Since 1998, prices have plummeted 50 percent, leaving more than a quarter of a million Nicaraguans destitute. Many live in makeshift roadside camps and some are suffering from malnutrition as a result of the reduced income.

On this once-a-year Global Exchange coffee harvest trip, you'll not only pick coffee beans (a task that begins bright and early each morning at 5), but you'll help the families at the cooperative depulp, ferment, wash, dry, and sort the morning's harvest. Participants must have at least basic Spanish language ability and be self-reliant people who are not afraid of challenging situations.

While the coffee you pick on this eight-day journey is important, your most important job—the place where you can make the most difference—awaits back at home. Being an advocate in your community for fair trade may include talking to the media, giving presentations, writing articles, and urging your local stores to offer fair-trade products. While they might cost more, knowing that farmers and craftspeople are being given a fair shake is worth a little extra expense.

You will experience life on an *upe* (coffee cooperative) in Matagalpa, a misty, mountainous region in the north of Nicaragua, and meet with community leaders. While you're there, you'll also get to visit such nature sites as the Yasica waterfall, hike the Poza Bruja Trail, and learn to cook typical Nicaraguan food.

The cost for eight nights' accommodation, all breakfasts and dinners, sightseeing excursions, the services of a translator, and transportation on a private bus runs $950.

HOW TO GET IN TOUCH

Global Exchange, 2017 Mission Street, 2nd Floor, San Francisco, CA 94110, 415-255-7296 or 800-497-1994, www.globalexchange.org.

build lifesaving lorena stoves in a remote peruvian village

SAN PEDRO DE CASTA, PERU

There comes a point in a person's life when you start asking yourself,
"What difference am I making in this world?"
—Gayle Harrod, Globe Aware volunteer to Peru

19 Perched high in the Andes, 11,000 feet above sea level, San Pedro de Casta is a traditional Peruvian village. Its 4,000 residents eke out a communal living here by farming the terraced fields carved into the slopes of the surrounding mountains, just as their ancestors have done for thousands of years before them.

Unfortunately, many of them also still cook just like their ancestors did—on three-rock stoves that pour smoke through their homes and cause life-shortening lung and eye problems. Asthma, emphysema, and other pulmonary problems are rampant in many Peruvian villages, not to mention the devastating effects of deforestation and erosion caused by chopping down all the trees that provide the wood for the stoves.

The World Health Organization reports that cooking and heating on open fires or stoves without chimneys is directly responsible for 1.5 million deaths per year worldwide—most of them due to acute respiratory infections in children under the age of five. The indoor air pollution that results from these methods of cooking and heating is also responsible for increased incidences of death linked to many diseases, including pneumonia among children and respiratory diseases, such as chronic obstructive pulmonary disease (COPD), among adults.

Globe Aware, a nonprofit based in Dallas, Texas, that offers what they call "mini Peace Corps assignments" in 14 countries, sends volunteers to San Pedro de Casta to work on community development projects ranging from repairing buildings, establishing irrigation channels for the schools, encouraging reforestation, and teaching English, computer skills, and first aid.

They also build rammed-earth adobe stoves that kill three birds with one small stone. A *lorena* stove that vents smoke through a chimney dramatically improves a family's health, reduces poverty (because it's energy efficient, it saves money—one-fifth of their incomes go toward harvesting and buying wood), and eases the burden on local forests. But perhaps the stove's finest feature is that it can be made easily and cheaply from local mud and sand. The stove's name, lorena, in fact, come from two Spanish words: *lodo* (mud) and *arena* (sand).

Besides building lorena stoves, Globe Aware volunteers work on a variety of community development projects in the village, from teaching English to planting

---

PISCO, THE NATIONAL DRINK

It wasn't enough for Chile to become world-renowned for its wine. Now, it's claiming ownership of pisco, the clear, Peruvian brandy that's drunk neat and in the infamous pisco sour. Both countries call pisco their national drink. It should be noted, however that Pisco Elqui—the village in Chile that now claims ownership of the beverage—was called La Union until 1936 when its name was changed by government order. Yet Chile produces more than 50 times the pisco that Peru produces annually.

On the other hand, Pisco, Peru, asserts that it has been making the rich grape brandy since early in the Spanish viceroyalty, which began in 1524 and ended in 1824.

Alas, the contentious pisco title is unlikely to be decided anytime soon. In the meantime, if you'd like to have a drink while you ponder the question, here's the recipe for a pisco sour.

1 part freshly squeezed lime juice
3 parts pisco
Ice
Sugar to taste
1 teaspoon egg white (for frothiness)

Combine the lime juice and pisco in a blender. Add sugar to taste. Add plenty of ice and blend. Spoon in egg white and blend again.

Some recipes use simple syrup instead of sugar and some include a dash of bitters, as well. Others use a cocktail shaker to blend the drink and discard the ice before serving the pisco sour. There are four varieties of pisco: pisco puro, pisco acholado, pisco aromático, and pisco mosto verde, with the latter being the most expensive.

trees to establishing irrigation channels. Since San Pedro de Casta is at a high altitude, you must check with your doctor before deciding to go if you have high blood pressure or a respiratory condition, or if you have ever had difficulty adjusting in higher altitudes.

Located four hours from Lima, this quaint, secluded village doesn't attract a lot of tourists. The few who do visit (there are only three tiny hotels, one of which doubles as the schoolteacher's house) are probably on their way to the plateau of Marcahuasi, a weird "forest of rocks" whose shapes, say the locals, change at various times of day.

Globe Aware plans a full week of activities, including horseback rides to Marcahuasi, visits to the cheesemaker and hatmaker, and Andean craft and cooking classes. You'll learn to make *hualquies* (pouches that are made for carrying coca leaves) and see Inca mummies at the local museum.

A one-week trip, including shared lodging in the central village lodge on Plaza de Armas—the town square—and three meals made with fresh veggies and beans from the surrounding hills, costs $1,250.

HOW TO GET IN TOUCH
Globe Aware, 6500 East Mockingbird Lane, Suite 104, Dallas, TX 75214, 877-588-4562, www.globeaware.com.

throw a christmas bash
for an indigenous village

COSTA RICA

Life's most persistent and urgent question is
"What are you doing for others?"
—Martin Luther King, Jr., clergyman and civil rights activist

20 A volunteer vacation with the Tropical Adventures Foundation is more like joining a family than taking a trip. No matter which of the Costa Rica-based organization's 15 projects you decide to undertake, just know that you'll probably feel connected to the families you work with forever.

Isaac Garcia started Tropical Adventures (TA) with American Scott Parlinsky, who serves as executive director of the organization. Garcia, director of volunteer services at TA, says, "Besides the sheer beauty of the country itself, I think people are really blown away by the authenticity, warmth, and generosity of the Costa Rican people. Almost 100 percent of our volunteers leave in tears, having made new friends for life. And a good majority of them come back to visit. It's really like we have created a big, international family. I love it!"

In 2007, Tropical Adventures decided to throw Christmas parties for the people in the Costa Rican communities where volunteers live and work. They figured that since the volunteers, who were joined at the hip with the host families they lived with, were going to send presents anyway, why not make it official and go all out? During the year, volunteers monitor sea turtles, work at iguana farms, teach English, garden, translate for tour guides, and help with injured monkeys. But because they live and eat with host families, who are doing the same work alongside them, they bond deep and fast.

The average Tico makes less than $500 a month. Obviously, there's not a lot left to put presents under the tree at Christmas. Tourists, with their disproportionately fat wallets, drive prices up and out of reach for local people. Presents received at the 2007 party were the first ones some children ever received.

CLUB MUD

After 400 years of peace and quiet, Costa Rica's Arenal Volcano erupted in spectacular, deadly fashion in 1968, killing 87 people. More moderate activity at the volcano hasn't really stopped since then, making it one of the 10 most active volcanoes in the world. It's a safe bet to think you'll get to see lava flows while you're here.

The glass half full aspect of living next to a volcano that spews a continuous supply of hot ash, steam, and lava, however, is the hot springs. There are a range of commercial hot springs you can soak in around the Arenal region, with settings ranging from basic to highly luxurious. Several local resorts, like the Baldi Hot Springs Hotel & Spa La Fortuna, Hotel Arenal Paraíso, and the Tabacón Grand Spa Thermal Resort, have hot springs on-site.

At our favorite hot springs, Eco Thermales, the temperatures of the four pools range from 91°F to 105°F. Run by a local family, it's secluded and only admits a hundred people per day. Doña Mireya Hidalgo, using a traditional, rustic kitchen, serves home-cooked Costa Rican meals in clay pots while howler monkeys look on. *Eco Thermales, near La Fortuna, 506 2 479 8484, $21 plus fee for dinner. Make a reservation in advance.*

The holiday parties, complete with presents, cakes, balloons, and, in one community, an inflatable bouncy slide, were such a rousing success that Pralinksy and Garcia and the rest of the TA gang have added it as a permanent volunteer project. As a volunteer, you'll help purchase, wrap, and deliver gifts, as well as plan activities and decorate. If you come for the whole holiday season, you'll also get to celebrate in several parts of the country.

In 2008, the parties centered on the theme of education. TA collected—or purchased with donated funds—items such as knapsacks, lunch bags, school uniforms, art supplies, pencil cases, pens, pencils, highlighters, markers, crayons, coloring books, Play-Doh, glue sticks, paper, notebooks, books, educational DVDs, English teaching materials, educational games, dictionaries (Spanish and Spanish-to-English), and geometry tools to distribute to the Costa Rican children.

Located on the Central American isthmus, between the Pacific Ocean and the Caribbean Sea, Costa Rica is one big outdoor playground. There are waterfalls, animals, beaches, volcanoes, hot springs, butterflies, jungles, rivers, and lots of friendly people. It's the oldest democracy in Latin America with more than a hundred years of political stability, all without a military. Tropical Adventures operates in the Central Valley, in Puerto Viejo on the Caribbean coast, on the Talamanca Indigenous Reservation, and in Guanacaste in the Pacific northwest.

If you look at the second word in this nonprofit's moniker, it should be no big surprise that volunteers also partake of such adventures as riding zip lines through jungle canopies, kayaking, river rafting, snorkeling, horseback riding, surfing swimming, and hiking.

A one-week stay, including accommodations and three healthful, hearty meals with a host family, runs $995. Tropical Adventures recommends staying at least two weeks, however, which runs $1,895. Additional weeks can be added for $299. The holiday project trip, like all TA trips, is flexible and can start and end at your convenience.

HOW TO GET IN TOUCH

Tropical Adventures Foundation, Apartado 8–7100, Paraiso, Cartago, Costa Rica, 506 2 574 4412, www.tropicaladventures.com; U.S. contact: 1775 East Palm Canyon Drive, Suite 110–341, Palm Springs, CA 92264, 800-832-9419.

work in an argentine soup kitchen

BUENOS AIRES, ARGENTINA

To ease another's heartache is to forget one's own.
—Abraham Lincoln, 16th President of the United States

21 A hundred years ago, Argentina was one of the wealthiest countries in the world. But by 2001, after a series of political and economic crises, the government was forced to default on $93 billion in debt, the biggest default in world history, plunging the country into a deep depression. After considerable upheaval, Governor Néstor Kirchner was elected president in May 2003. During his term, Argentina invested in public works, restructured its defaulted debt, paid off other debt, reworked utilities contracts, and nationalized some private entities.

In the past five years, Argentina has been enjoying economic growth again. Yet despite his popularity, Kirchner chose not to run for reelection as his term was drawing to a close in 2007. Instead, he supported the campaign of his wife, Senator Cristina Fernández de Kirchner. After winning the October 2007 election by a landslide, the senator became Argentina's first female president. She began her four-year term on December 10, 2007.

Unfortunately, Argentina's once-solid middle class has yet to fully recover from the fallout of the economic crisis. Many still live in poverty with limited access to education, health care, and good-paying jobs. The gap between the rich and the poor has become nearly as wide as the country that makes up nearly the entire bottom half of the South American continent is long.

That's the bad news. The good news is that Argentina, as a country, still possesses extreme natural beauty, a lively, refined culture, great restaurants, nightlife, and shopping. Only now, thanks to its once devalued currency, it's all the more affordable for those who still have money, or are coming from outside the country.

Despite Argentina's economic rebound, as many as a hundred Argentines die of malnutrition every day. For many of the country's 38 million people, soup kitchens—

which have sprung up everywhere—provide the only daily nourishment. In 2006, controversial activist Raúl Castells even opened a community kitchen in the middle of swanky Puerto Madero, the former docks turned "it" place to live. Visitors at

the Buenos Aires Hilton or local upscale restaurants could see a huge sign emblazoned with his slogan, *"Luchamos por una Argentina donde los perros de los ricos dejen de estar mejor alimentados que los hijos de los pobres,"* or "We are fighting for an Argentina where the dogs of the rich are no longer fed better than the children of the poor."

IT TAKES TWO

Confucius said a nation's character is defined by its dancers. Argentina, which invented the sassy, improvisational tango, certainly would have to agree. Historically, the now world-famous tango was one of the first dances where partners were actually allowed to touch each other (only the Viennese waltz and the polka came first). It is hard to separate Argentina's history from the brash dance that began in the disregarded periphery of the culture and gradually worked its way into polite society and, indeed, into the consciousness of the whole world.

The tango, in fact, was so popular in Argentina that after the 1955 coup that ousted Gen. Juan Perón, the new military government, in a knee-jerk reaction, imprisoned and blacklisted many tango artists with Peronist ties (perceived or real). In its antinationalist fervor, the new government imposed curfews, changed tango lyrics and titles, and banned meetings of more than three people. To the wealthy members of the new regime, gatherings of large numbers of dancers seemed suspicious, an obvious cover for political agitation.

After the 1983 fall of the military junta, a spectacular tango renaissance occurred. Today, a tango fan can choose from among three dozen *milongas* each day in Buenos Aires alone. A milonga, in case you're new to the addictive dance, are places where tango is danced. A milonga typically offers classes and a few demonstrations before the first *tanda*, three to five dances in a row, begins. Tandas are separated by a *cortina*, a musical break when the floor is cleared and new partners are chosen.

According to tango aficionados, there are numerous styles of tango, including Canyengue, Club, Salon, Fantasia, Liso, Milonguero, Nuevo, and Orillero. Ballroom tango comes in two styles, American and international. There's even a style called Finnish Tango, unique to that country, which was profiled by Morley Safer on *60 Minutes* in 1993.

On this volunteer trip sponsored by Center for Cultural Interchange, a Chicago-based nonprofit that organizes internships, language study, home stays, and volunteer programs in more than 30 countries, you will help prepare and distribute meals. You also will provide emotional support, legal assistance, and basic skills workshops to homeless people. A veritable United Nations of volunteers show up in Argentina every year to lend a hand and experience the passionate culture and people who are busy churning lemonade out of the lemons they were handed.

Cosmopolitan Buenos Aires, where you'll be volunteering, has French architecture, Italian heritage, and a nickname that gives away its European lifestyle: "The Paris of South America." In fact, Mom's Kitchen, the soup kitchen where you'll work, is in Recoleta, an area resembling Paris that is known for its squares, parks, cafés, and galleries. In your free time, excursions will take you to Rosedal, Buenos Aires' most famous park, to the bohemian San Telmo Market, and the Plaza de Mayo, the epicenter of Argentina's colorful political history.

For this project, the minimum commitment is three weeks, and you must want to work with the homeless population. An intermediate level of Spanish is required; Spanish lessons are available prior to the volunteer project in Buenos Aires for an additional fee. You'll live with a host family, and, except for Sundays, be provided with two meals per day. The fee for volunteering at the soup kitchen for three weeks is $1,490. For the maximum commitment of 12 weeks, the fee is $3,510.

Other Center for Cultural Interchange projects in Argentina range from two to twelve weeks and start at $1,290.

HOW TO GET IN TOUCH

Center for Cultural Interchange, c/o Greenheart, 712 North Wells Street, 4th floor, Chicago, IL 60657, 888-227-6231 or 312-944-2544, www .greenhearttravel.org.

collect butterflies in remote amazonia

HUAORANI RESERVE, ECUADOR

> When we try to pick out anything by itself,
> we find it hitched to everything else in the Universe.
> —John Muir, Scottish-born American naturalist,
> *My First Summer in the Sierra*

22 It takes four hours by motorized canoe to get to this remote biological research station in the Ecuadorian Amazon. And that's after you take a 10- to 17-hour bus ride from Quito to Coca, followed by a three-hour car ride to Rio Shiripuno. Remote might be an understatement, in fact, as the nearest telephone connection and Internet hookup are in Coca. At night, if you want to read over the data you have collected that day, you'll do so by candlelight, as there is no electricity.

The Shiripuno Research Center, located 45 miles southeast of Coca, is just outside the Yasuni National Park, a designated UNESCO biosphere. The Huaorani, the fiercely protective indigenous people of this region, still hunt monkeys, deer, and wild pigs with blow guns and poison-tipped darts. But when it comes to cataloging, and, hopefully, preserving biodiversity, this rain forest outpost is without peer. So far, Jarol Fernando Vaca and his volunteers at the Shiripuno Research Center have cataloged 600 species of butterflies and 450 species of birds.

Vaca, who was born in the Amazonian village of Misahualli, has been in love with nature since he was 14 and invited to help out with a local bird survey. By 16, he was guiding treks into his jungle homeland, serving as a naturalist at Yasuni National Park. With funding from National Geographic and the American Birdsong Association, he has been able to establish his own legacy at the biological reserve he started. Its mission? To stem the alarming decrease in butterfly populations whose habitats are being chopped down to the tune of a football field–size piece of jungle every second of every day.

EMBODYING ECOTOURISM

Not far from the Shiripuno Research Center is Yachana Lodge, an 18-room ecolodge built by American expatriate Douglas McMeekin, who started the project with three goals: He wanted to save the rain forest, create jobs, and establish a health clinic for the 8,000 people who live along the Napo River. Since 1994, Yachana (formerly Funedesin) has purchased and protected more than 4,300 acres of primary and secondary rain forest. Yachana is a Quichua word that means "a place for learning," and all of the foundation's endeavors live up to that moniker.

In 2000, as a way to create more jobs, McMeekin joined forces with Juan Kunchikuy, an Amazonian blowgun hunter, on yet another altruistic business. Yachana Gourmet (www.yachanagourmet.com) makes what they call jungle chocolates, fair trade treats made from cacao beans grown in the nearby rain forest. Yachana pays fair market price to the 1,200 small family farmers they've taught to grow cacao beans.

In May 2008, McMeekin told Nicholas Kristof of the *New York Times*, "People have to make a living . . . But they can chop down 50 acres of forest to make a pasture, or they can earn the same income by chopping down 5 acres and planting cacao."

In June 2008, Yachana was one of three winners in the Geotourism Challenge sponsored by Ashoka (www.ashoka.org) and National Geographic. Here's how they responded to one application question, "How does your approach support or embody geotourism?"

"The Yachana Technical High School opened in September 2005, addressing a need on a regional basis for a practical, hands-on education for poor youth from the Amazon region of Ecuador. It is the only school in Ecuador offering a degree in Eco-tourism and Sustainable Development, approved by the Ministry of Education. The Yachana Lodge opened in 1995 and now the two entities are combined under the umbrella of the Yachana Foundation. The school has 128 students, 80 percent indigenous, from five provinces and four ethnic groups. The students are involved in cultural programs for the Lodge guests. The newest program being our Amazon Culinary tour where our guests harvest and prepare Amazonian foods with our students. All of the students work in the Lodge as part of their education, interacting with our national and international guests. A cultural interchange that both groups enjoy. The school provides a large percentage of the food for the Lodge and the Lodge is the major supporter of the school. All of our guests visit our 4,300 acres of protected rain forest that is also the living classroom of the students." *Yachana Foundation, administrative offices: Vicente Solano E12–61 y Avenida Oriental, Quito, Pichincha, Ecuador, 593 2 252 3777, www.yachana.org.ec.; U.S. contact: 888-922-4262.*

Lepidopterists claim butterflies, often the first to suffer and disappear when natural habitats become stressed, are the proverbial canaries in the coal mines. Although butterflies, as a species, are generally well understood, the neotropical butterflies of this region, estimated to be as high as 4,000 different species, have yet to be properly documented, and studied.

As a volunteer at the Shiripuno Research Center, you'll rear caterpillars, collect field data, create trails, put up signs, and lead tours. During the first week of each month, you'll bring down butterfly traps, resupply them with food, and collect and identify all butterflies captured that month from the jungle canopy. During the other three weeks of your monthlong stint, you'll have the opportunity to participate in other surveys being conducted at Shiripuno, which range from medicinal plants to Amazonian birds. All volunteers are required to write and file field reports.

You'll be serenaded at night by tree frogs, entertained by seven species of monkeys, and given the chance to hike trails cut through the jungle by tapirs, peccaries, and jaguars. Every walk is a potential adventure, unpredictable and unlike the walk before.

If you don't have at least an intermediate command of the Spanish language, Ecuador Volunteer will bring your language skills up to snuff with a program before your volunteer stint begins. The monthlong program costs $1,280 and includes shared lodging in a dorm with mosquito netting and three meals per day. This is a rustic outpost, though, with no hot water or electricity.

HOW TO GET IN TOUCH
Ecuador Volunteer, Yánez Pinzón N25-106 y Av. Colón, Quito, Ecuador, 593 2 2557749, www.ecuadorvolunteer.org.

track jaguars

It was as if I was participating in a fascinating tropical biology lesson,
with an element of adventure in it.
—Dagmara Wróbel, volunteer with Ecovolunteer's Jaguar Project

23 Less than a thousand people per year get the privilege of seeing a jaguar—the largest cat in the Americas—in the wild. The Convention on International Trade in Endangered Species (CITES) claims there are only 50,000 mature breeding cats left. Conservationists believe jaguars, already endangered, stand a good chance of being wiped out completely in this region. These elusive cats' habitats are shrinking, even in the Pantanal, a 68,000-square-mile primordial floodplain of the Paraguay River, with swamps, grasslands, and forests on the edge of Brazil, bordering Bolivia.

One side effect of the the big cats' loss of habitat is that they are being tracked down and shot by maverick cattle ranchers who are trying to protect their livelihoods. The ranchers report losing as much as 5 percent of their herds each year to the spotted predator, so they couldn't care less about the hunting ban intended to protect the dwindling population of jaguars. As far as they're concerned, the Pantanal's population of 4,000 to 7,000 jaguars represents nothing more than an annoyance entering their pastures to feed.

Ecovolunteer, an international group with wildlife conservation projects in Africa, Asia, Europe, North America, and South America, sends volunteers here to work with scientists who are trying to determine accurate estimations of the area's predator population (besides the jaguars, there are also pumas and ocelots) and to figure out their territories and habits. By studying the behaviors of the jaguar, there's hope that the ranchers and the conservationists can devise some kind of win-win solution for minimizing predation losses. Ultimately, they hope to come up with a workable plan for the coexistence of cattle and jaguars.

As a volunteer on this important research project, you'll be on a private working ranch, or *fazenda,* with 5,000 head of cattle located near the town of Miranda. You'll spend days riding the ranges (usually on horseback), looking for hints of this lone cat's existence. Working alongside Ph.D. candidate Fernando Azevedo and his research staff, you'll capture jaguars, fit them with radio collars, and keep detailed records of their habits and movements. You will also be involved in helping the local people to improve their livestock management and to minimize the predation of livestock in private lands.

Normally you will be working about ten hours a day or night, depending on the animals' movements. You'll wake every morning to the call of endangered hyacinth macaws that roost in trees by the bunkhouse. You might pass endangered jabiru storks on your walk to the stables. While you're at the ranch, you'll probably see at least some of the following local denizens: anacondas, anteaters, armadillos, caimans, capybaras, coatis, crab-eating foxes and raccoons, egrets, giant otters, green parakeets, herons, howler monkeys, ibis, marsh deer, peccaries, toucans, red and green macaws, and storks.

Robin Mooney, who volunteered on the fazenda in June 2007, described sighting a jaguar with her team: "One of the highlights of this trip was when we interrupted a female jaguar feeding on a freshly killed feral pig. Although she darted into the bushes before we could get a good look at her, we knew she was still very close and was watching us as we examined the carcass. That afternoon we went back to set camera traps and were rewarded the next day with pictures of her when she came back to finish her meal. I didn't need to see her in person in order to appreciate her beauty and power. Just knowing that I had been in her presence was enough for me. After all, if jaguars were meant to be seen, they would never have survived this long."

You must have a working knowledge of English, Portuguese, or Spanish and be at least 21 years old for this project, which accepts up to four volunteers at a time. The two-week project, including simple accommodations at the research base and three meals a day, runs $1,062. Additional weeks can be added for $405 per week.

HOW TO GET IN TOUCH

Ecovolunteer (www.ecovolunteer.org) books trips for American and Canadian volunteers through the **Great Canadian Travel Company,** 158 Fort Street, Winnipeg, Manitoba R3C 1C9, Canada, 800-661-3830, www.greatcanadiantravel.com.

lead walks through a cloud forest

LA TIGRA, HONDURAS

Sentiment without action is the ruin of the soul.
—Edward Abbey, environmental author and essayist

24 The belt of cloud forest that stretches across Central America into South America is slowly shrinking. It's being cleared for cattle grazing, logged to provide fuel for heating and cooking, and paved over to make roads and hotels for tourists. While the cloud forests of Costa Rica and Guatemala have gotten the lion's share of the glory, Honduras is finally standing up to better publicize its own natural realms. In fact, the country has more virgin cloud forests than any country in Central America.

In the 1880s, the New York and Honduras Rosario Mining Company plowed a destructive road from Tegucigalpa to La Rosaria. Nearby San Juancito grew into a mining boom town, much to the detriment of the surrounding forests. After the

BEFORE THE SPANISH INQUISITION

Copán, the most artistically advanced of the known Maya cities, is 40 acres of archaeology heaven. Though Copán was discovered in 1570 by Diego García de Palacio, the ruins were not excavated until the 19th century. According to UNESCO, which designated it a World Heritage site in 1980, "The ruined citadel and imposing public squares reveal the three main stages of development before the city was abandoned in the early tenth century."

Located in Honduras near the Guatemalan border, the 250-acre site has more than 4,000 structures, including temples, stelae, plazas, huge pyramids, a central structure referred to as the Acropolis, a Maya ball court, miles of underground tunnels, and a hieroglyphic stairway. What's that last one, you ask? It's an enormous staircase with more than a thousand carvings representing the city's extensive history.

mine closed in the 1950s, the government stepped in to preserve the area's precious cloud forests. Today, 13 of the country's largest 40 cloud forests are protected in national parks, where they provide fresh, clean, and already filtered water.

As a biodiversity hot spot, Honduras is home to more than 700 species of birds, including the harpy eagle and the quetzal. It also has jaguars, ocelots, pumas, tapirs, giant anteaters, and mantled howler monkeys, many of which prowl La Tigra National Park, the country's first national park and its largest cloud forest park. Unfortunately, the park lacks funding and has a grand total of two park rangers at its lowest staffing levels. Even though visitors are limited to 70 per day, it still takes more than four hands to maintain a cloud forest, especially one with this much diversity.

Luckily, i-to-i, a British-based company with a U.S. office in Seattle, sends volunteers to help out at La Tigra. Volunteers lead nature walks, patrol for illegal logging, make and repair signs, and help clear the six hiking paths that zigzag through this insanely lush pocket of ferns, orchids, vines, and bromeliads, many of which exist nowhere else. La Cascada Trail, the park's longest at 6 miles, winds by a waterfall and crosses from one entrance of the park to the other.

You will also plant trees and tend those growing in a nursery, as the park is undergoing a major reforestation project in order to reduce the strain on its forests. Within La Tigra's confines, there are 87 communities, and all of them need wood to survive. The park has instituted a carbon offset program to supply firewood for the families' wood-burning ovens.

La Tigra is a short hop, skip, and jump from the capital of Tegucigalpa, also known as Tegus (pronounced Teh-GOOS), which has parks, museums, churches, and colonial architecture galore. Your humble residence at the park also provides the perfect launching pad for visiting Honduran crafts villages and the beaches and scuba diving haunts of the Bay Islands.

Volunteers live inside the park in the miner's camp hospital, which has been converted into a dorm. One week runs $965—every week thereafter is $270, with a maximum stay of 12 weeks—for dorm accommodations and breakfast and dinner each day.

HOW TO GET IN TOUCH

i-to-i North America, 458 Wheeler Street, Seattle, WA 98109, 800-985-4864, www.i-to-i.com.

ANOTHER THOUGHTFUL, COMMITTED CITIZEN: GRACE STEIN

Before Grace Stein turned 18, she had already spent two summers volunteering outside the United States. In 2007, before her junior year at Shining Mountain Waldorf School in Boulder, Colorado, she spent five weeks building a school in Nicaragua. Stein and the 13 teens she traveled with raised all the money they'd need to build the school and fund their expenses. They sent out letters, held auctions, and hosted music events. "We were recruited by the leader of the sister city program [Jalapa, Nicaragua, is one of Boulder's six sister cities]," she explained. "She showed a film at our school about people in Nicaragua who live on a landfill. I was crying by the end of it."

Still, Stein was a bit hesitant about taking the trip. "I was afraid I'd miss a lot by being out of the country," she said. "Plus, I'd never really been out of the country, not to a third world country anyway. I'd been to Mexico with my parents, but this was different. I wasn't sure how I was going to handle it."

She lived with a Nicaraguan family in a tiny house, slept on a wooden plank, ate beans and rice at every meal, and confronted cockroaches every time she went to the bathroom. "I loved that I was helping, that I was making a difference in the lives of these children," Stein said. "I came home from that trip and I knew what I was going to do in my life."

And as for those things she thought she'd miss out on? "When I got back, everyone and everything was exactly the same..." she said. "I've always been mature for my age and conscious of what's around me. But this really opened my eyes. I realized Americans aren't very full."

The Nicaragua trip gave Stein the confidence to go it alone for her 2008 trip to Peru's Sacred Valley to teach English. "My parents suggested I take a friend, but I wanted to be able to immerse myself in my own situation, to be responsible entirely for myself," she said. Through Projects Abroad, a U.K.-based company that organizes volunteer trips to 24 countries, Grace served as head English teacher in Pisac, near Cuzco.

"I had hoped to teach young kids, but I ended up teaching kids of all ages— some that were my age or older," Stein said. And she was surprised to see how appreciative they were. "They're grateful for everything. Even something small," she remarked. "I'd give stickers to boys who were 17 or 18 and they'd be over the moon. We'd be singing the theme song to *Titanic* and everybody would stand up and sing and dance. Kids here would never do that."

The trips have reshaped Stein's worldview. "Volunteering in other countries puts everything in perspective," she mused. "We're privileged in Boulder. Everyone has clothes and food and cell phones and computers. We hear about starving kids. But to actually see it is huge."

produce the news

Journalism can never be silent: that is its greatest virtue and its greatest
fault. It must speak, and speak immediately, while the echoes of wonder,
the claims of triumph and the signs of horror are still in the air.
—Henry Anatole Grunwald, former editor of *Time*

25 Thomas Jefferson said that given the choice of a
government without newspapers or newspapers
without government, he'd pick the latter.

The *Cocha Banner,* an English newspaper in Cochabamba, Bolivia, keeps the government honest and gives lin-
guistics students at the Universidad Mayor de San Simón the
chance to practice their English skills. Yet it also gives international
interns who are working journalists or contemplating journalism as a career or
study option the chance to gain some fantastic work experience abroad and add to
their portfolios while living in one of the most vibrant countries in Latin America.

The monthly newspaper was started by Projects Abroad, a volunteer organization
with projects in 23 countries, and it offers a mix of reviews, stories, poetry, and
letters. Volunteers who come to work on this project will write, take photos, and
work side by side with Cochabambinos who need someone proficient in English to
answer the language-learner's perpetual question, "How do you say…?"

Projects Abroad offers two-week- or monthlong print journalism internships.
Print interns will be involved in every aspect of producing a paper, from reporting
stories and interviewing people to writing and editing articles to designing and laying
out a publication. You'll work with local reporters and, if you're up for it, freelance
for *Los Tiempos,* the biggest Spanish-speaking newspaper in Cochabamba.

Volunteer Minato Kobori described his internship as follows: "I knew very little
about Bolivia and even less about journalism when I arrived…. I wanted to have a
totally new experience. I let the culture of Bolivia sink in everyday and at the same
time learned different things as a journalist. Every single day my eyes were opened."

Anyone who is fluent in Spanish can instead choose a broadcast internship that lets him or her work on-air at a local Cochabamba radio station. Radio Del Valle is based just ten minutes from the Projects Abroad office, and the station's owner, Dr. Antonio Revollo, welcomes two volunteers at a time. You must be confident enough to read articles on-air and compile your own stories. You'll also assist in the production booth, participate in live discussion programs, conduct interviews with local people, and research stories by traveling around the city and possibly to nearby villages to track leads for stories, which you then write and broadcast live.

Cochabamba, a pulsating urban hub 8,000 feet above sea level, has one of the world's best climates—sunny days and cool crisp evenings. There's lots of nightlife, gorgeous plazas, the largest outdoor market in South America (La Cancha), and a university that attracts students from all around the world. Plus you're never more than a short plane ride from Bolivia's infinitely varying landscapes.

Projects Abroad also offers teaching and health-care opportunities at its Bolivian headquarters. In your free time, you can trek in the Andes, relax at Lake Titicaca, visit volcanoes, or explore the jungles of Chapare, rich with wildlife. Volunteers get three hours of Spanish lessons per week with students from the university.

You'll live and eat with a host family. A two-week trip, including three daily meals and a bed, runs $2,395; it's $2,995 to stay for a month.

HOW TO GET IN TOUCH
Projects Abroad, 347 West 36th Street, Suite 903, New York NY 10018, 888-839-3535, www.projects-abroad.org.

help create
patagonia national park

AYSEN, PATAGONIA, CHILE

> Each of us, at some point in our lives, will come to realize that
> most of the ordinary things we take for granted are, in fact,
> almost never permanent and, in fact, often fragile.
> —Kris Tompkins, head of Conservacion Patagonica

26 Patagonia, a wilderness area covering the southern tips of both Argentina and Chile, exists in a mostly unspoiled state, at least for the time being. Less than 5 percent of this vast landscape of fjords, glaciers, and ancient forests is protected, however, which means that at any time a corporation could snap up the rest of it and *poof!* there goes the neighborhood.

Kristine McDivitt Tompkins, who retired at 43 as CEO (and one of the founders) of the Patagonia clothing company, decided in 1993 that it was about time to guarantee that future generations would be able to witness this wild and untrammeled land. Her husband Douglas Tompkins, former CEO and co-founder of the North Face and co-founder of Esprit, had founded Conservation Land Trust, through which they created Pumalin Park in southern Chile. In 2000, Kris Tompkins founded Conservacion Patagonica (CP), a land trust that's working to buy and preserve as much of the area as it can. Between them, they can claim more than 2 million acres of land placed into conservation in Chile and Argentina.

In 2004, the Tompkinses found the buy of the century—a 173,000-acre sheep ranch in Chile that borders three already protected national reserves. Estancia Valley Chacabuco, the 85-year-old ranch that CP purchased on a wing and a prayer, will join the neighboring reserves to be protected forever as Patagonia National Park. Like many other large landholdings in Patagonia, Estancia Valley Chacabuco once was used to raise sheep and cattle, a business that takes a heavy toll on land and wildlife. Between erosion, logging, roadbuilding, and the introduction of exotic plant species, the ranch needs a good eight to ten years of work to complete its Cinderella-like transformation.

Volunteers work in groups of six alongside gauchos and Chilean scientists documenting native plants, collecting seeds, digging out fence posts, and removing non-native plants that, in some cases, have taken over entire hillsides. There are also cattle and sheep to remove, visitors centers to build, and power to derive from renewable sources. Work groups camp in a work area for about four days, then have two rest days. Work usually begins at 9 a.m., with a break for lunch around 12:30 p.m. After lunch, work begins again between 2 and 3 p.m. and continues until 5 or 6 p.m.

When it's finished, the park, with its magnificent steppes, beech forests, and mountain peaks, will represent the full range of Patagonia's natural diversity: grasslands, Andean foothills, the Andes themselves, and arid and semiarid Patagonian steppes. It is home to more than a hundred fauna species including the four-eyed Patagonian frog, nearly extinct huemul deer, and guanacos—camelids that are similar to llamas.

Digging posts can be backbreaking work, but on days off, volunteers can indulge in everything from fly-fishing to wine imbibing to long-distance cycling and hiking. A minimum stay of three weeks is recommended. An extensive gear list on the CP website will help you prepare for your trip.

For $40 a day (you can stay up to three months), you'll get housing and meals. Most volunteers come between October and May, Chile's spring and summer months.

HOW TO GET IN TOUCH

Conservacion Patagonica, Building 1062, Fort Cronkhite, Sausalito, CA 94965, 415-229-9339, www.conservacionpatagonica.org. The volunteer coordinator can be reached at 56 65 970833.

SISTER, SISTER, ARGENTINIAN SISTER

Before Estancia Valley Chacabuco came on the market, Conservacion Patagonica (CP) was busy across the border. In 2001, the land trust purchased the 155,000-acre Estancia Monte León, an Argentine sheep ranch located on the southern Atlantic shoreline a few hundred miles north of the Strait of Magellan. CP crafted a master plan for the ranch's transition to a national park and, in 2002, donated the property to the Argentine National Parks Administration, creating the country's first coastal national park. Monte León is known for its remarkable richness and diversity of species, including Magellanic penguins, sea lions, elephant seals, leopard seals, and migratory seabirds.

protect the resources of the indigenous pemón nation

LA GRAN SABANA, VENEZUELA

The Indian way of life gave me some understanding
of original contentedness and happiness.
—Frederick Heine, volunteer with Peace Villages

27 Thanks to abundant oil reserves discovered early in the 20th century, Venezuela is a wealthy nation. It has excellent roads, modern architecture, and a well-developed tourism infrastructure. But not everybody has reaped the benefits of the oil boom, most notably the indigenous people who live in the Gran Sabana region.

The Pemón Indians, an ethnic minority who are fiercely protective of their cultural identity and traditional way of life, face all sorts of 21st-century problems. Their tropical forests once covered more than a third of the Gran Sabana, but after three centuries of logging, mining, and cattle farming, their forest has been reduced to small areas of trees amid giant swaths of grasslands that show little propensity for regeneration.

Venezuelans who live near the Gran Sabana often refer to it as Second Africa. This moniker is certainly an appropriate nickname: The region's expansive grasslands are interrupted mainly by islands of tangled jungle and enormous mesas that rise dramatically over the savanna. The Pemón call them *tepuis,* which means "house of the spirits."

Fundación Aldeas de Paz (Peace Village Foundation), a nonprofit located in Santa Elena de Uairén, the capital of Gran Sabana, sends volunteers to a Pemón village where they can learn about the culture, pitch in with such chores as gathering yucca, and offer ideas for developing sustainable tourism, such as ecotourism and organic agriculture.

Manfred Mönninghoff, the easygoing German who started the Peace Village Foundation, spent several years volunteering in Europe, Asia, and other countries in South America before settling in Santa Elena. His nonprofit now attracts volunteers from across the world who work with children, build green buildings, provide horse therapy, and even have their own community radio show.

If you choose to work with the Pemón, you'll be located in Chirikayen, a village named after the tepui that serves as its backdrop. Located in a picturesque valley within Gran Sabana National Park, it's a bumpy hour-and-a-half drive from Santa Elena. Projects are flexible and range from indigenous gardening, planting trees, and researching and protecting wildlife to working with children in the school and teaching English. You might also shore up the community's infrastructure by performing maintenance work, or even initiate an environmental education program. Whatever you choose, just know you'll get a rare front row seat onto contemporary indigenous issues.

Fritz Reuter, a Peace Villages volunteer from Austria, described his volunteer experience as follows: "As you quickly realize, the Pemón of Chirikayen do everything with a smile on their faces, they also have an enviable philosophy of *'compartir.'* Every man and woman is an integral cog in the wheel and everything is done together as a community—working, eating, worshipping and socializing."

Amenities are very basic in Chirikayen, so be prepared for a simple, rugged way of life. There is electricity in the village for roughly three hours a day when a generator is run. Clothes are washed in the river, so you'll need to bring eco-friendly toiletries and laundry detergent.

You'll stay in family-style accommodations with locals (possibly the village chief), sleep in a hammock, and share three traditionally cooked meals a day. Dishes you might be served include *pabellon*, stewed and shredded meat with rice, black beans, and banana; *cachapa*, a sweet corn pancake served with cheese; and *arepas*, cornmeal bread topped with cheese, ham, or chicken.

Donation (it's all tax-deductible) is $835 for a week, $990 for two weeks, and $1,140 for three weeks.

HOW TO GET IN TOUCH

Fundación Aldeas de Paz, Centro Comunitario, Lomas de Piedra Canaima via Sampai, Santa Elena de Uairén, Código Postal 8032, La Gran Sabana, Estado Bolívar, Venezuela, 58 289 414 5721, www.peacevillages.org.

create an hiv/aids awareness campaign

> I have learned more about love, selflessness and human understanding
> in this great adventure in the world of AIDS than I ever did in
> the cut-throat, competitive world in which I spent my life.
> —Anthony Perkins, American actor

28 Everyone from members of the G-8 to U2 frontman Bono is working on the African AIDS crisis. But what about addressing the issue closer to home? The country of Belize, where every third person lives in poverty, has the highest rate of HIV/AIDS infection in Central America, and the second highest rate in the Caribbean.

The Cornerstone Foundation, a grassroots nonprofit started in 1989, uses volunteers to get the word out about HIV/AIDS. Volunteers who choose the HIV/AIDS outreach program, one of several volunteer opportunities offered by Cornerstone, spend two weeks creating a community awareness project. They work with a team resource leader, but the program is purposely loose and unstructured, giving creative types lots of leeway to use their imagination. Past volunteers have done everything from painting a mural on the wall of the local football stadium to creating puppet shows, from posting flyers in bar bathrooms to hosting school poster competitions or organizing AIDS Orphan March activities. It's a golden opportunity for anybody looking to develop skills in project management and community development.

According to Cornerstone, "Belize is a small country with a total population of around 300,000. Because of the high unemployment rates, Belize has an extremely mobile population; people living in one district and working in another…. This movement makes it difficult to address prevention through behavior change communication, which requires several meetings with an individual."

That means that reinforcing messages of prevention is even more important. The school system in Belize focuses on abstinence-only sex education, which has been proven ineffective. The Youth Ambassador Program allows young volunteers to address prevention in a peer-to-peer way, in hopes that the students they talk to will, in turn, take the prevention message to the wider community.

Nestled between Mexico and Guatemala, Belize offers an intriguing mix of tropical forest, majestic mountains, and mysterious Maya temples. San Ignacio (locally known as Cayo), where you'll be located, is a pretty little town right across the Guatemalan border. Archaeologists, Peace Corps types, and adventure travelers mix with the town's diverse populations of Creole, Maya, and Mestizo.

Spanish lessons are included in the program, as well as canoe trips down the Macal River and rain forest hikes to the ancient Maya sites of Xunantuich and Cahal Pech. Cornerstone will extend your monthlong tourist visa if you're game to work with bush doctors and natural healers, who will introduce you to ancient rain forest medicines. Volunteers can also address women's, children's, and disability issues in Belize.

The two-week HIV/AIDS community awareness program costs $599 and includes shared accommodations, hot daily lunches, transportation to and from the airport, and organized tours.

HOW TO GET IN TOUCH

Cornerstone Foundation, 90 Burns Avenue, P.O. Box 242, San Ignacio, Cayo District, Belize, www.cornerstonefoundationbelize.org.; U.S. contact: 501-678-9909.

SPELUNKING, BELIZE-STYLE

Even a jaded adventurer like Indiana Jones would probably be impressed with Belize's Actun Tunichil Muknal. Also called the Cave of the Stone Sepulcher, it has the stalagmites, stalactites, limestone flows, intriguing rock formations, and bats that are typical of most caves. But if you're daring and fit enough (there's a stream near the entrance you have to swim through) to venture farther in, you'll also find not just shards of ancient pottery, but hundreds of complete pre-Columbian vessels embedded into the cave's walls. Not to mention several skeletons, presumably remains from human sacrifices.

Although no one knows for sure, archaeologists have suggested that the ceramic pots were carried underground to collect *zuhuy ha* (virgin water) for Mayan ceremonies. Getting to this ancient wormhole to the netherland, located about 10 miles south of the village of Teakettle, involves three stream crossings and a strenuous hike through the Tapir Mountain Nature Reserve.

save the rain forest

PERU

> Now when you cut a forest, an ancient forest in particular,
> you are not just removing a lot of big trees and a few birds
> fluttering around in the canopy. You are drastically imperiling
> a vast array of species within a few square miles of you.
> —Edward O. Wilson, American biologist and
> Pulitzer Prize–winning author

29 Most tourists go to Peru to see Machu Picchu and learn about the ancient Inca. That's a lucky break for this volunteer vacation. The more camera-toting tourists who head for Machu Picchu, the less who tromp through the jungles of the Amazon Basin, the most diverse ecosystem in the world. In fact, Puerto Maldonado, where the ProNaturaleza butterfly farm is located, escaped development for just long enough that most of its natives understand and carefully guard the complex relationship between all animals (not just the human ones) that live down the Madre de Dios and Tambopata Rivers.

If you'd like to join them in conserving their unique spot on the planet, consider one of the following volunteer opportunities.

ProNaturaleza Butterfly Conservation Project. If you're one of those people who keeps a list of butterfly sightings the way some Audubon types keep lists of birds, this is the project for you. Since 2002, ProNaturaleza, a prominent Peruvian conservation organization, has been running a riverfront butterfly farm near the Puerto Maldonado airport. The farm, formerly named Tropical Insects and now called Japipi, was started six years earlier by a couple of self-taught scientist-entrepreneurs who raised and sold butterflies (this southern Peruvian rain forest has more than 1,230 species) to museums, zoos, and private collectors all over the world.

Volunteers assist in butterfly research studies and in environmental education programs. Being located so close to the airport, the center stays quite busy with tours and butterfly walks. Japipi's volunteers are trained by the center's scientists to find caterpillars and their feeding plants in the wild.

Volunteer packages with the ProNaturaleza Butterfly Project or other conservation projects sponsored by the group can last anywhere from one week to three months and include personalized training, field manuals, and excursions. In the case of longer packages, your stay might include field trips to nearby protected regions such as Tambopata National Reserve, Bahuaja Sonene, and Manu National Park. ProNaturaleza, which was formed in 1984 to protect and find sustainable uses for Peru's natural resources, seeks volunteers for field projects all over the country.

ProNaturaleza, Box 18-1393, Calle Alfredo León 211, Miraflores, Lima 18, Peru, 51 1 447 9032 or 51 1 241 7981; Butterfly Center: 51 1 264 2736, www.pronaturaleza.org.

Reserva Ecológica Taricaya. With the highest canopy walkway in the Peruvian rain forest (125 feet tall), this 1,200-acre reserve run by Projects Abroad seeks

---

THEY DON'T ATTACK IF THERE'S NO BLOOD

Not far from Puerto Maldonado and the Taricaya center is Lake Sandoval, a beautiful rain forest lake, with massive schools of piranhas. People also swim in the lake, because, as a guide explains, piranhas wouldn't dream of attacking unless there's blood in the water. Some of the other unusual species in the Peruvian rain forest include:

- **Giant otters,** as big as 6 feet long. Supposedly, there are only a thousand of this mammoth species left, nine of which live in Lake Sandoval.
- **Hoatzins.** Emus and ostriches aren't the only birds that can't fly. Hoatzins use claws, two per wing, to climb trees. Their call is loud and wheezy and sounds like something a three-pack-a-day smoker might make.
- **Macaws.** The largest known assemblage of macaws in the world can be seen at the clay licks near the lake. These high orange cliffs attract hundreds of large macaws in a rainbow of colors, which come each day at sunrise to eat small balls of clay. Scientists speculate that the clay detoxifies the poisons of the seeds they ingest the rest of the day.

---

volunteers to assist with their important conservation work. Several species like the black spider monkey and the white-chested capuchin monkey became extinct before the group, led by Oxford biologist Stuart Timson, started the place from scratch in 2001. Staff and volunteers at the reserve are working hard to keep the same fate from befalling the endangered side-neck turtle, black caiman, and other rain forest species.

One of the reserve's biggest functions is educating the 18 ethnic groups that live in the Madre de Dios (and others who settled here in the early 1900s to farm rubber trees and Brazil nuts) about how to live sustainably rather than destroying the forest. They're experimenting with alternative food sources and have pilot farms for growing many of the plants being destroyed in the rain forest. The palmiche frond, for example, a popular roofing material, can be grown right at the center.

The Taricaya Center, located about an hour's boat ride on the Madre de Dios River from Puerto Maldonado, has an animal release program (jaguars, margays, and anteaters are just a few of the creatures now free to roam their protected habitat), a turtle protection project, a pilot mahogany farm, a medicinal plant garden, and much more. Volunteers build and monitor trails (more than 30 miles of them since its founding), patrol the reserve, help on the experimental farms, and record such wildlife as giant anteaters, pumas, black jaguars, red howler monkeys, green anacondas, white-lipped peccaries, a dwarf caiman (fully grown at only 3 feet long), and more than 350 other species.

You'll live with up to 30 other volunteers (and a resident spider monkey) at the Taricaya Center. A two-week stay is $2,995, a one-month stay is $3,695, a two-month stay is $4,645, and a three-month stay is $5,695.

Projects Abroad, 347 West 36th Street, Suite 903, New York, NY 10018, 888-839-3535, www.volunteer-conservation-peru.org.

europe

I am a little pencil in the hand of a writing God
who is sending a love letter to the world.
—Mother Teresa of Calcutta, Catholic nun
and founder of Missionaries of Charity

This chapter presents volunteer opportunities throughout Europe, ranging from working with dolphins in Scotland's Hebrides to refurbishing castles in Germany. You can tend gardens at castles and manor houses all over the United Kingdom, take orphaned children hiking in Kyrgyzstan, or play the part of a Viking ghost in Iceland.

European volunteer gigs, like the countries in which they take place, are culturally and historically diverse. The best part of embarking on a volunteer vacation is that you'll learn more about your dream country than you could ever get from a book, a nature show, or a tour bus. You will be right there, in the thick of things, working with the very organizations who are restoring Provence's medieval stone work, beekeeping on organic farms in Tuscany, excavating Roman forts, and assisting Romanian gypsies.

Although there must be a million ways to experience the sights, sounds, smells, and tastes of Europe, sometimes it can seem difficult to get away from ticking items off on the same-ole, same-ole tourist trail. Eiffel Tower? Check. Big Ben? Check. Acropolis? Check. As a volunteer, however, you will be able to immerse yourself in a new culture and experience day-to-day life as the Greeks or the Armenians or the Bulgarians or the Russians do.

protect indigenous greek wildlife

ISLAND OF AEGINA, GREECE

The bulldozer and not the atomic bomb may turn out to be the most
destructive invention of the 20th century.
—Philip Shabecoff, environmental journalist

30 Amid orange, fig, and pistachio farms on the tiny Greek island of Aegina sits a sprawling wildlife hospital that treats between 3,000 and 4,500 injured, poisoned, or orphaned wild animals every year. Coming on ferries from all over the Greek islands, the hospital's menagerie includes everything from baby foxes with broken backs to storks, pelicans, owls, blind cormorants, and a griffin vulture that survived 75 gunshot wounds.

With a patient load like that, it's not surprising that volunteers are welcomed with open arms. The busy nonprofit even converted part of its nationally recognized veterinary clinic, a former prison, into volunteer quarters complete with comfy bunk beds, kitchen, and a spacious living room where volunteers meet every morning for breakfast.

With dazzling views of the island's mountains and surrounding Aegean Sea, the clinic attracts animal lovers from all over the world who come to clean cages, prepare food (expect to chop up a lot of raw chicken and carry many heavy buckets of fish), administer medicine, and play with baby magpies, peacocks, and owls.

The roots of the Hellenic Wildlife Hospital (HWH) were planted in 1984 when university students in Thessaloniki rescued animals from an understaffed and unsympathetic zoo where animals were dying and being stuffed for display. By 1990, the most active of the rehabbers, many of whom are still involved today, opened the hospital on Aegina. In addition to animal rescue, HWH is committed to educating the public on the perils of overdevelopment and the importance of protecting wildlife. The center is open to the public and presents programs to schoolchildren throughout the islands.

Volunteers work six days a week from approximately 8 a.m. to 2 p.m. and are asked to commit to stay at least seven days, although it is not uncommon for some

MIRACULOUS DEEDS

Need a miracle? St. Nektarios, the protector of Aegina and one of the most widely known Greek Orthodox saints, built a monastery there with his bare hands, carrying stones, planting gardens, and praying for the nuns who requested his services. Located just 4 miles from the Aegina harbor, the monastery is probably the best regarded of the island's 365 churches. The locals built one church for each day, supposedly to protect them from pirate raids. Thousands of people visit the saint's tomb, located on the monastery grounds, to ask for blessings. Many of the faithful swear that if they put their ear to the tomb, they can hear his healing words. Although more than 2,000 miracles have been attributed to St. Nektarios, we'll limit ourselves to just two:

Born into poverty in 1846 in Thrace, Nektarios was sent by his parents to Constantinople when he was 15. He had no money for boat fare, but begged for a ride from a captain whose ship was about to leave the port. The captain refused and the boy walked away. Although the ship's engines were running, it refused to budge, despite the captain's every effort. Feeling guilty about rejecting the boy, the captain called to him to come back and jump on the boat. Just as Nektarios leapt aboard, the boat regained its power.

Next to the hospital bed where St. Nektarios died on November 8, 1920, lay a man who had been paralyzed for many years. The nurse and the nun who prepared Nektarios's body for burial accidentally set his sweater on the bed of the paralyzed man, who immediately gained strength, arose from his bed, and began shouting, "Hallelujah!"

---

volunteers to stay for months or even years at a time, developing into what they call "a big, happy family."

"Everyone is pulling the same rope at work as well as on time off," says Susan Maki, a HWH volunteer from Finland explaining the family bond that develops.

The highlight for volunteers and staff alike is when an animal of any kind, be it endangered or common, finds the strength to spread its wings and return to the wild.

There's no charge to volunteer at HWH. While meals are not included, the kitchen has an ample supply of basics such as pasta, rice, and bread.

HOW TO GET IN TOUCH

Hellenic Wildlife Hospital, Box 57, Island of Aegina, Greece 18010, 30 229 7031338, www.ekpazp.gr.

restore medieval stonework on castles, farms, and chapels

PROVENCE, FRANCE

Every breath you take of Provençal air is like
ten euros in the bank of health.
—Peter Mayle, author of *A Year in Provence* and many other books

31 Peter Mayle's 1990 best seller, *A Year in Provence*, turned this once little-known destination of unspoiled rural countryside, stone farmhouses, and ancient fortresses into a cliché. Almost.

Now, busloads of foreign tourists crowd the quaint villages, every gourmet store offers goat cheese tastings, every linen store sells calming lavender pillow sprays, and Mayle, forced to enter the "author protection program," decided to relocate.

Luckily, some things are impervious to trends. Since 1979, ten years before Mayle met the characters of his famous book, the Association for Regional Participation

SAY GOAT CHEESE

How can you govern a country which has 246 varieties of cheese?
—General Charles de Gaulle, France's first president

At every market in Provence, you'll find cheesemakers proudly selling their version of *un crotin de chèvre* (goat cheese), usually with four different ages from fresh (one to two days old) to *très sec* (a month to three months old).

Claudine and Yves Malbosc, who sell two varieties of the famous unpasteurized cheese from an outdoor market stall in St.-Martin-de-Crau, tend 70 Alpine goats, raising them on hay of the Crau (called *foin,* it is even flown to Saudi Arabia for racehorses), grains, oats, corn, and barley. Their Chèverie du Mas Doutreleau (open March to Dec., tel 33 4 90 47 08 95) offers private tours where you can meet the goats, learn about cheesemaking, and of course, indulge in samples. You might even catch Yves dancing with the goats.

and Action (APARE), a nonprofit based in Avignon, has been organizing volunteer work camps that to this day still offer a slice of authentic Provence.

From July through September, about three dozen of these work camps spread out across the lavender fields of the Provence countryside, bringing groups of 10 to 15 international volunteers together to restore and rebuild historic and cultural sites.

On one project, you might repair stone roadways at the base of Mont Ventoux. On another, you'll renovate a chapel in the Alpes-de-Haute-Provence or learn to rebuild a stone wall on a citadel overlooking Saint-Tropez. You'll work on huts once used by charcoal workers, gunpowder factories, pebble walls surrounding castles lived in by popes, and hermitages where spiritual seekers still come to find peace and insight.

And the best part? These two- to three-week gigs are not called work camps, but *chantiers*, which—like most things—sounds a lot more romantic in French. Make no mistake, however. You'll be wielding pickaxes, hoes, and cement shovels. A team leader and a technical advisor train each team in such traditional building techniques as dry-stone walling, stone dressing, and lime facing.

You'll start early in the morning, work for five or six hours, and have afternoons free to partake of Provence's well-known *savoir-vivre*. Wholehearted passion, whether from the region's chefs, vintners, artists, craftsman, or even the humblest stall keeper who will spend 15 minutes extolling the virtues of a particular melon, comes with the territory.

Perhaps you'll join other members of your team at one of Provence's famous outdoor cafés. With tables laid out beneath shaded awnings, these quintessential Provence gathering spots are where locals gossip, talk politics, play *boules*, or simply drift to a glass of Chateau St.-Pierre, one of the region's fabulous chilled rosés.

On weekends, led by your team leader, you'll pedal through fields ablaze with poppies, herbs, and olive trees, visit wine festivals and leather fairs, and partake of the colors, smells, and other delights that so inspired painters Vincent van Gogh and Paul Cézanne.

Three-week chantiers, including lodging (usually in a castle, barn, or village hostel), meals, insurance, and excursions, run 130 euros ($167).

HOW TO GET IN TOUCH

APARE, 25 Boulevard Paul Pons, 84800 L'Isle-sur-la-Sorgue, France, 33 4 90 85 51 15, www.apare-gec.org.

help build community or restore a castle

CZECH REPUBLIC

The man with the boots does not mind where he places his foot.
—Irish proverb

32 The Czech nonprofit **INEX-SDA** (Association for Voluntary Activities) organizes a wide range of volunteer work camps every year throughout the Czech Republic. These two- to three-week camps range from herb collecting on a country farm to assisting the handicapped in Prague. The nonprofit group, which was established in 1991, works with local organizations that need assistance through four programs: One to Another, Bridges to Nature, Hands and History, and Meetings in the Countryside.

Tasks vary from year to year, depending on community needs, but you'll be given full instructions when you arrive. Volunteers help children or teenagers to learn English by playing games and

CASTLES ON THE GROUND

Another well-known castle in Moravia is commonly known as the Archbishop's Chateau. The castle is located in the heart of Kroměříž and surrounded by lush baroque gardens considered to be among the best in Europe. The castle and gardens were designated as a UNESCO World Heritage site in 1998. The building includes a 275-foot tower, a hall where the 1848 Austrian Imperial Congress took place, and an extensive gallery with paintings by Titian, Chranac, and van Dyck. But perhaps its biggest claim to fame is that Czech director Miloš Forman used it as a stand-in for Vienna's Hofburg Imperial Palace during the filming of *Amadeus,* the award-winning movie (1984) about the life of Wolfgang Amadeus Mozart. The castle's main audience chamber was also used in the 1994 movie *Immortal Beloved,* during the piano concerto scene.

talking with them. At a summer camp in Lipová-lázně, they plan activities for the children, and may assist with water therapy, massage, and breathing therapy in the nearby caves. In Ústí nad Labem, volunteers help rebuild the community center and lead Roma children in singing, drawing, field trips, and other activities.

When you volunteer with INEX-SDA, you should arrive prepared to work outdoors in all kinds of weather—comfortable, waterproof boots are a must. Tasks include clearing invasive plants from protected areas, landscaping educational trails, tending and planting trees, cleaning up rivers and streams, and gardening. If your trip is in late summer, you might be harvesting apples and putting them by for winter. You will help clean, create, or maintain village public spaces. In 2008, volunteers helped construct a historical museum of Slovanian houses from natural materials.

If historical preservation is enticing to you, there are castles galore in the Czech Republic. INEX-SDA volunteers work at an archaeological work camp at the ruins of Hartenberg castle, clearing rubble and excavating, and on the grounds of the baroque castle at Bečov. They also work at ruins of castles around the Malse River in southern Bohemia. At the 13-century Zamek ("castle" in Czech) Kynžvart in the town of Lázně Kynžvart, volunteers work on the grounds, revitalizing a brook, repairing an old greenhouse, and removing invasive plants.

One unusual work camp takes at a place at a 15th-century castle in Střílky, a village in southern Moravia. The 64-room fortification near the town of Kroměříž was crumbling in the 1990s, when an international yoga association, Yoga in Daily Life, bought it and began renovating. They then opened an ashram and began offering classes. Volunteers tend the castle's sprawling gardens, help out in the kitchen, clean the meditation rooms, and generally practice the art of karma yoga—selfless service.

Depending on the location of their work camp, in their free time, volunteers may hike, swim, attend community events, and visit eco-farms, ruins, spas, and so forth.

Accommodations run the gamut from castles to cottages to hostels to tents (you may need to bring a sleeping bag). Meals are usually prepared by participants in shared kitchens, though there may be some canteen or restaurant meals provided. Some work sites do not have running water. All of INEX-SDA's work camps are free.

HOW TO GET IN TOUCH

INEX-SDA, Budečská 1, Prague 2, 120 00, Czech Republic, 420 222 362 715, www.inexsda.cz.

work with kosovo refugees

ALBANIA, KOSOVO, AND MACEDONIA

For once in my life, I won't live in an artificial bling-bling world.
—Lisa Holstenson, volunteer with Balkan Sunflowers

33 Wam Kat, the Dutch peace activist who started Balkan Sunflowers (BSF), a grassroots volunteer group, the first to work in Croatia's refugee camps after the 1999 NATO intervention that finally brought an end to the deadly struggle, is the perfect example of what one person can do. His near-daily electronic diary from Zagreb detailing the atrocities of the ethnic cleansing that was devastating innocent lives inspired people from around the world to send money, to show up, to say, "No, this is unacceptable." He covered the events long before CNN and the BBC arrived on the scene.

International volunteers began flocking to the political hotbed. As Kat, the father of three, remarks, "People came to realize that this was no political abstraction, but real people like you and me. They decided they wanted to help in a way transferring money could not."

Today, as the dust settles from this horrific chapter in world history, thousands of these "real people" still live in refugee camps, and still suffer the consequences of unbridled prejudice, a bombed-out homeland, and resources that are stretched thin.

Although Kat has since retired from BSF, the nonprofit he started is going strong with projects throughout Albania, Kosovo, and Macedonia. Volunteers are still needed, mainly to work with Kosovar kids by organizing soccer leagues, art projects, English lessons—anything "to make life easier and more fun."

"Trying to help these children regain their trust in the world and faith in humanity is part of our mission," says Sherine Zagho, an Egyptian volunteer with BSF.

Over the years, BSF volunteers have done everything from install playgrounds and restore parks to pass out teddy bears and host theater troupes. One volunteer translated Dr. Seuss books into Albanian. As another volunteer says, "They throw us in the deep end," which means it's up to you, the volunteer, to be creative, to come up with an idea and to implement it. Any idea is fair game. A BFS youth video program resulted in presentations at two of the world's leading film festivals—Sundance in 2001 and Cannes in 2007.

The volunteer commitment is normally six months, unless special arrangements are made, living with host families and sharing meals with them. The volunteer should raise money to support his/her stay in Kosovo and should check with Balkan Sunflowers on this amount, as it depends on current conditions and whether or not the project he or she joins has funds to support their participation.

As for the name Balkan Sunflowers, it was inspired by an earlier act of Kat's. In 1994, when sandbags were piled around the bunkers in Zagreb, Kat secretly added sunflower seeds to the heavy bags. In the spring, when the weather warmed the ground, the giant yellow sunflowers sprouted throughout Zagreb, creating a poetic antiwar statement.

HOW TO GET IN TOUCH
Balkan Sunflowers, Youth, Culture and Sports Hall #114, Luan Haradinaj Street, Prishtina, Kosovo, 381 38 246 299, www.balkansunflowers.org.

THE POWER OF ONE

When Wam Kat was 18, his doctor gave him one year to live. He decided right then and there, he'd squeeze an entire lifetime into that year. Thirty-five years later, he's still going strong. His list of exploits include:

- Co-founded the European Youth for Action (EYFA) environmental network to address the effects of acid rain on local forests.
- Smuggled computers, modems, and faxes into Eastern Europe to report on the as yet hidden political situation.
- Organized Ecotopia, a yearly summer festival to promote environmental awareness.
- Co-founded a mobile vegetarian kitchen, Rampenplan, that provided food and other services to political activists.
- Serves as a town councilman in Belzig, Germany.
- Published a political cookbook called *24 Rezepte zur kulinarischen Weltverbesserung*, which translates as *24 Prescriptions for Culinary World Improvement*.

excavate a roman fort, harbor, and village

MENORCA, SPAIN

Archaeology is the peeping Tom of the sciences.
—Jim Bishop, American journalist

34 Even though Menorca has more beaches than its bigger sister, Mallorca, it hasn't been a tourist destination for long. Until 1969, when the San Climent airport opened, the economic drivers of this laid-back Spanish paradise were dairy farming and shoemaking. By 1993, the entire 9-by-32-mile island was declared a biosphere reserve. Even those few tourists who do come tend to agree with the tourist literature that declares: "If the Mediterranean were a book, Menorca would be a beautiful poem read out in a whisper."

Menorca's strategic location in the center of the western Mediterranean Sea cast it as an important player in the annals of history. At one time or another, this Balearic Island was occupied by the Carthaginians, Greeks, Romans, Arabs, British, and French, all of whom left traces of their existence on the isle.

The Romans arrived in 123 B.C. and, for the 600 years that followed, Sanitja harbor on the north end of the island served a pivotal role in the immense Roman Empire, receiving ships from such far-flung locales as Africa, France, and Italy. This historic legacy is being uncovered, piece by piece, by archaeologists with the Ecomuseum de Cap de Cavalleria who are busy excavating an ancient Roman fort, village, and cemetery.

Every summer and fall, when the island's famous breezes aren't too brisk, volunteers show up from around the world to help preserve the island's natural and cultural history, while mastering important archaeology techniques along the way. Excavation projects range from the fort and Roman camps to clusters of Roman tombs outside the town of Sanisera. There are even two-week underwater explorations of the submerged ruins of Roman and medieval shipwrecks. In 2009, the underwater field school will explore waters near the port of Sanitja. In addition

HOLD THE MAYO

American literary genius Ambrose Bierce (1842–1914?) claimed that mayonnaise was one of the sauces that serves the French in place of a state religion. But he failed to mention that it wasn't the French, but the residents of Menorca who invented the rich, egg-based condiment in the first place.

In 1756, the Duke de Richelieu—along with 20,000 French troops—landed in Mahon, Menorca, to root out the island's British rulers. While there, the duke's chef happened upon the local *allioli* recipe, which he proceeded to duplicate and serve at the victory banquet back in Paris. *Mahonnaise,* as it was first called, was an instant smash success.

Other gastronomies the island is known for:

Spiny lobsters. Menorca's port of Fornells is so famous for its *caldereta de langosta* (lobster stew) that King Juan Carlos is said to sail over frequently to partake.

Menorca gin. Thanks to the British, who controlled the island twice during its long history, Menorca gin is the island's drink of choice. The 18th-century Xoriguer Gin Distillery, located at Moll de Ponent harbor, features enormous copper stills bubbling with the alcoholic drink's signature juniper berries.

Little-known fact: During the Punic Wars between Carthage and Rome, the Carthaginians recruited Menorca's famous Balearic slingers, slingshot mercenaries who could hit a forehead from a football field away. These formidable men were paid handsomely in wine and women. Today the island's residents are paid mostly in euros, for less heroic exploits.

---

to Roman ruins, the area has ruins of a Muslim mosque and English defense tower, leading experts to believe that divers may find vessels from these time periods.

Amateur archaeologists divide their two- to six-week stints between excavations and lab work, lectures, excursions, and dives—for those who choose the diving track. They stay in a dorm in the former capital of Ciutadella, a quaint town with winding cobblestone streets, ancient cathedrals, and lively squares.

Participating in the summer and fall fieldwork ranges from $1,750 (for two weeks) to $2,400 (for 20 days) and includes shared lodging, insurance, and three meals a day.

HOW TO GET IN TOUCH

Ecomuseum de Cap de Cavalleria, Apartado 68, 07740, Es Mercadal, Menorca, Balearic Islands, Spain, 34 971 359999, www.ecomuseodecavalleria.com.

clean fossils in portugal's first unesco-sponsored geopark

CASTELO BRANCO, PORTUGAL

I've seen and met angels / Wearing the disguise
of ordinary people / Leading ordinary lives
—Tracy Chapman, singer-songwriter, "Heaven's Here on Earth"

35 At last count, there were 57 geoparks (UNESCO-sponsored geological heritage sites) in Europe, Brazil, China, and Iran. According to UNESCO, "A Geopark is an area with a geological heritage of significance, with a coherent and strong management structure and where a sustainable economic development strategy is in place. A Geopark creates enhanced employment opportunities for the people who live there bringing sustainable and real economic benefit, usually through the development of sustainable tourism."

OOPS!

At Cape Espichel, south of Lisbon, there's a popular shrine to Our Lady of the Mule. According to a 13th-century legend, the footprints up the steep cliff were made by a giant mule that rescued the Virgin Mary from Lagosteiros Bay, carrying her up the cliff to safety. In 1976, a paleontology professor from Lisbon's Nova University identified the footprints, however, as those of a giant sauropod of the late Jurassic Tithonian age.

Other significant finds in Portugal include a nest with scores of black dinosaur eggs, several containing embryos, and one of the world's longest tracks left by giant plant-eating sauropods. Located in Serra d'Aire National Park, near the Roman Catholic sanctuary of Fatima, this spectacular find on the floor of a limestone quarry includes more than a thousand elliptical brontosaur footprints. This 482-foot track that looks as if a herd of dinosaurs passed through only yesterday was classified as a natural monument in 1996. It's one of a dozen such sauropod tracksites in Portugal, representing one-third of the world's total known Jurassic sites.

Located in Portugal on its border with Spain, Geopark Naturtejo—one of UNESCO's most recent additions to the global geoparks network—has a Trail of Fossils, an Ichnological Park, and a Paleontology Museum in the 750-year-old village of Penha Garcia. Volunteers come each summer to help maintain the 490-million-year-old trilobites and other marine fossils found here. They work with the Amigos do Geoparque, a group of locals working to preserve the paleontology found throughout their region's steep rose-and-gray jagged rocks.

Volunteers live in an old stone farmhouse near Penha Garcia with unforgettable views of Portugal's Beira Baixa plain. During their two-week work camp, volunteers maintain the paleontology museum, guide tours of the fossil trail, and clean million-year-old fossils.

In their spare time, they visit Gardunha Mountain, the historical village of Idanha-a-Velha, and Monsanto—an ancient, fortified hillside village built amid gigantic boulders. They kayak, go bird-watching, cook traditional Portuguese bread, and swim in Penha Garcia's natural swimming pools.

Every other year, Geopark Naturtejo also plays host to the weeklong, all-green Boom Festival (www.boomfestival.org). This global art, music, and culture celebration attracts young electro-raving campers from all over the world. This completely sustainable festival is held on the sun-drenched shores of Lake Idanha-a-Nova during August's full moon and uses generators powered by recycled fuel, solar power, biological water treatment systems, and composting toilets.

In 2008, Geopark Naturtejo won the "Educational Programmes" award at the Skål International Ecotourism Awards. Skål International is an association that supports tourism around the world.

The two-week work camp, including meals and accommodations in the Penha Garcia farmhouse, is free.

HOW TO GET IN TOUCH
Geopark Naturtejo, Rua Conselheiro Albuquerque, No. 4, Cave C, 6000-161 Castelo Branco, Portugal, 351 272 320 176, www.naturtejo.com.

support icelandic arts by playing a ghost or a viking

ICELAND

Not only must we be good, but we must also be good for something.
—Henry David Thoreau, author and transcendentalist

36 Ask Icelanders about ghosts and elves or what they call the *huldufolk* (hidden folk) and 80 percent will tell you they believe in them. Half of Icelanders claim to have spoken to an elf and one out of four have seen one. The main road from Reykjavík to Selfoss bears left for no apparent reason a few miles beyond Hveragerði to avoid an elf hill. And Icelandic streets, even new ones, are aligned to avoid elf hills and dwarf rocks. Attempting to build over a huldufolk site is asking for trouble: Bulldozers will fail and hammers will break, so you'll save yourself loads of heartache if you just go around it.

Unsurprisingly, during the summer when tourists come to this volcanic land resting on the edge of the Arctic Circle, hidden folk and ghosts play an important role in connecting visitors with Icelandic lore. In Stokkseyri, a village of 500 on the south coast, there's even a Ghost Museum—complete with a Ghost Bar made from driftwood where the American rock band Foo Fighters drank ghost shots (Sea Ghost, Móra Milk, and Skotta, to name a few) with local garage band Nilfisk.

Since many of the villagers spend their days fishing, somebody has to play the specters and apparitions that haunt visitors who come to Stokkseyri to kayak and enjoy the black-sand beach. Veraldarvinir, a nonprofit that arranges dozens of work camps throughout Iceland each summer, recruits volunteers to play spirits in the Ghost Museum's maze. For three weeks, volunteer actors live in Stokkseyri, assist the museum staff, and play the parts of shepherd ghosts Starkaour and Egill, nude ghost Vigfus Eriksson, the schnapps-quaffing Brennivin ghost, and many others.

If you'd rather play a Viking, Veraldarvinir sends volunteers to the town of Hafnarfjörður, a much larger town near Reykjavík, to work in its Viking Village. And, yes, you'll wear a Viking costume, display ancient Viking arts and crafts, and, if you're up for it, demonstrate battle skills of the brave and adventurous Vikings who settled Iceland around A.D. 874.

As for being a troll, everyone knows that trolls, like elves, are invisible (except when they want to be seen). Veraldarvinir volunteers in Reykjanes, near the meeting of the Eurasian and American continental plates, are helping Nordan Bál, a well-known Icelandic art group, build a "home for trolls," a cave with oversize furniture, dishes, and other necessities for 10- to 12-foot-tall trolls. The cave is near the former NATO base which has been turned into a center of art and filmmaking.

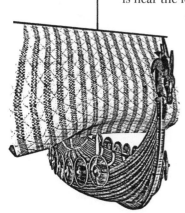

Nonactors can volunteer for other Veraldarvinir work camps that clear brush, organize festivals, and work with children.

These two- and three-week work camps run from 80 to 130 euros ($100–$165), including food and lodging (bring a sleeping bag).

HOW TO GET IN TOUCH

Worldwide Friends - Veraldarvinir, Einarsnes 56, 101 Reykjavík, Iceland, 354 55 25 214, www.wf.is.

FIVE MORE THOUGHTFUL, COMMITTED CITIZENS: THE HILDEBURNS

Charles and Colleen Hildeburn didn't want their three children thinking that everyone in the world lived like they did in Orinda, California, an affluent suburb of San Francisco's East Bay. For several years, they talked about taking their kids, Jane, 17, Chase, 15, and Mary, 12, overseas to show them the developing world. They wanted the kids to appreciate what they had in America, but also to realize that they, as global citizens, had a responsibility to uplift the rest of the world.

"We'd been scheming for months about the possibilities of taking some time off to show the real world to our children," Charles says. "We enjoy relative luxury compared to a lot of the rest of the world and we wanted the kids to experience what the rest of the world was experiencing. We had both spent time overseas and felt we'd gained a lot from those experiences."

Their dream was to spend an entire year traveling, volunteering, and exposing the kids to other cultures. "I didn't want us to travel with a selfish, please me, entertain me attitude," Colleen says. "More than seeing the world, I wanted us to go in the spirit of how we could bless people along the way."

In April 2008, their volunteering adventure simply fell into place. Colleen stumbled on a relevant Bible study lesson: "You cannot stay where you are and go with God." Then Charles, an international stockbroker for Merrill Lynch, was offered early retirement. ("I qualified by exactly ten days," he says.) The kids, albeit hesitantly at first, agreed to take a year off from school. They rented out their home for ten months and hit the road.

The Hildeburns trolled the outdoor markets in the Côte d'Azur, France, hiked through the Swiss Alps, biked through Ireland, punted the River Thames in England, and played Family Von Hildeburn in Salzburg, Austria.

They also did lots of good works along the way. They taught English to children at a summer camp outside Warsaw, Poland, through Global Volunteers, a Minnesota-based nonprofit featured throughout this book. "It was really great, being able to work together as a family," Charles says. "We taught English in the morning and the kids were able to participate in all the activities with the camp kids in the afternoon. Our family got as much or more than the Polish kids."

Twelve-year-old Mary agrees: "There are so many people who need help. No point in just sightseeing when we could be helping the people who live there. Even though I am giving to others, I always feel like I get more out of it."

In Spain, the Hildeburn family volunteered for La Gota de Leche (A Drop of Milk), a nonprofit that serves breakfast to 50 at-risk children each morning. In Patagonia, they helped build a Bible college. In Peru, they worked in an orphanage that assisted adolescent mothers who make crafts. Along the way, their blog (www.5blest.blogspot.com) kept their friends abreast of their activities.

work for britain's national trust

LOCATIONS THROUGHOUT ENGLAND, WALES, AND NORTHERN IRELAND

The need of quiet, the need of air, the need of exercise, and … the sight
of sky and of things growing seem human needs, common to all men.
—Octavia Hill, one of three philanthropists who started
Britain's National Trust

37 Britain's National Trust runs approximately 450 working holidays every year offering volunteers a chance to do everything from herd goats to paint lighthouses to garden the grounds of a famous Elizabethan manor.

Founded in 1895, Britain's National Trust was set up to thwart uncontrolled development and guard the country's threatened coastline, countryside, and historic buildings. Its popular working holidays range from two to seven days, from outdoor farm chores such as hedgerow laying to indoor activities like serving as a temporary room steward at a 16th-century Tudor island castle. Because the options are so many and diverse, we'll list just a sampling from the trust's wide variety of vacations categories to whet your appetite:

Maintain a historic estate: Attingham Park, a 3,800-acre estate with an 18th-century mansion and a medieval deer park, uses volunteers to lay and plant hedge, make corridors for wildlife, and practice traditional countryside crafts.

Weed and prune celebrated gardens: Volunteers spend six days weeding, pruning, and creating bonfires from their cuttings at the celebrated gardens of Sissinghurst Castle, once the home of writer Vita Sackville-West and her husband, Sir Harold Nicolson.

Scrub a Gothic chapel: The chapel at Clumber Park in Sherwood Forest requires a yearly scrub—volunteers clean everything from candlesticks to choir pews. You'll stay in a converted gardener's cottage on the 3,800-acre estate.

Coppice beautiful woodlands: The trust owns 2,100 acres of land around Stonehenge, one-third of the World Heritage site, and volunteers are needed to coppice the nearby hazel woodland. Coppicing, in case you're not familiar with that verb, is a method of cutting down trees where their stumps are encouraged to

grow thin stems that are used to make brushes, hurdles, and besom brooms. You'll bunk at the Stourhead Estate in Stonehenge's renovated stables.

Survey sand lizards and nightjars: Hindhead Commons, one of the trust's first acquisitions, uses volunteers to survey sand lizards and nightjars, clear paths, and monitor vegetation amid stunning landscapes of lowland heath. You'll stay at the restored Swan Barn Farm, tucked away in the Surrey Hills.

The trust's working holidays at more than a hundred beautiful locations throughout England, Wales, and Northern Ireland average about £60–£175 ($90–$270) per week, plus a £5 ($7.70) transferring fee for out-of-country volunteers, and include food and lodging. In most cases, you'll stay at one of the trust's 31 base camps, which range from farmhouses and cottages to converted sheep shearing sheds. After completion of your working holiday, you'll get a National Trust admission card allowing free admission to all properties owned or managed by the trust for an entire year.

HOW TO GET IN TOUCH

National Trust Central Volunteering Team, The National Trust, Heelis, Kemble Drive, Swindon SN2 2NA, England, 44 1793 817632, www.nationaltrust.org.uk.

restore medieval castles, churches, manors, and rectories

WEIMAR, GERMANY

> Unless someone like you cares a whole awful lot,
> nothing is going to get better. It's not.
> —Dr. Seuss, children's book author, *The Lorax*

38 Thanks to eccentric King Ludwig II, and Walt Disney, who copied his Neuschwanstein for Cinderella's digs, everybody knows about Bavaria's castles. But other regions of Germany—Thuringia, Saxony, and Altmark, to name a few—also have castles, and many of them could use some tender, loving care.

Enter Offene Häuser (OH), a group of innovative do-gooders who not only restore such German castles as Lorha, Oberau, and the Ollendrof Water Castle, but they invite anyone from anywhere to show up and help. That's why they called themselves Open Houses, as in open doors, open attitudes, open arms.

Formed in the mid-1980s to renovate castles, churches, rectories, and manors in what used to be East Germany, this group headquartered in Weimar, the town where Goethe made his name, believes property—or at least their property—should be open to the public. And their international work camps, organized throughout the year, consider the goal of creating community and new ideas to be as important as the historic restoration work they're undertaking. They see construction and the maintenance of historic buildings as a way to bring people together, to facilitate learning, and to encourage an exchange of ideas. The aim is to fill the old rooms with new life, free from economic restraint, bureaucracy and institution, something a mere craftsman's work cannot achieve.

Volunteers can choose between technical building camps, art camps, general work camps, and family camps, all which take place communally with jobs ranging from chopping wood to clearing horse stables.

Part of their vision, stated on their website, is to "offer shelter to all who come to us with the will to join. Anybody without warning, night or day, can turn up at the door, walk in and stay for a day, a week, a month—as long as he is prepared to join his efforts to those who are already there."

Each year, this idealistic group sponsors skilled carpenters, stonemasons, bricklayers, and other tradesmen from foreign countries for what they call European Craftsmen Exchanges. These several-months-long apprenticeships give eastern Europeans the chance to travel to a new country while helping restore important historical monuments. These skilled volunteers also teach nonskilled volunteers from around the world the ropes of, say, making a mortise or replacing a warped beam from the Middle Ages.

ODE TO A GREAT IDEA
(THE VISION FOR OPEN HOUSES)

Open Houses –
room open for those
who come along.

Open Houses –
no empty buildings, but places with visible and invisible traces of history,
places which have grown and decayed
during the centuries,
which were shaped by those
who lived there long time ago
and those
who left only yesterday,
places which will be shaped
by each of us
who lives there
or who comes as a guest.

Open Houses –
room
which wants to be filled
with dreams and ideas,
with meetings and exchange,
by people of different backgrounds,
different cultures,
different generations,
different ideas and visions.

Besides renovating castles, Open Houses also offers volunteers the chance to learn rammed-earth construction (their volunteers helped build a simple clay Chapel of Reconciliation near the Berlin Wall), ecological farming, and theater. In 2008, volunteers at a three-week work camp held in the 11th-century Lohra Castle created an improvisational theater piece and then took it on the road. Open Houses believes that such performances help reconnect people with magic and the possibility of transformation. Volunteers have also made films, hosted concerts, and created art celebrating peace and justice.

Many of OH's work camps, art workshops, exhibitions, and concerts take place at the Lohra Castle, a complex of 20 buildings located next to a beautiful forest overlooking the Harz mountain range. The medieval fortification includes a tower from the 11th century, a 12th-century Romanesque chapel, a manor from the Renaissance period, and stables and granaries from the 19th century.

Participation in two- to three-week work camps runs 25 to 40 euros ($30–$50) per week and includes insurance, seminars, lodging, and meals—although everyone shares cooking duties.

HOW TO GET IN TOUCH

Offene Häuser (Open Houses), Goetheplatz 9 B D, 99423 Weimar, Germany, 49 3643 502879, www.openhouses.de.

conduct surveys of dolphins and whales

ARGYLL ISLANDS, HEBRIDES, SCOTLAND

When we protect our oceans, we protect our future.
—Bill Clinton, former President of the United States

39 If you're afraid of heights, you might want to turn the page. This eight- to eleven-day volunteer vacation in and around the 550 islands of Scotland's Hebrides asks participants to look for dolphins, whales, and 22 other species of cetaceans from the crow's nest of a 53-foot schooner, the *Silurian*.

With a team of eight, you'll ply the waters off Scotland's west coast, enjoying spectacular scenery, honing your sailing skills, and recording the cetacean abundance (a third of the world's species) that make their way through these warm waters of the Gulf Stream. You're apt to spot anything from the blue whale to the tiny resident harbor porpoise—that is, if you're not too distracted by the area's sea lochs, towering mountains, and medieval clifftop castles.

The Hebridean Whale and Dolphin Trust (HWDT) uses volunteers each spring and summer to assist with its long-term studies into the distribution, behavior, and ecology of the area's cetaceans. The research collected since the trust was formed in 1994 is potent ammunition for area conservation efforts. The data help the trust with its goal to protect endangered whales and dolphins, which are under increasing threat from offshore oil exploration, marine pollution, drowning in gill nets, and uncontrolled tourism.

Volunteers, five of whom are used on each trip, are trained to observe and collect data, conduct acoustic monitoring, deploy hydrophones, and help run the research vessel.

HWDT also turns the *Silurian* into a floating classroom two weeks a year, using volunteers to run the seven-day education programs at various Scottish ports in the area. If you choose to volunteer during those two weeks, you'll set up equipment, stock the touch tank, and perform necessary duties such as inflating life-size dolphin decoys as teaching tools.

TOM, DICK, OR HARRY WHALE

For a mere £150 ($230), the Hebridean Whale and Dolphin Trust will let you name your own minke whale—they've photographed 82 in Scottish waters over the past few years. You'll get an 8-by-6-inch mounted print, HWDT membership, a species fact sheet, and exclusive naming rights for one of the sleek, pointy-headed whales that circle the *Silurian* each summer. Though you won't have the privilege of naming new species, unlike naming record-holding scientist Charles Paul Alexander (he discovered 10,000 species of crane flies), perhaps these examples by scientists who did will provide inspiration:

- Carl Linnaeus, the Swedish scientist who came up with the classification system, named an ugly, insignificant weed after a critic: *Siegesbeckia.*
- Rousseau H. Flower discovered a worm he named *Khruschevia ridicula,* after former Soviet leader Nikita Khrushchev.
- A colleague of Richard Fortey, senior paleontologist at the Natural History Museum, who loved the '70s punk band The Sex Pistols, named an ancient trilobite species *Sid viciousi* and *Johnny rotteni* after Sid Vicious and Johnny Rotten.
- G. W. Kirkaldy, a scholar Lothario, celebrated romantic conquests through naming, including a variety of plant insects for which he used the Greek suffix, *chisme,* pronounced KISS-me. Thanks to Kirkaldy, there are now bugs called *Polychisme, Marichisme, Dollichisme* and on and on.
  - In 2005, Quentin Wheeler made a political statement by naming slime mold-eating beetles after then President George W. Bush and company: *Agathidium bushi, A. rumsfeldi,* and *A. cheneyi.*

Either way, you'll live aboard the *Silurian,* sharing one of four cozy cabins and cooking and cleaning duties with the research vessel's three permanent staff.

And as for the crow's nest? Never fear. HWDT also offers volunteer opportunities at lower altitudes in the home office in Tobermoy on the Isle of Mull. Landlubbers can do everything from create teacher resource kits to clean and assemble bones.

Eight to eleven days aboard the 53-foot ketch, including meals, your own berth, training, and equipment runs £750 to £950 ($1,150–$1,450), depending on the month of travel. The seven-day educational tours run £585 ($700).

HOW TO GET IN TOUCH

Hebridean Whale and Dolphin Trust, 28 Main Street, Tobermory, Isle of Mull, PA75 6NU, Scotland, 44 1688 302 620, www.whaledolphintrust.co.uk.

document a vital historic district in the cradle of christianity

GYUMRI, ARMENIA

Without an architecture of our own we have
no soul of our own civilization.
—Frank Lloyd Wright, American architect
and proponent of organic architecture

40 A 1988 earthquake, the fifth in the 20th century alone, destroyed nearly 80 percent of the buildings in the ancient Armenian city of Gyumri, killing 25,000, injuring 12,000, and leaving a half million homeless.

After two decades of living in shipping containers turned into makeshift homes, the brave souls of Gyumri are slowly rebuilding their city. But in an age of homogenization, globalization, and cultures being stripped of their individuality, the Armenian people are smart enough to ask, "How can we stay true to our historic roots?"

To help out, American architect Jane Greenwood, associate dean of the College of Architecture, Art, and Design at Mississippi State University, is busy developing what she calls an "Armenian pattern language," a prototype, if you will, that clearly spells out the country's unique architectural style. It refers to architect Christopher Alexander's seminal 1977 work, *A Pattern Language*, which espouses building in harmony with geography, climate, and culture. According to Armenian history professor Gevork Nazaryan, "beauty through simplicity [represents] one of the trademarks of Armenian architecture."

Greenwood is creating workshops, writing papers, and helping public officials develop design guidelines to preserve Gyumri's Kumayri Historic District, an open-air museum with more than a thousand 18th- and 19th-century homes, many built with indigenous red and black tuff (a form of volcanic rock), classic churches, and plazas. It's the only place left where you can see an authentic Armenian village.

Armenia, the smallest of the former Soviet states and perhaps the most reluctant to claim independence after the U.S.S.R. collapsed in 1991, is a landlocked country of deep river gorges, mountainous steppes, and wild green pastures. It shares borders with Iran, Turkey, Azerbaijan, and Georgia. Having adopted Christianity as early as A.D. 301, Armenia has hundreds of temples, medieval monasteries, and churches.

International volunteers fly into Armenia and, after learning the historical, political, social, and cultural context of this country in the southern Caucasus mountains, work with Greenwood to create a one-of-a-kind architectural language. Last summer, Greenwood's volunteers adopted seven historic homes that survived the earthquakes and documented them via drawings and photographs. They also spent time with Armenian

I'D LIKE TO MAKE AN ARMENIAN TOAST

Armenians are rightfully proud of their brandy, considered to be the best in the world, and have a thing about making toasts. These tributes to every member of the family, from the grandfather to the smallest newborn, often start at breakfast and continue throughout the day. Following are several other little-known facts about Armenian brandy.

- Armenia is the world's largest producer of brandy.
- During the International Exhibition in Paris in 1900, Armenian brandy, in a blind taste test, received the Grand-Prix and the legal right to be called "cognac," not brandy.
- The most famous Armenian brandy, Ararat, is named after the well-known biblical mountain where Noah finally hit land. (Although Mount Ararat used to be on Armenian soil, it is now located in Turkey.) The Yerevan Brandy Company (YBC) has been producing Ararat since 1887.
- YBC was the official brandy purveyor of the imperial Russian court.
- When the government sold its most well-known company in 1998 to the French company Pernod Ricard for $30 million (it's still produced in the capital city of Yerevan), protestors lined the streets.
- During the Yalta Conference, Winston Churchill was so impressed with the Armenian brandy given to him by Joseph Stalin that he ordered 400 bottles to be sent to him every year.
- Boris Yeltsin liked Yerevan brandy so much that he was honored with his own barrel in the factory's cellars.
- Several brands (Erebuni, Kilikia, and Noah's Ark) are unavailable through retailers and can only be obtained by special order.

families, recording oral histories, sketching, and measuring floor plans, all tools that will help Greenwood and her students at Mississippi State University create a historically accurate architectural syntax.

Daily tasks include cataloging digital images, measuring and sketching architectural artifacts, writing field reports, and producing presentations and booklets. Volunteers who can translate Russian or Armenian into English are especially valuable for these projects.

Free time on this expedition includes exploring ancient monasteries, visiting outdoor markets, and an excursion to Etchmiadzin, the Armenian equivalent of the Vatican.

This 13-day Earthwatch expedition, including double lodging at the Berlin Art Hotel—an 11-room, European-style hotel filled with art by Armenian painters and sculptors—and three traditional Armenian meals a day, costs $2,440.

HOW TO GET IN TOUCH

Earthwatch, 3 Clock Tower Place, Suite 100, Box 75, Maynard, MA 01754, 800-776-0188 or 978-461-0081, www.earthwatch.org.

help russia's less fortunate in a historic city

YAROSLAVL, RUSSIA

I really just suddenly saw the world for what it is—so much bigger than me or my community, or even my country, and that was revealing.
—Trish, volunteer with Cross-Cultural Solutions

41 Many souvenirs from Russia feature a bear, said to represent the character and power of the Russian spirit. But it's in Yaroslavl, a picturesque city 155 miles north of Moscow, that the Russian bear first made his name. It was in 1010, in fact, that Kievian prince Yaroslav the Wise supposedly wrestled a bear and decided to mark the feat by building a fortress.

Today that city on the banks of the majestic Volga and Kotorosl Rivers is about to celebrate its thousand-year anniversary and has been designated a UNESCO World Heritage site. As the unofficial capital of Russia's Golden Ring, a symbolic circle of ancient towns with some of Russia's oldest architecture, Yaroslavl is one of the most beautiful and historically preserved cities. Home to the country's oldest and best public theaters, dozens of picturesque cathedrals, gilt-domed churches, and a vibrant artistic community, it is also the base for Cross-Cultural Solutions' (CCS) volunteers in Russia.

According to past volunteers, working in Yaroslavl with Russian CCS director Nadia Savelieva and her warm-hearted team of translators and other staff is a life-changing experience. As volunteer Andrew Navratil explains, "Working with the children was amazing—I felt like I had a real impact on their lives and I grew as a person ... I wanted to learn more about Russian culture, about the political system, and about the orphanage system. I accomplished this through the guest lectures, Russian lessons, talking with the translators, and doing some independent travel on the weekends."

Volunteers, who live and eat in a comfortable hotel near the city center, choose between working with children, the elderly, or people with disabilities. They either

COLLECTING TIME AND TUNES

Russia, the largest country in the world, spanning two continents, 11 time zones, and 6.5 million square miles, has hundreds of national museums. But it wasn't until its emergence from behind the 70-year-old Iron Curtain that private museums were allowed.

The first such museum, located in a fin de siècle merchant's house on the Volga in Yaroslavl, is the Museum of Music and Time. Owned and operated by professional magician John Grigoriyevich Mostoslavsky, the museum attracts hundreds of cruise passengers from ships trolling the Volga between Moscow and St. Petersburg. He began collecting small bells, gramophones, records, clocks, accordions, harmoniums, irons, and religious icons back when it was still illegal to amass a private collection, starting with a bell he received as a young man.

Mostoslavksy enjoys leading visitors around his museum, demonstrating the noises generated by his decades of secretive collecting by cranking the gramophones, playing the organs, ringing the bells, and pumping the pedals on a Story & Clark player piano.

Born in 1942 to Jewish parents who fled the Nazis, Mostoslavsky spent his life performing magic on the road, all the while illegally collecting a reliquary of Russia's gentried past. And he admits that under the Soviets, he did spend some time in jail.

His museum has the Cupid-emblazoned gramophone he once used in his magic act, as well as German and French clocks, dozens of Swiss music boxes, and an Odessan street organ that, when cranked, emits a circus tune. *Museum of Music and Time, 33a Volzhskaya Embankment, Yaroslavl 150000, Russia, 74 85 232 8637.*

spend their days in an orphanage, leading craft projects and teaching English, or at a hospital, where they befriend women with mental health challenges. Kam Santos, director of communications for CCS, says, "Volunteers work in orphanages or transition homes. Many of these are understaffed and under-resourced. Volunteers might paint a mural or help the kids put on a theater show. Local interpreters help the volunteers design a program, but volunteers run the show. One of the biggest tasks is serving as positive role models."

When volunteers are not working, they have time to enjoy the city's rich legacy of architectural masterpieces, including the Church of St. Elijah the Prophet, built on the spot where the "wrestling match" took place. It was later made the focal point of Catherine the Great's historic vision of urban planning, along with the Epiphany Church—replete with frescoes and paintings by Russia's simple peasant artists—and the Monastery of the Savior, whose white walls dominate the center of town.

Volunteers are also invited to attend Russian culture and language classes, take excursions to local villages, and hear guest speakers on Russian history, politics, traditions, and cuisine. They might hear a local psychologist discuss Russian fairy tales, for example, or meet a World War II survivor. They can take in a production at a local puppet theater, attend the ballet, or visit markets where old women haggle over cheese and sausage. It's also entertaining to simply walk the tree-lined streets, where Yaroslav's huge student population (this ancient town has 18 scientific research and project institutes, 10 higher educational establishments, and a university and academy) stroll in and out of cafés.

Cost for a three-week volunteer post in Yaroslavl, Russia, including lodging and meals at the same hotel where you sleep, runs $2,994 to $3,219.

HOW TO GET IN TOUCH

Cross-Cultural Solutions, 2 Clinton Place, New Rochelle, NY 10801, 800-380-4777, www.crossculturalsolutions.org.

take at-risk kids to the kyrgyzstan mountains

BISHKEK AND OSH, KYRGYZSTAN

The mountains give kids independence and confidence.
—Garth Willis, founder of the Alpine Fund

42 The Alpine Fund, a small nonprofit in the former Soviet country of Kyrgyzstan, takes at-risk kids from Kyrgyzstan and Tajikistan on hiking trips in the mountains. It was started in 2000 by American climber Garth Willis, who hiked most of Kyrgyzstan back in 1995, learning Russian and working as a U.S. government aid worker during the three years he was there. He runs the nonprofit on a shoestring budget of less than $20,000 a year. If it wasn't for the volunteers, who teach computer skills, English, and AIDS prevention to children from area orphanages and street bazaars (in addition to leading the overnight camping trips), Willis would never have been able to help the thousands of children whom he has helped.

A small, impoverished nation of five million people, Kyrgyzstan is 95 percent mountains—ideal for sightseeing, but murder for an economy seeking development. To better provide for their families, many adults end up emigrating in search of work, leaving children, more than 50 percent of the population, at home to fend for themselves. As Willis says, "Just about every kid in Kyrgyzstan is at risk." Children living in orphanages are often required to leave when they reach the age of 16, leaving them with few options.

Volunteers come, usually for two months or longer, to help Willis keep the commitment that he made to the children who, he says, "get gifts from foreigners and then never see them again." Volunteers help Willis offer twice-weekly physical training at the orphanage and lead weekly hiking expeditions into the mountains overlooking Bishkek, Kyrgyzstan's capital. Fifteen kids go on each trip that includes camping and trash collecting, plus learning survival skills, discipline, and respect for nature.

"These kids are surrounded by beautiful mountains and they never get to go up them," Willis says, emphasizing that "soft aid" to these Muslim countries is more effective at cementing international relationships than military might. "We give them something to look forward to. In the schools, the teacher-student relationships are very rigid, Soviet-style," he remarks. "And here are we, adults who play soccer with them, hike with them, and yell at them to make sure their backpacks fit correctly. Once they realize that we are coming every week, it isn't hard to earn their trust."

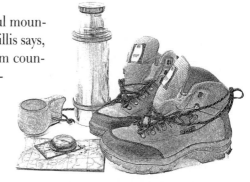

When they're not in the mountains, volunteers teach English and computer classes, usually holding a one-hour lesson in each discipline twice each week. Providing Internet access is another way that the fund helps expand the young people's education and opportunities in Kyrgyzstan.

A FAIRY-TALE ENDING?

The fairy tale of Sleeping Beauty was first published in 1697 by Frenchman Charles Perrault, but it's possible (not that I'm accusing anyone of plagiarism) that he absconded with the tale of a princess doomed to prick her finger from a legend in Kyrgyzstan. Way back in the 10th or 11th century, when Balasagun—now a ghost town in Kyrgyzstan's Chui Valley—was a bustling stop on the Silk Road, a local king was warned by a witch that his one and only daughter would be bitten by a scorpion on her 16th birthday. The king, having the power and authority of most kings, built a 150-foot tower to protect the precious princess, who the witch also predicted would die. But alas, legend tells us that despite his best efforts, the servant who delivered her food each day unwittingly carried in a scorpion amid a plate of grapes on her 16th birthday. And unlike Sleeping Beauty, who merely fell asleep for a hundred years, this princess died.

The remains of the tower, Burana, lie 50 miles from Bishkek. Some believe that it was a minaret that stood nearly 150 feet tall, though the structure was reduced to about 80 feet by earthquake damage. The site also includes a museum, some grave markers and mausoleums, the ruins of a castle, petroglyphs, and stone sculptures known as *bal-bals*. It is such a landmark in Kyrgyzstan that it has been featured on postage stamps.

The Alpine Fund also offers local children internships, jobs, and other leadership opportunities. Those who really excel in the program get a chance to continue their education. One way that you can help—without even traveling to the mountains of Kyrgyzstan—is by donating money to the Alpine Fund's Path to the Summit Scholarship (PASS), which helps young people with leadership abilities to get through college. PASS will support tuition at a local university, plus a stipend to cover living expenses, clothes, and school supplies.

Most important, all of the programs sponsored by the Alpine Fund give the young people here hope that they can create brighter, more prosperous futures for themselves and their families.

Volunteers, Willis says, are asked to stay for two months or longer (although it's not written in stone), giving them time to figure out how to best run the programs, get to know the youth, experience a culture from the inside, and explore a region with amazingly beautiful mountains. Volunteers who are interested in doing more for the fund can help in the office with fund-raising, writing grants, and updating the organization's website.

Although there is no charge to volunteer with the Alpine Fund (there's so much to do that Willis would never charge), volunteers are responsible for their own housing, transportation, and living expenses, which Willis says average about $250 a month.

HOW TO GET IN TOUCH

The Alpine Fund, Box 583192, Minneapolis, MN 55458; Kyrgyzstan contact: Ahunbaeva 119A #502, Bishkek, Kyrgyzstan, 966 312 47 16 35, www.alpinefund.org.

assist europe's marginalized gypsies

TARLUNGENI, ROMANIA

cause there's good deeds
and there is good intention
they're as far apart
as heaven and hell
—Ben Harper, singer-songwriter, "Ground on Down"

43 Romania officially joined the European Union on January 1, 2007. While this event provided an enormous economic boost for the former Iron Curtain country, its Roma people, who have long suffered discrimination, have reaped few, if any, of the benefits.

In the United States, Gypsies, as Roma are generally known, elicit an image of romance and intrigue. In Europe, however, the stateless ethnic group has endured a long history of persecution. Adolf Hitler killed 500,000 Gypsies during his genocidal frenzy; they were the only ethnic group besides Jews to be targeted.

Since the Roma left India at the beginning of the last millennium, they have been deported, homeless, stateless, and forced into incarceration. In Romania, they worked as slaves for 400 years until 1864, when the inhumane practice was finally abolished. Even today, Roma are often scapegoats for most anything that goes wrong in the country. Most Romanians, eager to modernize and catch up to the rest of Europe, view their horses and carts as an embarrassment and their sometimes noisy nighttime parties as a disruption.

Although the Roma have spread out across Europe, Romania has the largest population—more than two million, 63 percent of whom live below subsistence levels. Thanks to widespread discrimination and stigma, large numbers of Roma still lack schooling, jobs, proper housing, and basic nourishment. They live in crowded, ramshackle huts and get passed over consistently for jobs and benefits provided to the rest of the population.

VAMPIRE-INSPIRED TOURS

Braşov is located in Transylvania; unsurprisingly, there are tours inspired by Count Dracula. Although Dracula is a fictional character popularized in Bram Stoker's infamous, eponymous novel, he was inspired by a well-known figure from Romanian history. Vlad Dracula, nicknamed Vlad Tepes (Vlad the Impaler), was a ruler of Wallachia between 1456 and 1461. Important historical places to learn about Vlad Tepes are the 14th-century town of Sighişoara (the house where he was born is now a restaurant and museum of medieval weaponry); the Snagov Monastery (where he was allegedly buried after his assassination, www.snagov.ro); the village of Arefu, Braşov (where Vlad led raids against greedy Saxon merchants); and, of course, Curtea Domneasca, Vlad's palace in Bucharest; and Bran Castle—sometimes called Dracula's Castle—a clifftop fortress where Vlad was briefly imprisoned that once served as the royal family's home and is now a museum (www.brancastlemuseum.ro).

Globe Aware (GA), a Dallas-based nonprofit that dispatches volunteers to 14 countries, offers a unique chance to help these marginalized people. Working with a nongovernmental organization in the fairy-tale medieval town of Braşov, Romania, Globe Aware gives volunteers the chance to build homes, mentor children, and help with a multitude of necessary tasks, determined by the Roma themselves. According to Chris Saucedo, Globe Aware's office manager, "We just do whatever the community feels that they need. We don't like to get too specific, because we want the community to decide what is best for the community on each project. We have built stoves and taught English in the past. The best thing is to look on our website."

Volunteers stay in a community center (designed by student architects from four European universities) in Tarlungeni, on the outskirts of Braşov.

The seven-day post with Globe Aware runs $1,390 and includes lodging in the dorms in the community center and three meals per day.

HOW TO GET IN TOUCH

Globe Aware, 6500 East Mockingbird Lane, Suite 104, Dallas, TX 75214, 877-588-4562, www.globeaware.org.

ECOVOLUNTEER

save the rare, 5,000-year-old breed of karakachan dogs

PIRIN MOUNTAINS, BULGARIA

What is the nature of a species that knowingly and
without good reason exterminates another?
—George Small, author of *The Blue Whale*

44 Cruella de Vil has nothing on the Bulgarian Communist Party. Not only did the communist government that ruled Bulgaria from 1944 to 1989 sell the pelts of Karakachan dogs to make fur coats, but they took them away from their owners and crossbred them with St. Bernards, shepherds, and other breeds to distill their unique characteristics.

For 5,000 years, these dogs protected the sheep and goat herds of Karakachan nomads who summered near the Aegean and Black Seas and wintered in Bulgaria's wide alpine meadows. During communist rule, when livestock was seized and Karakachan nomads forced to settle down, these faithful dogs that served their masters so well all but died out.

By 1990, when Bulgaria finally became free, Sider Sedfchev, a graduate student in Sofia, tried to find a purebred Karakachan to breed with the Karakachan pet he had grown to love. It proved to be a difficult task. He and his brother hiked Bulgaria's mountains in search of communities that still had a pure strain of the dogs that immigrated to Bulgaria with their nomadic masters. It soon became apparent how rare the ancient breed had become. Sedfchev started Semperviva, a nonprofit working, along with the Balkani Wildlife Service, to restore the nearly extinct breed. As both groups are well aware, the rare breed of dogs play an important role in the natural, cultural, and historical heritage of Bulgaria.

Although the dog breeding project began in the backyard of Sedfchev's grandparents' home in Sofia, it has since moved to Pirin National Park, a World Heritage site in southwest Bulgaria with pine forests, waterfalls, 70 glacial lakes, and hundreds of endemic and rare species.

Volunteers who come in from across the globe feed and care for the dogs, whose populations have thankfully been restored to several hundred. In addition to the dog project, Semperviva is also working to insure the legacy of Karakachan horses, a small, hearty horse also used by the nomads, and Karakachan sheep, a long-haired sheep whose wool is used in Karakachan handicrafts.

Volunteers, working through Ecovolunteer, spend a week or more (some stay for several months) on this important biodiversity project. They alternate between a home in the village of Vlahi that serves as a dog and sheep breeding station and a sheepherder's hut in the Pirin Mountains. While tracking sheep and wild horses, volunteers work on horseback. Duties include feeding dogs, bottle-feeding lambs, making cheese and yogurt from sheep's and goat's milk (the long-haired Kalofer goats are another local breed being revived by the group), and leading horseback riding tours of beautiful Pirin National Park.

On those trips through the alpine mountains of Bulgaria, volunteers camp out and spend evenings around the fire listening to shepherds' stories. Spring—when puppies, lambs, and foals are born—is perhaps the busiest time, but volunteers are useful throughout the year.

This volunteer trip that includes meals and lodging (in the beautifully restored village home and in shepherd huts on mountain treks) runs 439 euros ($555) for a week with discounts for consecutive weeks.

HOW TO GET IN TOUCH

Ecovolunteer uses the **Great Canadian Travel Company** to book trips for American and Canadian volunteers, 158 Fort Street, Winnipeg, Manitoba R3C 1C9, Canada, 800-661-3830, www.ecovolunteer.org.

work on an organic farm

FARMS ACROSS ITALY

It's good for a city girl to get her hands dirty.
—Pamela Newton, WWOOF volunteer in Italy

45 Whether you want to pick olives, keep bees, grow vegetables, or harvest medicinal herbs, there's an organic farm in Italy that needs your help. For a mere 25 euros ($30), you can join World Wide Opportunities on Organic Farms (WWOOF) Italia and receive the list of more than 250 Italian farms that will provide you with a bed and three square meals in return for five or six hours of work a day.

The beauty of a vacation with WWOOF Italia is that the farms on the list, spread across Italy from Aosta to Puglia, are far from the well-known tourist paths. Not only do you learn about organic and biodynamic farming in some of the most serene settings in Italy, but you get the rare chance to meet real down-to-earth Italian families. Away from the big tourist traps, you'll find farms where olive trees are still pruned by hand, where milk arrives warm in pails, and where goats and a new litter of puppies share the same 300-year-old stone barn.

And as for those three squares a day? It's Italy, after all, where food is practically a religion. You'll come in from the fields to find steaming bowls of rigatoni with pesto sauce and fresh grated parmesan or smoky chestnut flour cakes, served with fresh sheep's milk ricotta and honey. In Italy, it should go without saying, there is true respect for the art of growing, cooking, and eating food. Eating locally isn't a catchphrase here—it's a way of life.

WWOOF, a worldwide organization with branches in most of the world's countries, was started in 1971 by Sue Coppard, a London secretary who recognized the need for a city girl like herself to experience the countryside. She organized a trial weekend at a farm in Sussex for four people she met through a classified ad. Her experiment was such a success that WWOOF quickly spread from England across the globe. Although WWOOF international provides loosely followed guidelines, each country hosts its own list of farms and runs its operation separately.

WWOOF Italia was started in 1999 by Bridget Matthews, a British expat who got tired of city life. She bought a farm in Tuscany in the late 1980s and, with a couple partners, organized the WWOOF organization ten years later. It has grown from 89 farms and 182 WWOOFers, as volunteers call themselves, to 283 farms and nearly 2,000 WWOOFers per year.

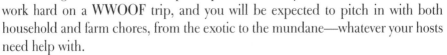

As Matthews points out, it's a win-win for everyone involved. Volunteers learn about organic farming and green living and get a rich cultural experience while doing so, and their hosts get much-needed help. Keep in mind that you will work hard on a WWOOF trip, and you will be expected to pitch in with both household and farm chores, from the exotic to the mundane—whatever your hosts need help with.

The variety of farms on WWOOF Italia's list range from a tiny farm near Castagneto Carducci where volunteers keep bees and make tinctures from wild echinacea to a 1,235-acre vineyard owned by a famous Italian artist. There's everything from mountain refuges an hour's walk from the main road with no phones or electricity to goat and sheep farms on the island of Sardinia. There's even a castle on the list.

WHAT'S IN A NAME?

WWOOF is a suspiciously canine-sounding acronym for an organization whose name has gone through several incarnations in its first decade of existence. The WW in WWOOF originally stood for Working Weekends. Then the first two words were changed to Willing Workers. Finally, those two words starting with the letter *w* ended up being World Wide, after immigration authorities in some countries suspiciously eyed WWOOF, apparently viewing it as a clandestine migrant worker organization.

WWOOF can be used in every part of speech.

- As a verb: "I plan to WWOOF next summer in Italy."
- As an adjective: "Welcome to our Sicilian WWOOF farm."
- As a noun: "I am a WWOOFer and I'm making plum preserves."
- As a gerund: "My WWOOFing last summer was both delicious and educational."

You might find yourself rounding up sheep on horseback in Molise in southwest Italy, tending deer in Tuscany, cultivating bamboo in the Umbrian hills, helping butcher a pig to make salami and sausage near Rome, or tying up grape vines or picking olives near Florence.

The best times to volunteer are in the spring (March to June), for the preparation of the vegetable garden, pruning, and spreading manure, and in the autumn (September to early December), for the grape and olive harvests. But any time of year is fine, as there is always work to be done on an organic farm.

GET PERMISSION

Italian immigration law requires that every person entering the country apply for a *permesso di soggiorno* (permit to stay) within eight days of arriving in the country. If your visit will last longer than eight days, you have to present yourself at the local police station with your passport and request permission to stay in Italy.

Most tourists skip this formality, but if you're coming to WWOOF it is wise to take care of it immediately after you arrive in Italy to avoid any problems with your status during your stay.

Once you submit the WWOOF membership fee, the only charge for a WWOOF vacation, you'll get the list of farms and contact information. You're in charge of making contact with a farm and setting up all the details. Most host farms welcome volunteers for two weeks or longer. Some farms will welcome families with older children, but you must confirm this with your hosts.

Work hours will vary greatly, depending on time of year and the project you're working on. If you don't speak at least rudimentary Italian, you should choose a farm where your hosts speak English.

Accommodations will also vary from farm to farm, though most have a room for WWOOFers. On some farms, you will stay in tents (you may need to bring your own sleeping bag and tent).

HOW TO GET IN TOUCH

WWOOF Italia, c/o Bridget Matthews, Coordinator, 109 via Casavecchia, 57022 Castagneto Carducci, LI, Italy, 32 90 806 234, www.wwoof.it.

middle east

Rain does not fall on one roof alone.
—Middle Eastern proverb

Saadi Shirazi, a 12th-century Middle Eastern poet, said that human beings are all members of one body, created from one essence. He said that when one member is in pain, the others cannot rest.

That's why volunteering in this part of the world is so important. None of us can afford to rest as long as the Middle East continues to bleed.

Violence only begets more violence. And while volunteers cannot change long-held animosity overnight, they can lay down a stone or two in a path that leads to reconciliation. By starting a dialogue, by holding out a hand, by saying "I'm interested in learning more about you and about your culture," volunteers can put a toe in a door that desperately needs to be wrenched opened.

The problems in the Middle East are hard to look at, marked as they are by terrible violence and mistrust. But somebody has to try. That somebody might as well be you.

In this chapter, you'll find lots of opportunities for healing the Middle East— from picking olives with disenfranchised Palestinians to turning abandoned army bases into schools and gardens, from protecting endangered monk seals to painting a mural on a wall.

And one of these days, if we all continue to believe in, and to strive for, a new reality, those walls—the real ones, the figurative ones, even the ones with the beautiful paint—might just come down for good.

assist iraqi refugees

DAMASCUS, SYRIA

I came to Syria to bridge a gap between me and someone not like me.
—Sally Tawfik, volunteer from Middle East Fellowship's 2008 Damascus
Summer Encounter

46 The American invasion of Iraq and the ongoing war drove five million Iraqis to flee their homes, the largest Muslim exodus since the creation of Israel in 1948. Scattered now throughout Egypt, Jordan, Lebanon, Syria, and Turkey, displaced Iraqis—one out of every five citizens—struggle daily to survive.

Middle East Fellowship (MEF), a U.S.-based nonprofit supporting indigenous organizations and churches throughout the Middle East, sends volunteers to work with Iraqi refugees. They organize Refugee Response Teams to meet with refugees and humanitarian groups working on their behalf in Syria, Jordan, and Lebanon, and host summer trips to Damascus, Syria, where many displaced Iraqis live.

The goal is to provide person-to-person encounters that MEF hopes "will build lifelong relationships and break down false stereotypes" that run rampant among most Americans. Anna Mazhirov, a Duke University English major who traveled to

ONE SIZE FITS ALL

According to Guinness World Records, a Damascus suburb claims the world's largest restaurant. Bawabet Dimashq (Damascus Gate in Arabic), a 6,014-seat eatery with waterfalls, searchlights, an in-house mosque, and reproductions of archaeological ruins, dethroned Bangkok's Mang Gorn Luang restaurant (a mere 5,000 seats) in 2008. The family-owned Damascus Gate employs 1,800 people in the busy summer season—including more than 500 chefs, who can prepare 25 to 30 helpings of hummus in one minute flat.

The $120-million restaurant opened in 2005, and its 26,000-square-foot kitchen prepares Indian, Chinese, Gulf-Arab, Iranian, Middle Eastern, and Syrian food. One item not on the menu? Alcohol, of course. Perhaps you can settle for an apple tobacco hookah.

Damascus in 2008 says, "Americans have no idea . . . how rich Syrian history is, how well-formed Syrian character is, how open the people are. . . . They have no idea how far [the reality] is from what they've built up in their minds from the media."

Another MEF volunteer, activist Kelly Hayes-Raitt, wanted to put a human face on the so-called enemy through the 2008 journey that she describes on her blog, Violating Sanctions: An American Woman's Listening Tour through the Axis of Evil (www.peacepathfoundation.org). Hayes-Raitt describes children whose parents were shot, whose cars and houses were burned, and who tell their stories matter-of-factly.

The yearly summer volunteer excursions, called Damascus Summer Encounter (DSE), are one- to two-month trips divided between volunteer work, study of the Arabic language, meeting with local leaders, and side trips to Aleppo, Hama, the Krak des Chevaliers Crusader Castle, Palmyra, and other cities and sites of historical and cultural significance.

Each summer, 30 to 60 DSE volunteers work at youth summer camps, assist orphans (especially by providing English instruction) or senior citizens (by offering basic care), or help local grassroots agencies find funding and update their websites.

At the summer youth camp, held on a hill outside Damascus at St. Paul's Church, 300 children—whose families are Sunni refugees who have congregated in Jeramana, a rapidly deteriorating section of the city—dance, draw, sculpt, play, and get tutored in English, math, and Arabic.

Tasks at the Greek Orthodox Patriarchate's Iraqi refugee program range from delivering food and school kits to families to composing letters and updating the refugee website. Participants in the Middle East Fellowship film interviews, conduct evaluations, and write articles, take photos, and update blogs for Middle East Window, MEF's online magazine.

Cost for Damascus Summer Encounter, including lodging at St. Elias Monastery (the Greek Orthodox monastery within walking distance of Bab Sharki, one of the seven gates to the Old City of Damascus), two meals a day, and Arabic language courses, is $1,950 for one month and $3,365 for two months.

HOW TO GET IN TOUCH
Middle East Fellowship, Box 1252, Brea, CA 92822, 714-529-1926, www.middleeastfellowship.org.

take school groups rock climbing, camping, and snorkeling

DUBAI, UNITED ARAB EMIRATES

You are here to enable the world to live more amply, with greater vision, with a finer spirit of hope and achievement . . . and you impoverish yourself if you forget the errand.
—Woodrow Wilson, former U.S. President

47 When filming the geopolitical thriller *Syriana,* actors George Clooney and Matt Damon expected to stay in the Emirate of Dubai for four days. Instead, they ended up staying for four weeks, enjoying the dramatic desert landscape that conjures up more outdoor adventures than an L. L. Bean catalog. In the enormous sandbox that is Dubai, tourists can do everything from speed down huge dunes on a sandboard to kite surf to barrel over dry riverbeds in a 4x4—an activity locally known as wadi bashing.

Changing Worlds, a U.K.-based travel company, recruits volunteers to teach outdoor adventure to the students in Dubai's many international schools, more than 30 at last count. It's a tough job, but, as the old saying goes, somebody has to take the wealthy private school students camel trekking, canoeing, rock climbing, ballooning, deep-sea fishing, and speeding around the desert in dune buggies.

They call it outdoor education and any school in Dubai worth its pedigree offers it as part of the curriculum. It develops character, fosters a spirit of discovery, and builds self-reliance. Not to mention, it's a lot more fun than dodgeball.

Volunteers, who stay for six months, design and implement outdoor adventure packages and take students out in "the field." In this case, the field is represented by the Hajar mountains, the beach town of Fujairah, and the endless miles of golden sand dunes and wadis that surround the city with its dramatic, high-tech skyline. Among other things, you'll plan educational forays to the Dubai Desert Conservation Reserve, a 55,600-acre refuge that protects the Arabian oryx, a rare species of antelope, and snorkeling expeditions to the Gulf of Oman.

Volunteers work five days a week, helping out at torch-lit dinners in Bedouin-style camps in the evenings. As a glitzy cosmopolitan city, Dubai offers lots of possibilities for your free time, from scoring bargains at traditional souks or flashy malls to indoor skiing.

Cost for the six-month post that usually starts in the fall (it's way too hot in the summer) runs £1,995 ($2,955) and includes lodging in a simple apartment and a 2,000-dirham (£140 or $205) per month food allowance.

HOW TO GET IN TOUCH

Changing Worlds, 11 Doctors Lane, Chaldon, Surrey CR3 5AE England, 44 1883 340 960, www.changingworlds.co.uk.

teach english or give swimming lessons to children

AMMAN, JORDAN

When the story of these times gets written, we want it to say that we did all we could, and it was more than anyone could have imagined.
—Bono, lead singer of U2 and activist

48 Forget the Foreign Service! If Dave Santulli, founder of United Planet, has anything to do with it, each of us will become our own diplomat. We need to develop personal relationships with people from all over the planet, people who may not look like us or follow the same customs, but who love their families, want happiness, and share more commonalities than might be apparent at first glance.

After working in Japan for many years and traveling to more than a hundred countries, Santulli came to the conclusion that world peace would only be possible once each of us walks in the shoes of our foreign brothers and sisters.

He started the nonprofit United Planet (UP), which offers Volunteer Quests, both short-term (one to twelve weeks) and long-term (three months to a year), to nearly 30 countries to facilitate what the organization calls "Relational Diplomacy—recognizing that the relationship between people of diverse backgrounds is the basic building block for uniting the world."

Like most of the volunteer nonprofits, UP offers a wide variety of volunteer options, from working in an orphanage to empowering women to saving the environment. The Jordan Quest, a two- to twelve-week opportunity to work with children, is offered in Amman, a capital city of two million in the country's northwest hills. Volunteers can teach English through a local nongovernmental organization, or work at a school for children with special needs, teaching English or arts and crafts, or helping physical therapists with such tasks as swimming lessons.

In addition to the Jordan program, United Planet offers short-term volunteer opportunities in 14 countries and long-term ones in 29 countries, and it doesn't stop there. The Cultural Awareness Project brings the shoes we're trying to walk in to America, letting fifth graders meet a Japanese *koto* (zither) player or the Lions Club hear about suicide bombers from a Palestinian who lived through an attack by one. It harnesses the Internet to get people from 150 countries talking to each other about everything from table manners to superstitions. On the autumnal equinox, a day on which the sun shines equally on all the Earth's people, Santulli and company host United Planet Day, a day for everyone to share their history, arts, and culture.

Jordan volunteers live with host families, and take Arabic and cooking lessons and excursions (included in the price) to Petra, the Dead Sea, and Mount Nebo.

Four-week volunteer posts in Jordan start the first and third Saturday of every month and cost $2,395, including a room with a host family and breakfast and dinner.

HOW TO GET IN TOUCH
United Planet, 11 Arlington Street, Boston, MA 02116, 800-292-2316 or 617-267-7763, www.unitedplanet.org.

PAY IT FORWARD

Volunteer vacations don't come cheap. Even on free ones, volunteers still have to get from their homes to the place where they will provide their elbow grease. Because the elbow grease is going to a good cause, volunteer vacations are often tax-deductible, and friends, colleagues, and other supporters who can't volunteer themselves often get vicarious pleasure from chipping in on expenses. Here, compliments of United Planet, are six fund-raising schemes.

- **Create an online fund-raising page.** Not only does this spread the word about your quest, but it allows sponsors to donate on the website.
- **Contact your local media.** Let your community know all the details about your project; it might entice sponsors to chip in.
- **Create a letter-writing campaign.** Craft a letter explaining why you've embarked on this life-changing mission, why the project is important, and how they can help support it.
- **Send e-mail updates.** Create a list and keep people posted on how your fund-raising efforts are going.
- **Host a fund-raising event.** Offer to babysit, wash cars, or do yard work in return for a donation. You could also host an event, like a dinner.
- **Apply for scholarships and grants.** Check with your school or local foundations to see if they can offer support for your journey.

INTERNATIONAL PALESTINIAN YOUTH LEAGUE AND ALTERNATIVE INFORMATION CENTER

turn a military base into a school and garden

BETHLEHEM, ISRAEL

Jesus Christ wouldn't be able to leave Bethlehem today unless
he showed a magnetic ID card, a permit and his thumbprint.
—Christian university student quoted by Jamil Hamad in *Time*

49 Mary and Joseph came into Bethlehem on a donkey. You'll probably come by taxi after being stopped at a daunting three-story concrete barricade crowned with razor wire. An Israeli soldier with an assault rifle will examine your papers and decide when and if to open the sliding steel door to let you in.

Such is the reality of everyday life in the birthplace of Jesus, a town the Prince of Peace could scarcely recognize—divided by religion, history, and years of bitter fighting. Christians, who once represented 90 percent of Bethlehem's population of 35,000, have mostly left town, no longer willing to live with the myriad cultural shifts and inconveniences brought about by the Israeli occupation and Islamic extremism. Still, their fearless leader, the one tourists come to honor, would never want them to give up—on peace, on love, on bridging the chasms that rip apart his hometown, and, indeed, the world.

Every December for the past several years, the International Palestinian Youth League (IPYL) and the Alternative Information Center (AIC), a joint Palestinian-Israeli political advocacy and grassroots activist organization, have sponsored an international work camp in Bethlehem. Volunteers from all over the planet come to this holy place to celebrate Christmas with Palestinians and to spruce up a former Israeli army base that has been turned into a residential village. IPYL and AIC are building a school, a hospital, a youth house, and a series of gardens there.

And while the work is extremely important in a city whose economic vitality has been depleted by the wall—an ominous gray snake started in 2002 that will eventually stretch 436 miles through the West Bank—the real mission of the project in Eish al Ghurab is to build bridges of understanding between people of various cultures.

Besides painting, farming, and cleaning, volunteers learn about Palestinian culture, tour such well-known spots as the Church of the Nativity, visit Bethlehem's three refugee camps, and watch documentaries at AICafe, a coffee shop run by AIC. They also spend time with Palestinian politicians, authors, and families who have been stuck in stateless limbo for generations. Many speak in wistful tones about their former homes, towns that have been erased from Israel's maps.

The two-week camp, including accommodations in a secure apartment in Eish al Ghurab, runs $530 and includes meals that you and other volunteers will cook together.

HOW TO GET IN TOUCH

Volunteers can secure their place in these camps through **Volunteers for Peace,** 1034 Tiffany Road, Belmont, VT 05730, 802-259-2759, www.vfp.org.

mentor a budding entrepreneur

MOROCCO

*I never thought I'd be living off a street where there's a stall selling watermelons
in between one that sells live chickens and one that sells DVDs!*
—Ceri Evans, Morocco volunteer

50 One out of every three people in Morocco is 14 or younger. That means a lot of people are soon going to be young adults who need jobs.

On this volunteer gig, administered by Projects Abroad, a U.K.-based business with more than a hundred volunteer projects across the planet, entrepreneurs are invited to spend a month or more mentoring brilliant under-30s who have a great idea for a business, but don't know how to find the starting line.

Budding entrepreneurs literally apply for mentors, detailing their business idea, their plan for making it work, and their dreams of what it might become. Volunteer entrepreneurs (and you don't have to be a billionaire like Virgin founder Richard Branson or Microsoft co-founder Bill Gates to qualify—you can simply be an astute manager) also fill out paperwork, advising where they'd like to offer their services.

Any of the 24 developing countries where Projects Abroad (PA) has in-country managers is fair game—from Moldova to Fiji to Rabat, Morocco. You might mentor Vijaya Prakash, who wants to expand his organic farm in southern India, or Richard Brown, who hopes to send players from his football (soccer) academy in Ghana to teams in Eastern Europe, or Fernando Rosenberg, who hopes to offer ecotourists expanded knowledge of the wild through his rain forest lodge in southern Peru.

Partnership in Enterprise (www.partnership-in-enterprise.com) was launched by Peter Slowe, the geography professor who started Projects Abroad, Britain's largest volunteer travel company, and Nick Wheeler, who founded Charles Tyrwhitt Shirts—an upscale London shirtmaker with nearly a half million customers and branches in Kuwait, Madrid, Mumbai, New York, Paris, and Singapore.

Slowe and Wheeler decided the best way that they could help developing countries was to unleash their citizens' ideas, encouraging them to think and act in enterprising ways. Partnership in Enterprise volunteers help the young Moroccan population spot opportunities, marshal resources, and turn their ideas into reality.

Because Projects Abroad has an active volunteer operation running in Rabat, it's easy to slot a business mentor into the country. Morocco's PA director Saad Rbiai, a former psychologist for the Peace Corps and a coordinator for the U.S. State Department, sets mentors up with a host family in a traditional *riad* with inner courtyards and a maze of staircases within the peach walls of the old city.

Like all PA volunteers, business mentors share meals with their host families, giving them an authentic Moroccan experience. Host families speak Arabic and French; one family member usually speaks English as well.

The PA office is located in Rabat's Agdal district near the Mosque Badr. Partnership in Enterprise volunteers are invited to network with other PA volunteers, who are in the country working in orphanages, teaching English, and coaching soccer.

Cost for this monthlong Partnership in Enterprise volunteer gig is $3,995 and includes all meals and accommodations.

HOW TO GET IN TOUCH
Projects Abroad Inc., 347 West 36th Street, Suite 903, New York, NY 10018, 888-839-3535, www.projects-abroad.org.

LIGHTS, CAMERAS, ACTION

Morocco's King Mohammed VI is an avid movie buff and has even been known to help out the foreign film producers who swarm to this unlikely country for big shoots. For Alexandre Aja's horror remake *The Hills Have Eyes,* the king lent some hunting trailers from the royal palace.

Several movie studios, including Dino de Laurentiis' CLA Studios with its two large, sound-proofed, air-conditioned shooting sets, 20 makeup rooms, and four set construction workshops, make Morocco a popular port of call for big shoots that require sand or monumental sets.

Here's a partial list of movies that have been filmed in Morocco:

- *Alexander*
- *Babel*
- *Black Hawk Down*
- *Gladiator*
- *Hidalgo*
- *Kundun*
- *Lawrence of Arabia*
- *The Man Who Would Be King*
- *The Mummy* and *The Mummy Returns*
- *The Sheltering Sky*
- The TV mini-series *The Ten Commandments*
- *Troy*

save the world's last mediterranean monk seals

MERSIN, TURKEY

I would feel more optimistic about a bright future for man if he spent
less time proving that he can outwit Nature and more time tasting
her sweetness and respecting her seniority.
—E. B. White, Pulitzer Prize–winning author

51 When Christopher Columbus arrived in the New World, Caribbean monk seals were nearly as abundant as sand. After several hundred years of hunting them for their oil and building hotels over their sunning beaches, Caribbean monk seals haven't been spotted since 1952. On June 6, 2008, the National Marine Fisheries Service declared this shy marine mammal officially extinct.

Luckily, it has some cousins—the Hawaiian monk seal (there are roughly a thousand left) and the Mediterranean monk seal, with 400, at most, hanging on for dear life. In fact, the Mediterranean monk seal is one of the six most endangered mammals on the planet.

One of the monk seal's problems is that its historical habitat on the southeast coast of Turkey is mighty gorgeous. Hotel developers are lustily eying the beaches and caves where it gives birth. And because the seal swims the seas between Greece, Syria, and Turkey, it's difficult to get governments to uphold international protections.

That's where you come in. You'll work with scientists from the Middle East Technical University's Institute of Marine Sciences (METU-IMS), collecting data about global climate change, studying the seals' behavior, patrolling their protected waters, and promoting fishing methods that don't interfere with the seals' needs and habitat. Dynamite fishing, though illegal, is still being used in this area.

This important conservation project began in 1994, when a team of METU-IMS scientists conducted a brief survey along the shoreline that uncovered the most prolific breeding monk seal colony in Turkey. They wasted no time setting up the

TIPTOE THROUGH THE TURKISH TULIPS

Everyone knows that tulips originated in Holland, right? Well, no, the cup-shaped blooms are actually endemic to Turkey, along with 9,000 other species of flowers. The first tulips didn't get shipped to Holland until 1593, when a Belgian trader imported bulbs from Istanbul. In fact, the name "tulip," or *tulband* in Turkish, comes from the Turkish "turban," and the flower was a popular motif in decorative arts of all types in Turkey for centuries. Scholars believe the Turks cultivated tulips as early as A.D. 1000. They even named an important historical era—the years 1700 to 1730—the tulip period.

When the showy flower first appeared in Holland, a Dutch botanist tried to use them for medicinal purposes, such as treating gout, and to provide a cheap, albeit unpleasant tasting, source of nutrition. Although the botanist's experiments bombed, the tulips became popular among the Dutch, actually far too popular.

In the ensuing tulip frenzy during the early 1600s, some Dutch tulip bulbs sold for more than houses. According to Jon Mandaville, associate professor of history and Middle East studies at Portland State University:

> "In Holland, one day in the early 1630s... a single Viceroy tulip bulb changed hands. Its price, paid in kind, was as follows: two loads of wheat, four loads of rye, four fat oxen, eight fat pigs, twelve fat sheep, two hogs-heads of wine, four barrels of eight-florin beer, two barrels of butter, 1,000 pounds of cheese, a complete bed, a suit of clothes and a silver beaker. The whole was valued at 2,500 florins. About the same time, one bulb of Semper Augustus was sold for twice that sum, plus a fine new carriage and pair."

In the end, however, the market was irrevocably affected by a brisk trade in tulip futures. When the market for tulip bulbs ultimately collapsed, hundreds of Dutch families found that their assets were wiped out.

research project, using volunteers to help with finances, data collection, and good-will among the locals.

Although they were soon able to establish the area near Mersin as a marine protected region, they knew from experience that a law alone does not guarantee the safety of an endangered animal. Rather, that animal's habitat must be restored and then protected, and everyone—from government officials to local fishermen—

must understand that protecting the monk seal is good for all concerned. To help reinforce those ideas, volunteers share information with tourists and give lectures at secondary schools about the precarious plight of the local monk seals.

While in Turkey, volunteers will have ample opportunities to gain hands-on marine biology experience by collecting data to support scientific research, such as tracking non-native species in the Red Sea and documenting the effects of global climate change. Other tasks may include monitoring the health of the shore habitat, taking photographs, snorkeling to conduct a visual fish census, experimental fishing, and monitoring and planting sea grass *(Posidonia oceanica).* They may also patrol the marine protected area to guard against illegal fishing practices, such as disturbing monk seal breeding areas, using explosives, bottom-trawling, or purse-seining—using a huge net with a drawstring closure between two boats to capture a larger catch.

Since the Mediterranean monk seals are identified and monitored based on photographs captured by remote cameras set up in the breeding caves, volunteers may also work on archiving photo data collected by the teams that are tracking the seals' behavior. The marine project team includes a project manager, four marine biologists, and a sociologist, plus one volunteer.

During much of this four-week project, volunteers live on the sea in a three-cabin research vessel recording data on not only the monk seals, but also on dolphins, two species of endangered turtles, an endangered sea urchin, birds, weather, and even boats that pass into the seals' marine habitat. If you go during whelping season, between August and December, you'll get the chance to monitor the breeding caves through infrared cameras, observing this annual ritual and counting new pups. If you're very lucky, you might even get to see one of the seals.

Working with a fishing cooperative in the village of Meydan, less than three miles from the Syrian border, volunteers get the chance to immerse themselves in Turkish culture, language, and food. They sometimes help the local fishermen prepare their catch to be sent to Istanbul.

Cost for the four-week project is $2,070 and includes accommodations and delicious Mediterranean meals.

HOW TO GET IN TOUCH

Global Vision International, 252 Newbury Street, Number 4, Boston, MA 02116, 888-653-6028, www.gviusa.com.

GUDRAN ASSOCIATION FOR ART AND DEVELOPMENT
save a fishing village

EL MAX, EGYPT

Our sense of life is the same, so why are we so apart?
—Muhammed Hosni, volunteer with Gudran

52 In 2000, husband and wife team Sameh El Halawany and Aliaa El Gready devoted themselves to saving one of Egypt's last fishing villages. El Max, an impoverished community on the outskirts of ancient Alexandria, was in danger of being razed.

Most of El Max's 9,000 residents made their living through fishing, a career that has been becoming ever more difficult. Wedged between a military base and a petrochemical factory, the trench—as they call the canal that leads to the ocean where they fished—was becoming more polluted by the day.

Instead of focusing on El Max's problems, something that often happens in situations like this, Halawany and El Gready decided to focus on what was right with El Max, and on what is possible in this independent-minded town that supplies 35 percent of the fish for Alexandria, a city of seven million people.

As artists, the enterprising duo wanted to uplift the village through art. They hoped not only to beautify the simple concrete homes along the canal, but also to beautify the souls and dreams of the despairing people. Could we use art, they wondered, use sculpture, painting, theater, and drama to encourage pride of place, collaboration, entrepreneurship, and nonviolence?

With a $3,000 grant from the Ford Foundation, they bought a building next to the canal and turned it into the Gudran Art Center, a place to hold art and music classes and all kinds of performances. At first, they appealed to the adults, but that idea went about as far as a one-legged camel, since El Max's grownups had a tendency to fear change, like grownups everywhere, and their sense of belief had dimmed and run dry.

So they turned to the town's children, inviting them to come in to experiment with paint and other materials and see what they could make. They chatted with fishermen in coffeehouses and enticed women to come out of their homes to display

Middle East | **149**

their embroidery and other crafts. And that grassroots approach began to change everything about life in the traditional village.

One by one, the cement block buildings situated along the canal were renovated, plastered, and painted in bright colors. Sculptures sprang up, music began being played on the streets. Life poured back into the town. Art, they found, was a potent form of cultural resistance.

Even the children's parents began to take aesthetic pride in their town. "Before" and "after" pictures of their homes serve as perfect metaphors for the villagers whose newly instilled pride helped them realize they could fight back against the government and corporations that were encroaching on their sacred fishing grounds.

Today, Gudran runs daily art workshops for children and adults, literacy programs, and public health campaigns. It hosts an Internet hub for youth and trains craftspeople to market and sell their work.

Wafaa Aly, whose colorful fabrics, skirts, and shirts are now sold in Gudran galleries, says the program enabled her to improve herself with art. "I've started to see," she says, "that there is something called a future that I should work for."

Every year, Gudran hosts three-week artistic work camps where international volunteers with an artistic bent (and as Gudran's founders are quick to point out, "everyone has art in them") come to work with the community to create art and inspire beauty.

In her online diary at Artthrob (www.artthrob.co.za/04nov/diary.html), South African artist and writer Sue Williamson describes how in the fall of 2004 she spent two and a half weeks with a group of artists in El Max. She recounts some of the pitfalls encountered along the way: "Since my work often involves listening to what people say, I find not being able to speak Arabic a major stumbling block, so I try to learn a bit, making lists of words each day and pinning them on my wall at night." Ultimately, her Gudran project ended up being "painting the statements people made about living in El Max on the outside of their houses." Further attempts to relocate El Max households were now met by homes painted in English and Arabic with such slogans as "We are like fish—we cannot live away from the sea."

Jean Christophe Lanquetin, a French scenographer and artist, installed a sculpture

The creative lifeblood of the fishing village of El Max pumps from the Gudran Association for Art and Development, a collective of artists, writers, film-makers, and dramatists who decided to abandon the galleries and theaters and instead connect art to the streets and souls of Egyptian communities. Although Gudran's name means "walls" in Arabic, it's meant as walls to paint, not to divide.

In a 2007 interview with writer Michelle Chen, Gudran program organizer Abdalla Daif remarked, "Development is just learning how to accept change ... How can you reach change without imagination? ... Development is to be able to change your life, to reach a better future.

"So, here is where the art arrives," he says. "To improve the imagination space."

on the flat roof of a home across from the Gudran Art Centre. Another French artist, Gilles Touyard, created a "monument to love" constructed of wire rings and helium balloons.

Volunteers may make kites, perform theater, and paint murals. But Halawany and Gready are very clear that there are no rules, no titles, and no punishment in Gudran's programs. Just a lot of creative work done together.

Program organizer Abdalla Daif says, "You're not discussing political stuff, or religious or cultural differences. You just get together and begin to paint. So, art here is really the neutral space, the neutral area for dialogue."

Cost for the three-week art camps, including lodging in cottages by the beach and such simple meals as bread, fish, and fava beans, runs about $370.

HOW TO GET IN TOUCH

Gudran Association for Art and Development, Tolombat El Max Street, El Max, Alexandria, Egypt, 20 1011 70800, www.gudran.com.

ANOTHER THOUGHTFUL, COMMITTED CITIZEN: IAN MCKILLOP

After reading an article about international volunteering in Canada's *Globe and Mail,* Ian McKillop, a risk analyst from Halifax, Nova Scotia, decided to spend his next vacation helping others instead of just taking a break from work. He mentioned his holiday plans at his office and before he knew it, 12 co-workers from Flagstone—a global reinsurance company—offices around the world had decided to join him. David Brown, Flagstone's chief executive officer, even decided he'd pay for it all.

In May 2008, Flagstone sent 13 employees from nine offices in four countries to Costa Rica to build trails through a rain forest, work in a butterfly garden, and paint the community center in Quebradas, a remote community in a biological reserve.

"We called our trip 'Flagstone without Borders,'" McKillop says. "Working together for a common cause was a life-changing experience for all of us."

Enlisting the help of United Planet, a U.S.-based nonprofit that offers what they call Volunteer Quests in 50 countries (see p. 136 for more on one of United Planet's projects in Jordan), McKillop and his team met up in Costa Rica to work together in Quebradas.

"I thought that this endeavor would be a great opportunity for team building—a chance for people from our different offices around the globe to get to know one another, put a name to a face, and at the same time, help a community in need," McKillop explains.

The Flagstone volunteers lived with Costa Rican families, sharing humble meals and life experiences. "They kept apologizing to me for not having more to offer me, but what they offered me was priceless," says Alison Thomson, a Flagstone employee from Switzerland.

Rennika Trott, an administrative assistant in Flagstone's Bermuda headquarters, agreed: "This is the best thing I've ever done in my life. It opened my eyes to a whole new world."

McKillop, who created a 12-page report about the two-week trip, complete with color photos, says corporate social responsibility is even more important for a global company like Flagstone with offices in nine countries. "It's imperative that people see the divide," he says. "There are lots of people who want to alleviate themselves from poverty, but don't have the means and opportunities to do it. A small little push is all people sometimes need."

As for next year's vacation? McKillop is already planning Flagstone without Borders, Redux—either to Siem Reap, Cambodia, or the Carpathian Mountains of Romania.

maintain an israeli military base

MILITARY BASES THROUGHOUT ISRAEL

A short period on an army base is good therapy.
—Ira Zimmerman, U.S. volunteer with Sar-El

53 You'll live in barracks, wear an Israeli Defense Force uniform, and work side-by-side with the 18- to 21-year-old Tzahal soldiers who will think you've lost your mind for choosing (they have no choice—all Israeli citizens are drafted at 18) to take a tour of duty with the Israeli Army.

Granted, your tour is shorter (three weeks compared to three years for men, two years for women), and you won't be on the firing lines (volunteers aren't even issued weapons). Yet you can feel good that you've helped defend an independent state that has enormous importance not only for the region, but for the world.

Thousands of volunteers come every year, from all over the world, to test communication equipment, pack intelligence maps, build fences, and clean medical supplies. This allows the conscripted soldiers to spend their days doing the higher level jobs for which they are trained and saves the Israeli Army millions of dollars.

Sar-El (a Hebrew acronym that means "service for Israel") began in 1982 when Israel was in the midst of the Galilee war. Since the majority of able-bodied Golan Heights settlers were tied up defending their country, their farm fields, ripe with crops, were going unpicked. Dr. Aharon Davidi, former head of IDF Paratroopers and director of the Golan Heights settlement, sent a recruitment team to the United States to beg for help. Within a couple weeks, some 650 volunteers showed up to save the crops.

The volunteers decided the once-in-a-lifetime chance to support this little country they loved should be continued. The following year, Sar-El was officially founded as a nonprofit, nonpolitical organization. Today, it brings in volunteers from 30 countries, many whom return year after year.

And as for why they travel as far as 5,700 miles to "join the army," Janna Walsh, a volunteer from Richboro, Pennsylvania, explains it like this, "In my 'real' life as a consultant, the work I do takes a very long road before it benefits anyone directly.

CAN'T KEEP A GOOD CITY DOWN

Each Sar-El "tour of duty" includes off-base excursions and usually one of those tours takes volunteers to Jerusalem, a controversial religious hub divided into three sections. One of the world's oldest cities, high in the Judean Hills, it has been around since 4000 B.C., and was founded by King David.

The city's biggest claim to fame, however, may be its astounding resiliency. In a 2004 book, *Jerusalem Beseiged: From Ancient Canaan to Modern Israel,* George Washington University professor Eric H. Cline uncovered "at least 118 separate conflicts in and for Jerusalem during the past four millennia—conflicts that ranged from local religious struggles to strategic military campaigns and that embraced everything in between."

According to Cline, despite often being called the city of peace: "Jerusalem has been destroyed completely at least twice, besieged twenty-three times, attacked an additional fifty-two times, captured and recaptured forty-four times, been the scene of twenty revolts and innumerable riots, had at least five separate periods of violent terrorist attacks during the past century, and has only changed hands completely peacefully twice in the past four thousand years."

At my base, I was scraping Israeli mud from hand suction pumps that had been used—and would be used again—by medical corpsmen to save a soldier's life."

During the work week (Sunday through Thursday), you'll be on duty from roughly 8 a.m. to 4 p.m. A *madricha* (liaison in Hebrew) will see to it that you get your fatigues and boots, daily assignments, off-base excursions, and a chance to hoist the blue-and-white Magen David at the early morning flag-raising ceremony. Evenings are often filled with activities and presentations on such topics as the Hebrew language, Jewish holidays and traditions, and social and political issues in Israel. Just don't expect to talk politics over lunch with soldiers, as political discussion is strictly forbidden.

Weekends are free to sightsee, attend military functions, and take part in weekly Shabbat. Cost for a three-week Sar-El "tour of duty" is $80 (returning volunteers pay only $50) and includes shared accommodations in a spartan barrack, three kosher mess hall meals per day, and the privilege of temporarily joining the Israeli Army.

HOW TO GET IN TOUCH

Sar-El recruits volunteers in the United States through **Volunteers for Israel,** which has 11 regional offices. Find out which one handles your state by calling 866-514-1948 or visiting www.vfi-usa.org/contactus.html.

help palestinian farmers bring in the olive harvest

SALFIT, WEST BANK

Even if you are at war with a city … you must not destroy its trees
for the tree of the fields is man's life.
—Deuteronomy 20:19-20

54 Farmers in America stress over weather, fuel costs, and the roller-coaster ride known as average price per bushel. But compared to the difficulties faced by Palestinian olive farmers, these issues seem almost petty.

The Palestinian farmers in the West Bank, like farmers everywhere, depend on their crops to feed their families. Yet they also worry about whether or not they'll even be allowed access to their own olive groves. Most of these groves, after centuries of being in the same family, are now surrounded by Israeli settlements. Many years, it's difficult for farmers to even see their crops, let alone pick them.

The farmers deal with harassment, blocked roads, and checkpoints with armed soldiers. Just getting from their homes to their fields, often blocked by concrete barriers, walls, and fences, can entail endless delays and questioning.

Since September 2000, more than a half million Palestinian olive and fruit trees have been bulldozed and destroyed by the Israelis. Those that remain are deemed to be in what the Israelis call "closed military zones." And these aren't just any old olive groves. The Palestinian olive groves that go back generations are among the world's oldest, some dating back as many as 2,000 years.

Every year, Zaytoun ("olive" in Arabic), a U.K.-based nonprofit that helps marginalized Palestinian farmers and their families harvest and sell their olives, hosts trips for volunteer harvesters. Working with the International Women's Peace Service (IWPS) that has a base in the Hares settlement, Zaytoun recruits volunteers and IWPS arranges the housing, the meet-and-greets with farmers, and a celebration of the harvest's end.

Volunteers not only physically pick olives alongside Palestinian farm families, but also negotiate their safe passage and provide witness for the farmers and their crops.

An Israeli soldier is less likely to point a gun at a Palestinian teen if an international team is looking on.

Volunteer Jenny Bell describes her Zaytoun trip as follows: "In 2006 I went to see with my own eyes the Palestinian olive harvest in the West Bank under occupation. As a country woman myself I could not believe how difficult the Israeli government has made it for farmers and the population as a whole to live a normal life and pick their own olives from their own trees. The sufferings inflicted on ordinary families in that country are a disgrace and a cause for shame. I believe Israeli security depends on Palestinian economic viability and we must work together to achieve this."

Harvest volunteers may share the problems of daily life with Palestinians, but they also get to experience legendary Palestinian hospitality. Along the way, they learn the *dabkeh,* an ancient Middle Eastern dance, and share bread baked in a *taboun,* a traditional oven heated with pressed olive pits.

Zaytoun sells fair-trade olive oil pressed from the Palestinian olives in Great Britain; one reviewer described it as "in the rich nourishing class of the best of the fruity Sicilian, Cretan, and northern Spanish oils."

Cost for the ten-day trip runs approximately £60 ($88) per day.

HOW TO GET IN TOUCH

Zaytoun, 33 Carronade Court, Eden Grove, London N7 8EP, England, 44 845 345 4877, www.zaytoun.org.

SOAP FOR THE QUEEN

The soapmakers of the West Bank's Old City of Nablus can't imagine why anyone would make soap out of animal fat. They proudly make their soap out of all-natural virgin olive oil—70 percent, in fact—and consider its production a treasured art.

The virgin olive oil is mixed with water and a salt compound, and the mixture is cooked over low heat for around five days. It's then poured over a large area on the floor, cut into individual blocks, and stamped with the traditional nablusi seal. But before it can be packaged and shipped, it's stacked into towering pyramids and left to dry for up to 30 days.

As early as the tenth century, Nablus's famous olive oil soap was exported across the Arab world and as far afield as Europe. *Sabon nablusi* was reputedly the soap of choice for England's Queen Elizabeth.

ANOTHER THOUGHTFUL, COMMITTED CITIZEN:
MATT HARDING

Matt Harding, a Connecticut-born video game designer, didn't set out to uplift the planet. In fact, if it wasn't for his traveling companion saying, "Hey, do that weird dance you do," one day in 2003, he'd probably be back at a desk, designing the next game adolescent boys can't get enough of.

The weird dance is a kooky arm-flapping, marching step that those same adolescent boys perform at middle school sock hops. His buddy videotaped him performing it on the streets of Hanoi. And then in Tonga. And then the Philippines, Mali, and the Panama Canal. His sister, who was trying to keep up with her vagabond brother, asked him to start a website so she could follow his progress around the world.

The video on the resulting website, "Where the Hell Is Matt?," showing a grinning Matt bouncing up and down in 69 countries, spread from computer to computer like a virus, achieving an unplanned side effect. It made people smile. And if you don't think making people smile is a noble cause, you haven't read a newspaper lately.

While Harding would be the last person to call himself a do-gooder, he is aware that his little four-and-a-half-minute video (and two more he's filmed since then) shows a different view of the world.

"All we see on the news media is misery and people suffering," he says. "It's important to know those things, but it's also important to realize that's not the whole picture. It [the video] shows people having fun."

So far, Harding's three videos have been viewed more than 30 million times on YouTube and brought him a weird sort of fame. Not only has he been interviewed by everyone from the *Washington Post* to Jimmy Kimmel, but Visa hired him to do a TV commercial, Stride Gum asked to sponsor him, and NASA featured one of Harding's three dancing videos on their Astronomy Picture of the Day website. Titling it "Happy People Dancing on Planet Earth," NASA stated that "few people are able to watch the above video without smiling."

"We're bound together on this planet in ways it's hard for us to even understand," says Harding, who is highly amused by the videos' success. "It shows that people in other countries aren't the enemy, they're just us in different costumes."

What's more, the underlying, if unplanned, message of unbounded human joy and connection comes across loud and clear without being preachy. "There are no words on the video and I'm not trying to get anybody to do anything," Harding says. "It just makes people happy."

See Harding's attitude-changing videos at www.wherethehellismatt.com.

CHAPTER
5

africa

It's one thing for Oprah or Bono to do these big things.
But normal people can make a difference, too.
—Susan Nordenger, who has made numerous volunteer trips to Africa

Africa is the poorest continent on the planet. Millions of people die there each year from completely preventable causes. This should have every last one of us up in arms. We should be marching in the streets protesting the fact that thousands of children die each and every day simply because they have no access to clean water. The millions of African children who have lost parents to AIDS should prevent us from sleeping at night.

But no, most of us just switch the remote to *American Idol* and pretend it's a problem *over there*.

Thankfully, over there has moved into the hearts of thousands of volunteers who head to Africa every year to build homes, hug AIDS orphans, and coach soccer teams. Still others volunteer to work on wildlife conservation projects, monitor elephants, count sharks, and bottle-feed nyalas.

Dozens of organizations offer volunteer trips to Africa, not to help "the poor unfortunates," but to allow everyday people from developed countries the chance to make new friends, to immerse themselves in a new reality, and to finally see what the world is like beyond a 26-inch plasma screen. And the funny thing that happens when these volunteers return home? They realize they're the ones who have been helped the most.

jump-start woman-owned businesses

Go where your best prayers take you.
—Frederick Buechner, author and minister

55 The United Nations and the World Bank bandy about the dollar-a-day statistic when describing poverty. In Benin, for example, they report that 30 percent of the population makes less than a dollar a day, considered the absolute minimum income required to provide nutrition, clothing, and shelter.

But what if you could help a person make $2 a day? What if decisions on community development came not from the World Bank, USAID, and other foreign organizations and foundations, but in the very slums where the poor live and struggle to survive?

That's the idea behind this volunteer program, which aims to lift women out of poverty by giving them a little training and a bit of financial help to start a small business, to give them their first chance at a slice of capital pie. It doesn't take a lot of money to create huge changes, either. African women who gain access to even a hundred dollars and a little technical assistance have proven to be quite savvy when it comes to showing entrepreneurship, forming associations, starting savings accounts, and demonstrating to their children a renewed sense of dignity, pride, and hope for the future.

Even though the Benin Constitution guarantees equal rights to women, the reality is that women are frequently denied basic human rights in Benin. They are often forced into marriage, not allowed to inherit property, and wracked by the effects of female genital mutilation. In addition, education, which is free for boys, often bears costs for their sisters.

VOODOO POLITICS

Sixty-five percent of Benin's nearly seven million people practice voodoo. There's a National Day of Voodoo (January 10) and a government-sanctioned National Voodoo Bureau, both of which were established in the 1990s under President Nicephore Soglo. When Mathieu Kerekou, the former Communist dictator who outlawed voodoo during his 18-year reign, ran for reelection in 1996, he flip-flopped on the ban, eventually going so far as to mix up an unnamed white voodoo powder to ensure his success. It apparently worked, and he served as president until 2006.

Although outsiders, who arrived in Africa wishing to supplant voodoo with their own religions, often have equated voodoo with witchcraft, in Benin there's no such thing as zombies or dolls stuck with pins—often the markers of voodoo in Western popular culture. (Animal sacrifice, however, is actually a voodoo practice.) Instead, voodoo, also known as vodou, is an ancient spiritual tradition with dozens of deities. Most adherents of voodoo have one or two personal deities.

According to a 2004 report by National Public Radio's John Burnett, the religion remains a centerpiece of spiritual life for millions of West Africans. Janvier Houlonon, a tour guide in Benin and a lifelong voodoo practitioner, told him, "Voodoo is older than the world. They say that voodoo is like the marks or the lines which are in our hands—we born with them. Voodoo are in the leaves, in the earth. Voodoo is everywhere."

The Center for Cultural Interchange (CCI), a Chicago-based nonprofit that organizes good works across the planet, coordinates with a social action project at a community center in Porto Novo, Benin, that provides microloans to help women start small basic businesses. Members gain experience handling money and raising farm animals.

The center, which currently serves around 200 people, also offers educational workshops—including radio programs—on malaria prevention, agricultural and environmental topics, computer skills, and HIV/AIDS prevention. An on-site pharmacy provides medication for people living with HIV/AIDS.

As a volunteer with CCI, you'll help women with little money or education become the architects of their own economic progress. By honoring, elevating, and supporting them in their fight against poverty, you'll empower them to develop their potential and become a powerful force in the lives of their families and communities.

CCI also works with a women and children's center in Porto Novo, which has a nursery, an orphanage, and both primary and secondary schools. At this nongovernmental organization started in 1993, volunteers organize youth groups, educate young mothers, and work on community campaigns and outreach programs, such as malaria prevention, importance of clean water, sex education, and support for those living with HIV/AIDS. Volunteers may be called on to tutor, mentor, counsel, or lead skills workshops for the women and children at the center. During the months of August and September when the students are on vacation, volunteers are needed to plan and lead daily recreational activities.

A tiny but vibrant country tucked between Nigeria and Togo, Benin is best known for its fishing villages on stilts, for its mud fortresses, and for being the birthplace of voodoo. As a former French colony, it's not unusual to see Beninois walking down the street with a baguette under one arm and a French newspaper under the other. The capital, Porto Novo, where you'll be working, was founded in the 16th century by Portuguese settlers. It has several museums, including the former palace of King Toffa (*R*.1874–1908), known as the Musée Honmé or the Palais Royale, which gives a glimpse of what royal life was like.

An intermediate level of French is required for this volunteer vacation, which includes a three-day orientation to Beninois culture and the project you will be working on. French lessons are available prior to the volunteer project for an additional fee.

You'll live with a host family, share two meals a day with them, and pay $1,550 for your one-month volunteer post.

HOW TO GET IN TOUCH

Center for Cultural Interchange, c/o Greenheart, 712 N. Wells St., 4th fl., Chicago, IL 60657, 888-227-6231 or 312-944-2544, www.greenhearttravel. org; www.cci-exchange.com.

open your heart to aids orphans

LIVINGSTONE, ZAMBIA

Being unwanted, unloved, uncared for, forgotten by everybody,
I think that is a much greater hunger, a much greater poverty
than the person who has nothing to eat … We must find each other.
—Mother Teresa of Calcutta, Catholic nun and
founder of Missionaries of Charity

56 Even though the son of Zambia's first president, Kenneth Kaunda, died of AIDS in 1987, the growing epidemic was kept under wraps for way too long. For nearly 20 years after the first case was diagnosed, the government, the Zambian press, and especially those dying of the disease, disavowed the large pink elephant sitting in the corner.

The devastating result of this hush-hush approach? One out of five adults in the country were infected with HIV by the early 1990s. An open, public effort to combat HIV/AIDS didn't happen until 2002, when Parliament finally passed a national AIDS bill. By 2004, the government declared it a national emergency and former President Kaunda became one of the nation's most committed AIDS activists.

Today, it's estimated that 600,000 Zambian orphans are paying the price for this stealth approach to the AIDS epidemic. Travellers Worldwide (TWW), a U.K.-based volunteer organization that organizes more than 300 volunteer projects in 21 countries, sends volunteers to work with the children left behind when the disease claims their parents.

TWW's founder, Jennifer Perkes (she started the company with her husband Phil, who died in 2004), has funded scholarships, books, food, and even roofs at a school for orphans in Lusaka, the capital of Zambia since 2002. On TWW's website, you'll see photographs of grateful students holding signs expressing their thanks.

Lusaka's Thandiwe Chama—who at age eight led 60 barefoot children to the school demanding their right to an education—won the 2007 International Children's Peace Prize. As a result, all children were taken into the Jack CECUP School, which is one of the local schools supported by donations from Travellers (see sidebar p. 165). Following her impressive speech during the Children's Peace Prize ceremony in 2007, a library was offered to the school. Chama is now 17 years old and writes a human rights blog at http://thandiwechama.blogspot.com.

Twenty percent of Zambian children under 17 have lost one or both of their parents to AIDS. As a result, many young people are homeless, live under bridges, or try to maintain a household by themselves. Those lucky enough to find a bed in an orphanage still struggle to secure health care, education, and even food.

Travellers sends volunteers to orphanages in Livingstone, a quaint colonial town that serves as the gateway to Zambia's many safaris and wildlife adventures, including Victoria Falls. The town was first documented in 1855 by explorer David Livingstone (as in, Dr. Livingstone, I presume) and turned into an official town in 1905 when the railway bridge across the Zambezi was completed.

Volunteers in orphanages may rock babies, prepare food, feed children, bathe them, wash their laundry, clean the building, or organize a soccer game or an impromptu sing-a-long. In the schools, volunteers—who usually work with a teacher on staff—may be asked to teach a variety of subjects, including math, science, drama, dance, art, music, and, of course, English. In fact, since many of the children are reluctant to practice their English, engaging them in speaking English is a primary function for volunteers. Sports-minded volunteers can coach basketball, cricket, football (soccer), rugby, or volleyball.

HOW I WROTE OFF MY SUMMER VACATION

If the fee you pay for a volunteer vacation is used to support research or another noble cause, it may qualify as a charitable contribution. The Internal Revenue Service (IRS) isn't keen on subsidizing taxpayers' fun and games, though. Travel costs qualify for a tax deduction only if the trip has no significant element of "personal pleasure, recreation, or vacation," and various other conditions apply. Be aware that if you tour the country before or after volunteering, you forfeit the right to deduct transportation costs. Consult your tax professional or an IRS representative to see if any part of your trip might qualify for a tax deduction.

COMMUNITY EDUCATION

The official name of the school is Jack CECUP School. The acronym CECUP stands for: Community Educational Centre for the Under Privileged. The Jack CECUP School started with 32 students in one tiny room. It now has more than 450 students, who are taught in three rooms. The school has a number of activities, which include football, netball, drama, poetry, choral music, cricket, cultural dances, Anti AIDS Club, Anti Drugs Club, Environmental Conservation Club, Child Rights Club, Book Club, and traditional games. The school also has one school computer for the children to use.

The school assists orphans, which includes children who have lost one parent or both parents. It also takes students whose parents are alive, yet are unable to meet their demands and cannot afford to enroll their children in either government or private schools.

Run by local volunteers, Jack CECUP School is considered a self-help school and is registered with the Zambian Ministry of Education as a service school. Students here, whose ages range from 6 to 16 years, are classified according to three types:

- **Never-beens:** Children who have never had a chance to attend a government school and who will no longer be accepted at a government school due to age limits.
- **Dropouts:** Children who failed to proceed to junior secondary or in any other grade due to various factors, including the lack of school uniforms, shoes, books, or school supplies.
- **Pull-outs:** Children who once attended government or private schools, but were forced out due to the loss of the main breadwinner or parent who used to sponsor them.

In their free time, they're free to kayak and canoe, take elephant-back safaris, visit Zambia's 19 national parks, or bungee jump off the highest commercial bridge in the world.

This trip, with accommodations in a hostel featuring an Internet café, a large garden, a swimming pool, and a bar that attracts an international clientele, plus two meals a day, runs £775 ($1,225) for two weeks, £1,295 ($2,280) for four.

HOW TO GET IN TOUCH

Travellers Worldwide, Suite 2A, Caravelle House, 17/19 Goring Road, Worthing, West Sussex BN12 4AP, England, 44 1903 502 595, www.travellersworldwide.com.

collect important marine data

CAP TERNAY RESEARCH STATION, MAHÉ, SEYCHELLES

In the end we will conserve only what we love. We will love only
what we understand. We will understand only what we are taught.
—Baba Dioum, Senegalese poet

57 The Seychelles is an archipelago nation of 115 islands in the Indian Ocean that between 1994 and 2005 lost 42.5 percent of its coral and half of its 134 fish species due to unsustainable fishing practices and the effects of global climate change. The Nature Conservancy, an Arlington, Virginia-based conservation organization, is working with local governments in the Seychelles to establish new marine protected areas and strengthen existing ones in the region.

According to National Geographic News, in 1998, El Niño sparked the worst coral bleaching event in recorded history, destroying 16 percent of the world's coral reefs. In the Seychelles, the damage was particularly devastating. The inner islands suffered the brunt of the damage, losing more than 90 percent of their staghorn, elkhorn, and table corals.

Unfortunately, the Seychelles Ministry of Environment doesn't have the staff, the time, or the resources to monitor the problems in its troubled waters. Yet you can do your part to help. Global Vision International (GVI), a British-based company with a U.S. office in Boston, sends volunteers to a marine station in Mahé, the largest of the islands, to fill the gap. Volunteers, all certified divers, spend five weeks conducting research that will help this island nation create plans for their valuable coral's survival. Not a diver? No worries. Come four days early, bring 360 euros ($500), and GVI will arrange the necessary training.

As a GVI volunteer, you'll collect data on coral and fish species, conduct whale shark migration surveys, and research turtles, dolphins, octopuses, and lobsters. After learning research diving and marine survey skills, you'll work on a team, participating in six to ten dives per week. You'll rotate between diving and nondiving projects and will collect, review, and input data and help keep the camp running, from cooking and cleaning to operating the compressor and filling scuba tanks.

Located 1,000 miles off the east coast of Africa, the islands that form the Seychelles are scattered across 500,000 square miles. The research center is located in Cap Ternay Marine National Park, on the west coast of Mahé—the Seychelles' main island. You'll also spend time at a satellite camp on Curieuse Island, a lushly vegetated outcropping near Praslin that has more giant hundred-year-old tortoises than humans.

On weekends (expect to stay busy and be quite tired out Monday through Friday), you can explore the islands and experience the Creole culture of the Seychelles—a mix of African, Asian, and European influences. You might choose to catch up on some well-earned sleep or visit the Internet café. Every Saturday night, the base hosts a lively party.

Five weeks, including dormitory accommodations and meals at the Cap Ternay Research Station, plus a zipline canopy tour, is $2,520.

HOW TO GET IN TOUCH

Global Vision International, 252 Newbury Street, Number 4, Boston, MA, 02116, 888-653-6028, www.gvi.co.uk.

coach a kids' soccer team

Many of us have surrounded ourselves with the excess of Western society
and have found that this emphasis on self and things is unfulfilling
and unrewarding and creates a vacuum inside.
—Cliff Lewis, volunteer with Projects Abroad

58 A kid in Senegal grows up with one of two dreams: a) to be the next Youssou N'Dour, the Senegalese singer and percussionist that *Rolling Stone* described as follows, "in Senegal—indeed, in much of Africa—N'Dour is perhaps the most famous singer alive," or b) to play soccer for the Senegal Lions, the national football team that in 2002 pulled a surprise upset by defeating the reigning world champion France in the opening game of the World Cup.

Projects Abroad, a U.K.-based nonprofit with bases in 23 developing countries, sends volunteers to Senegal to help nurture those dreams—not so much to encourage kids to play professional soccer, but to use the popular sport to foster cooperation, hope, discipline, and respect.

In a country where less than 30 percent of children can read and write, football (as they call soccer) plays an important role in the development of young people's values. From street players to those aspiring to follow in the fleet footsteps of Senegalese football star Aliou Cissé, soccer brings people together and builds strong communities. Besides the obvious physical and mental benefits that any sport provides, being coached by an adult who cared enough and believed in them enough to travel across the globe can mean the difference between hope and despair.

Senegal's national motto is "One people, one goal, one faith." Nowhere is that spirit more evident than on the football field, however modest that field may be. Volunteers, working with team managers, set up training drills and fitness sessions, and coach teams in already established leagues. They help young football players (there are under-12, under-14, and under-17 leagues) develop their skills in ball control, maintaining possession, passing, and dribbling.

Projects Abroad's Senegal base is located in the island town of St. Louis, four hours north of the hectic capital city, Dakar. With palm trees, sandy streets, donkey-drawn carts, mosques, and French patisseries, St. Louis is a fascinating mélange of many cultures. It's located on a long, rectangular island in the middle of the Senegal River.

Between national parks—one with the largest pelican breeding grounds in the world—and sandy beaches, wild countryside, a vibrant music scene, and thriving cities, Senegal offers something for everyone. It's a great place to improve your French, study colonial architecture, take in local nightclubs, or visit the nearby Mauritanian desert.

A monthlong volunteer post, living with a host family and sharing three tasty onion-, garlic-, and ginger-based Senegalese meals (expect *chebujen*, the national dish of fish and rice, and fish *maffe*) per day, runs $2,895. Projects Abroad even puts out a monthly newsletter from Senegal called *The Spirit of St. Louis*.

HOW TO GET IN TOUCH
Projects Abroad (U.S. Office),
347 West 36th Street, Suite 903,
New York, NY 10018, 888-839-3535,
www.projects-abroad.org.

FAIR TRADE CASHEWS

Aliou Cissé, a famous Senegalese football player who plays for France (that traitor), has a first cousin named Ibrahima Cissé who never left Senegal. Instead, Ibrahima Cissé started a company that, he hopes, will alleviate poverty and halt massive deforestation. Working with former Peace Corps volunteer Jeffrey Chatellier, Cissé started Green Caravan (www.organiccashewnuts.com /greencaravan.htm), a fair-trade company that sells organic cashews and solar dried organic mangoes.

Like coffee beans and cocoa, cashews grow abundantly in Africa—more than 16,500 tons are shipped from Senegal alone every year. Until recently, Senegal's cashews (grown mainly in the southern region of Casamance) were exported raw, which brings in less profit. Since Green Caravan operates under fair-trade agreements, it pays reasonable wages to workers, ensures a safe working environment for them, and guarantees fair prices to producers.

build a grain bin in one
of the world's poorest countries

KANSONGHO, MALI

*You will go home absolutely overwhelmed by what you saw,
who you met, what you've learned, and how your heart has expanded.
You will be inspired to exceed your own expectations of yourself.*
—Jim, Tandana volunteer in Ecuador

59 Remember Maslow's hierarchy of needs? Well, when you're down on rung one, just trying to survive, reading, writing, and 'rithmetic aren't necessarily high on the agenda. In Mali, where less than 12 percent of the population know how to read, economic activity is largely confined to farming and fishing. Women get up at 3:30 in the morning to fetch fuelwood and buckets of water, much of which comes from the Niger River, much of which is contaminated.

With 72 percent of the population living on less than a dollar a day and an 88 percent illiteracy rate, Mali is third from the bottom on the UN's Human Development Index.

Yet, despite Mali's overwhelming problems, Anna Taft, founder of the Tandana Foundation, says her organization's mission is one of cross-cultural education—making friends with and learning from a handful of the 12 million people in this landlocked country. The name Tandana, in fact, is a Quechua word meaning "to gather together" or "to unite."

Anna started the Tandana Foundation after teaching at a grade school in Panecillo, Ecuador. The four months she spent teaching and living with an Ecuadorian family were followed by other projects throughout the Andes, which led her to start the nonprofit that has the goal of giving people of all backgrounds an expanded sense of possibilities. Tandana offers scholarships to kids in Ecuador and grants to villages in Mali, in addition to taking volunteers to both countries.

IT JUST TAKES ONE (OR TWO)

The influence of a beautiful, helpful character is contagious,
and may revolutionize a whole town.
—Collier Graham, British jazz composer

Mary Graham may just be one person, but because of this young American woman there are villages in Mali that now have solar power and clean water. Along with co-founder Kristin Johnson, whom she serendipitously met at a New York City restaurant as she was launching PSP, Graham started Practical Small Projects (PSP), a nonprofit based in Williamsburg, Virginia, in 2005 to foster sustainable enterprise in the impoverished country.

After attending a solar energy workshop in Mexico, then seeing how Nicaraguans were able to generate income by setting up microenterprises using solar energy, she was inspired to introduce this type of work in Mali, Africa. With a budget of between $150,000 and $200,000 and a grand total of two employees (Graham and Johnson), PSP founded Afriq-Power.

This Malian nonprofit brings potable water, electricity, and infrastructure to remote villages and can produce as many as a thousand solar panels per month. Together, the two groups have installed water pumps and brought electricity to dozens of villages. In turn, villagers have started businesses that allow them to stay in their remote villages and earn a living.

At Banco School, where a 35-watt solar module (Mali's first one) and water pump were installed by Graham, Afriq-Power head Daniel Dembélé, and 15 locals they trained as technicians, students went from 6 out of 36 passing the national exam to 36 out of 37. Clearly, electric lights increase the students' productive hours, allowing them to study after dark, when the day's chores are finished.

Graham expressed her pride in the case study she wrote describing the impressive results of the Banco project, "When I left Mali I realized that with less than $6,000 that I managed to raise, we completed the following: 1) The development of a local enterprise manufacturing solar panels and cookers locally; 2) The completion of 7 locally constructed panels; 3) The installation of two of the locally made panels in Banco that powered 6 lights and a solar pump; and 4) The construction of 6 solar cookers. We could not help but be proud that such a small amount of money involved in this project is in stark contrast to the hundreds of thousands of dollars that characterize most development projects." *Practical Small Projects, 4801 Courthouse Street, Suite 300, Williamsburg, VA 23188, www.practicalsmall projects.com.*

In Mali, Tandana has created school gardens and tree nurseries, built a well, and is working on a book of folktales to benefit the villagers that shared their stories.

After several days of touring, including a stop in Tombouctou (Timbuktu), volunteers with Tandana's latest project will travel to Kansongho and work with villagers to build a grain bin and anti-erosion dikes. Both of these projects will help contribute to food security for the local people.

Among the places you will visit is Mali's Dogon Country, home to about 350,000 Dogons and one of the country's most popular tourist destinations thanks to the striking scenery around the Bandiagara Escarpment, a 90-foot, nearly vertical cliff. Its crevices hide the homes of the ancient Tellem people who, according to legend, flew to reach their dwellings. Designated a UNESCO World Heritage site, the region has caves, overhangs, and elaborate, ancient mud buildings.

Not only will you ride camels into the Sahara, but you'll sleep in the desert under the stars (if only for one night), travel the Niger River by *pinasse*, and visit the tiny outpost of Ende, famous for its mudcloths, indigo cloths, woodcarvings, and other Dogon crafts. Along the way you'll meet fishermen, nomads, wood-carvers, and textile producers.

The 16-day trip, including lodging with a local family and food, runs $2,500.

HOW TO GET IN TOUCH

The Tandana Foundation, 2933 Lower Bellbrook Road, Spring Valley, OH 45370, www.tandanafoundation.org.

ELEPHANT – HUMAN RELATIONS AID
track and map desert elephants

DAMARALAND, NAMIBIA

Take nothing but pictures.
Leave nothing but footprints.
Kill nothing but time.
—Motto of the Baltimore Grotto, a caving society

60 Northwest Namibia—known as Damaraland—is one of the most isolated and scenically spectacular places on the planet. In a good year, the Namib Desert, a 15-million-year-old land of arid mountains, gets around 3 inches of rain. Drought, as they say, happens.

Miraculously, the desert elephants that roam this stark, lunarlike landscape are increasing in number, returning home to habitats they have not frequented for hundreds of years. At first blush, this sounds like good news.

But for the indigenous farmers who toil to scrape out a living in this remote and unforgiving landscape, the elephant herds are simply competing for precious water. The elephant population has grown from 52 about 20 years ago to more than 600 now. Less than 6 percent of this wide, reaching land is protected as wildlife habitat, so farmers reach for their rifles and think mainly of defending their resources when

BUSH SKILLS FOR BEGINNERS

While you do not need any special training to work on this project, Elephant – Human Relations Aid will teach you the following skills:

* **Camp craft:** cooking over a fire, bush camp setup, safety, and hygiene
* **Bush craft:** tracking, approaching dangerous animals on foot, animal behavior, bush walking, navigation, map reading, and using a GPS
* **Elephant identification:** compiling identification kits on elephants
* **Traditional building skills:** constructing walls, fences, and other traditional structures.

NO SNOW REQUIRED

The Namib Desert is not only the oldest desert on the planet, but it also has some of the world's largest dunes. Thrill seekers come to speed down these shifting mounds of sand on traditional Swakopmund "sandboards" or snowboards that have been adapted for desert use. They either slide down headfirst, maxing out at about 50 mph, or they carve the sand standing up, snowboarding style (best attempted by those with some experience with surfing or snowboarding).

Alter-Action, a company in Swakopmund that rents out specially adapted boards, has even set up runs that range from Little Nellie and Brigit, the bunny slopes of sandboarding, to Lizzie and Dizzie, the black diamonds of the desert. The only problem? The dunes shift so quickly that it's impossible to install lifts, which means adrenaline seekers are forced to trudge to the top by foot. *Alter-Action, P.O. Box 3992, Swakopmund, Namibia, 264 81 128 27 37.*

---

these giants they consider nuisances inadvertently damage windmills, water pumps, and wells.

In 2001, Johannes Haasbroek, fresh from his work with Damaraland's black rhinos, decided to step in to arbitrate. The Elephant – Human Relations Aid (EHRA) project was launched to respond to the escalation in competition for natural resources between the desert-dwelling elephants and human inhabitants of the northern Erongo and Kunene regions. The Gandhi of desert elephants, Haasbroek started EHRA to find a way humans and elephants could live peacefully together.

The movements and habits of the expanding wild elephant population, still adapting to their newfound freedom, are largely unknown. By tracking the elephants, EHRA and its volunteers provide important data that Namibia's Ministry of Environment and Tourism can use to effectively manage the herds and avoid conflicts between farmers and elephants.

Volunteers on this two-week project (you can stay up to three months, however) work from remote field camps in the vicinity of the Brandberg—Namibia's highest mountain—and the ephemeral Ugab River, immersing themselves in pioneering conservation work. They track and map wild elephants, but they also mend fences, both figuratively and literally. Starting early in the morning, before the desert heat becomes unbearable, volunteers construct fences that protect windmills and other structures that thirsty elephants tend to get into.

Besides working to protect scarce supplies of water, volunteers here also support local schools, doing everything from building them to teaching students the importance of preserving ecosystems—even broaching the idea that maybe, just maybe, elephants could become an economic asset. Volunteers have even been known to teach local women the fine art of making paper from elephant dung. Your duties will vary according to the needs of the project and those of the local community: You might be on camp duty one day and help build a tourist camp the next day.

Sandwiched between the Skeleton Coast and Etosha National Park in the east, the harsh stretch of burned mountains and rugged semidesert known as Damaraland has been described by some as the land God created in anger, and by others as the last great wilderness on Earth. You'll share its open plains and grassland with giraffes, gemsboks, springboks, hyenas, lions, leopards, baboons, and ostriches.

You'll camp under the stars, eat meals around a campfire, and pay just $720 for a two-week stay.

HOW TO GET IN TOUCH

Elephant - Human Relations Aid, P.O. Box 2146, Swakopmund, Namibia, 264 64 402 501, www.desertelephant.org; U.S. contact: c/o Doreen Niggles, P.O. Box 272, Wainscott, NY 11975.

bottle-feed orphaned lion cubs

VICTORIA FALLS, ZAMBIA

> The more clearly we can focus our attention on the wonders and realities
> of the universe, the less taste we shall have for its destruction.
> —Rachel Carson, American author and environmentalist

61 In 1972, when *Living Free*—the sequel to the influential, Oscar-winning 1966 movie *Born Free*—was released, more than 200,000 lions roamed the African continent. Between feline tuberculosis, poaching, and diminishing habitat, that number today has dwindled to fewer than 15,000. If something isn't done soon, this icon of Africa could well be extinct.

That's why Amanzi Travel, a British-based travel company, offers volunteers the chance to work with, and hopefully save, the "king of beasts." Gemma Whitehouse named her company Amanzi after the lion cub she helped rear on her own volunteer vacation to Africa. So it's fitting her company would give its customers the same chance.

A former international marketing director in the United Kingdom, Whitehouse offers adventure expeditions, luxury safaris, and more than 30 volunteer vacations to Africa, one of which includes babysitting lion cubs. She likes to say, "Everyone at some point in their lives deserves to do something amazing."

On this volunteer vacation with a work base at Thorntree Lodge near Livingstone, you will, for all intents and purposes, be the pride for orphaned lion cubs, ranging in age from several weeks to 18 months. You'll bottle-feed tiny cubs and take the older ones for walks in the bush, giving them a chance to observe, smell, and feel the wild and improve their hunting skills. You'll also be involved in feeding, cleaning, and data-collecting that will enable the lion rehabilitation center to better care for the animals until they're released into the wild, the ultimate aim for each of the cubs there.

Located along the Zambezi River within Mosi-oa-Tunya National Park, this project is close to the park's namesake, Victoria Falls. The locals call the falls Mosi-oa-Tunya, which means the "smoke that thunders." Designated a UNESCO World

Although some people prefer to take in the majesty of Victoria Falls from the safety of the viewing platform, excitement addicts may choose to microlight overhead, white-water raft below, or bungee jump betwixt and between.

And if you happen to time your visit to coincide with a full moon, you can view a lunar rainbow. Victoria Falls is one of just four places in the world where they occur. Also known as moonbows, these spectacular arcs attract thousands of people to the national parks on both sides of Victoria Falls (Mosi-oa-Tunya National Park in Zambia and Victoria National Park in Zimbabwe). The parks stay open late just for the spectacle. The light of the full moon is refracted through the same mists that cause the perpetual rainbow during the day. If you go during January through March, when the water is highest, be sure to take a raincoat.

Also within striking distance of Victoria Falls are Matobo National Park (where you can see rhinos), Hwange National Park (it's roughly the size of Belgium), and hippo-dodging canoe and kayak trips down the Zambezi.

Heritage site in 1989, this enormous cataract also consistently appears on lists of the world's seven natural wonders compiled by authorities ranging from ABC to CNN to the *Guardian* newspaper.

Another activity for volunteers here is giving conservation lessons at nearby schools and providing assistance in Mosi-oa-Tunya National Park, where you'll walk dung transects and take game censuses, perhaps of elephants or buffaloes. Other species found here include African wild dog, greater kudo, and waterbuck.

Volunteering at Mosi-oa-Tunya, including simple but comfortable shared rooms in the volunteer house in Livingstone (there's even a swimming pool) and three meals a day, runs £1,195 ($1,785) for two weeks or £1,895 ($2,830) for four weeks.

HOW TO GET IN TOUCH

Amanzi Travel Limited, No. 4 College Road, Westbury on Trym, Bristol BS9 3EJ, England, 44 1179 041924, www. amanzitravel.co.uk.

rebuild a storm-demolished coastal town

VILANCULOS, MOZAMBIQUE

Volunteer work has revolutionized my life.
It has, in the best possible, most dramatic and rewarding way,
turned my life inside out and upside down.
—Ashley Judd, actress

62 Mozambique, which was exploited for centuries by Portuguese colonialists, emerged from decades of civil war in 1992 as one of the world's poorest countries. While humans have caused problems in the country, nature has not always been kind here, either.

Vilanculos, a popular beach destination on Mozambique's Indian Ocean, had just recovered from devastating floods that left 80,000 Mozambicans homeless and 30 dead when it was socked again by Cyclone Favio, a powerful storm that delivered its knockout blow on February 22, 2007. The roofs of the hospital, the schools, and 80 percent of the homes were blown off like the seeds of a dandelion.

African Impact (AI), a family-owned, Zimbabwe-based travel company that offers volunteer excursions in 12 African countries, provided much of the initial relief work. And they're still there, rebuilding homes, working in rural orphanages, and teaching English, all with the help of their trusty volunteers.

The homes in Vilanculos, four out of five which lost their roofs, were lucky in contrast to their more remote neighbors. In the rural areas outside of Vilanculos, people live in thatched huts, many of which were completely flattened by the storm's fury. AI, based in Vilanculos, is currently building about two new homes in these rural areas per month. Building simple, rustic structures can be backbreaking work, but volunteers find it extremely rewarding interacting with throngs of curious children who come to watch and challenge workers to pickup games of soccer.

At the orphanage, volunteers provide English and Portuguese instruction with visual aids and an interpreter, participate in developmental play with the children, engage them in sports such as Frisbee and soccer, provide one-on-one attention, and teach crafts, such as making rag rugs and shell mobiles or decorating pots. In the community-based project, volunteers teach in a rural preschool using songs, games, and crafts; teach English, life skills, and soccer to youth; and assist an outreach program that empowers local women who are HIV positive by teaching them trade skills. You'll also have the opportunity to learn some basic Portuguese and Xitsua—the local Mozambican language.

Stuart Neath, an AI volunteer from the United Kingdom, said, "The whole experience was absolutely incredible. It was uplifting, rewarding, challenging, grounding, heartbreaking, and soul-destroying in equal measure. To see the absolute joy on the faces of the children when we arrived to spend time with them, or their excitement at being given some new clothes, or the opportunity to do something creative, was incredible."

With its white-powder beaches, rugged bush interior, and pulsating Afro vibe, Mozambique has quickly become the getaway pick for such stellar somebodies as Leonardo DiCaprio and Britain's Prince Harry. Vilanculos, where the AI volunteer camp is located, is a short boat ride from Bazaruto Archipelago, a UNESCO World Heritage site where dolphins, humpback whales, and whale sharks breach. The warm, clear water and teeming reefs around the archipelago's four islands,

Benguerra, Bazaruto, Magaruque, and Santa Carolina (also known as the Paradise Islands), are nirvana for divers.

AI hosts what they call cultural days, when volunteers are introduced to Mozambique's traditions of dancing, drumming, and singing. You also can learn how to cook traditional Mozambican cuisine. You'll get the chance to take triangular-sailed Arab dhows through the postcard vistas of Bazaruto while flying fish skim across the water. There are also opportunities for scuba diving and snorkeling, game-fishing (black marlin season runs from October through January), and playing beach volleyball.

A two week-stay runs $1,400 (four weeks is $2,090) and includes a shared beachfront bungalow, complete with garden, swimming pool, fire pit, kitchen, and three squares a day.

HOW TO GET IN TOUCH
African Impact, P.O. Box 1218, Gweru, Zimbabwe, www.africanimpact.com; U.S. contact: 877-253-2899.

ANOTHER THOUGHTFUL, COMMITTED CITIZEN:
WARREN STORTROEN

After 37 years of sitting in an office, Warren Stortroen, 77, a former insurance claims manager, is making up for lost time. Since 1996, when he volunteered for his first Earthwatch project, a survey of the long-tailed manakin's mating habits in Monteverde, Costa Rica, he has helped out on 54 scientific expeditions, averaging 4.5 a year.

"I guess you could say I'm addicted," says the St. Paul, Minnesota, native, as he gleefully lists the five Earthwatch research projects he picked for 2009—dolphins in Greece, Roman ruins in Italy, coastal ecology in Bahamas, sustainable coffee in Costa Rica, and prehistoric pueblos in New Mexico. And while he's committed to ecology, sustainability, and citizen activism, he says the real reason he volunteers on so many Earthwatch expeditions is that they're just so darned much fun.

"The biggest selling point for me is the other volunteers. I've met so many like-minded, enthusiastic people," Stortroen says. "Usually you don't know anyone before you go, but it doesn't take long before you're instant friends. I've got Earthwatch pals all over the world, from Australia to the Netherlands."

Indeed. On a recent archaeological excavation to England, Stortroen's fellow volunteers began calling themselves "Warrenites" in honor of his veteran status. Although the Warrenites don't have T-shirts or a fan site yet, they did make plans to meet up again on a dig in New Mexico after viewing photos their namesake brought from the prehistoric pueblos project he'd volunteered on—four times.

The leader of the Warrenites says he's probably most proud of the giant glyptodont, a three-million-year-old Volkswagen Beetle-size armadillo, that he found on an Earthwatch fossil hunt in an ancient arroyo outside San Miguel de Allende, Mexico.

"Not a bad find for my first project there," he says.

He also found an amber fertility amulet in Jamaica, the teeth for a wooden effigy in Turks & Caicos, and a neolithic child burial pot in Angkor Wat, Cambodia.

In between Earthwatch stints, Stortroen volunteers for Friends of the Mississippi, collecting native seeds for habitat restoration on the banks of the lower Mississippi. He also spent five summers controlling forest fires and blister rust for the U.S. Forest Service.

"Before I retired, I started looking around for things I could do that were meaningful and adventurous," he says to explain his volunteer fanaticism. "I used to travel with the Science Museum of Minnesota, but now, I think those trips would seem pretty tame. Instead of listening to some guide tell me about it, I'm there with major scientists doing it myself.'"

support a ghanian doctor

COMMUNITIES THROUGHOUT GHANA

Success in life has nothing to do with what you gain in life
or accomplish for yourself. It's what you do for others.
—Danny Thomas, actor

63 If you were an oddsmaker picking which of Africa's 53 countries has the best shot at escaping the poverty that perpetually plagues the continent, Ghana would be a good bet. The first country in sub-Saharan Africa to gain independence, it's largely free of civil conflict, enjoys a multiparty democracy, and is well endowed with natural resources, including a new oil field discovered in 2007.

But like the rest of Africa, Ghana suffers from disease, poverty, and a not-yet-developed infrastructure. Seventy percent of Ghana's poor live in rural areas without access to medical care. And unfortunately, many Ghanaian doctors, eager for bigger rivers to fish, choose to practice outside the country. In fact, there are more Ghanaian doctors practicing in Europe and North America than in Ghana itself.

Elghana, a volunteer organization based in Kumasi, works with 19 hospitals and clinics around the country to help those doctors who have stuck around. Elghana also sends volunteers to work at orphanages, schools, and other community projects.

COFFINS TO DIE FOR

If you drive cabs for a living, you might as well step into the hereafter in a giant wooden taxi. Or at least that's the thinking in Ghana, where a coffin is the last word in style. Fifty years ago, a Ghanaian angler was buried in a 7-foot fish and started the trend. Preachers are buried in Bible-shaped coffins, soccer players in 7-foot black-and-white balls.

Today, there's an endless variety of silly, hand-sculpted coffins on the market from Ferraris to Nokia cell phones to 7-foot Star beer (Ghana's most famous suds) bottles. Want your own? If you like, eShopAfrica (www.eshopafrica.com) will sell you a giant reminder of your mortality for $1,500.

Although the government pays for 80 percent of people's health care, the other 20 percent of the cost can be mighty hard to come by in a country where nearly half the population makes less than a dollar per day. Women, particularly, bear the brunt of inaccessible health care. Less likely than men to receive education, health benefits, or even a voice in family decisions, women in Ghana work nearly twice as many hours as men and spend three times as many hours transporting water and goods. Lack of medical care for them can be deadly.

As a volunteer on this Elghana project, you will support local doctors and nurses, often accompanying them on rounds. Depending on your level of expertise (trained medical personnel may be called upon to diagnose illnesses and perform surgery), you will offer first aid and injections, assist in deliveries, record patient histories, and provide community health education on such topics as safe water and eating balanced meals. The clinic equipment is basic and the medicines available are limited, but you'll be working alongside some of the most ingenious health-care providers in the world.

Formerly known as the Gold Coast, Ghana has stunning beaches and scenery, but it's the warmth of the people and the vibrancy of their culture that will make the biggest impression. If you're new to Africa, Ghana is a good introduction. It's safe, English is the official language, and the people are welcoming, appreciative, and eager to exchange ideas. As volunteer Lena Gilliland says about her time in Ghana, "My life has changed completely."

Elghana will gladly arrange visits to such popular destinations as Mole National Park, the Cape Coast beaches, Kakum National Park, and Adidome Island. You can take a canopy walk, a cruise on Lake Volta, or a safari with elephants, antelope, monkeys, warthogs, and baboons within arm's reach.

Volunteers are invited to spend from two weeks to six months (past volunteers—who are always on hand to answer questions—recommend staying as long as you possibly can) with positions open any time of the year. You'll receive a thorough orientation upon arrival in Ghana and live with a host family, sharing three daily meals which include such Ghanaian specialties as palm-nut soup, okra stew, *fufu* (cassava porridge), and *kenkey* (maize dumplings). Two weeks runs $800, a month $1,000.

HOW TO GET IN TOUCH

Elghana, Block H, Plot 11, W/Patasi, Kumasi, Ghana, 233 24 4889146, www .elghana.com.

help marginalized batwa potters sell their wares

KIGALI, RWANDA

> How wonderful that no one need wait
> a single moment to improve the world.
> —Anne Frank, child writer
> who perished in the Holocaust

64 When it comes to Rwanda, the complex and lethal relationship between the majority Hutu and Tutsi tribes gets all the attention. The Batwa people, the last remnants of the hunter-gatherers who for thousands of years had central Africa all to themselves, have been all but ignored. This pygmy group, sometimes known as the Twa, are being squeezed out as the forests they once lived in get chopped down due to encroaching development, logging, and agriculture. This indigenous tribe has no representation in local or national government and, after being forced off their land, no viable source of income.

In 2001, the Forest People's Project, a British nonprofit that assists indigenous tribes around the world, came up with Dancing Pots—a project to help market the Batwa's traditional handicrafts—in partnership with a Rwandan nongovernmental organization then called CAURWA (Communauté des Autochtones Rwandais). Through the NGO's current incarnation, COPORWA (Communauté des Potiers au Rwanda), Dancing Pots works with 14 pottery groups and has a pottery market in central Kigali. The group is actively looking for new ways to sell the Batwa's pottery, which were selling for a measly nickel when the project began. As the first certified fair-trade organization in Rwanda, the goal of Dancing Pots is to find a sense of respect and an income for this marginalized society.

Because they were stereotyped by other Rwandans as "morally, physically, and intellectually deficient," the Batwa suffered disproportionately during the 1994 genocide, losing some 30 percent of its population to the violence. Today, there are only about 33,000 Batwa left in the country, representing less than one percent of the population of Rwanda as a whole. As more and more forests are cut down, the Batwa find it difficult—make that impossible—to maintain their traditional way of life, which was seminomadic and completely based on the forest. Many have ended up begging on the streets. Three out of four can't read, and many Batwa children, suffering from intense prejudice, have little or no access to education. The average Batwa income is $82 per year, one-fourth the dollar a day level the UN considers poverty.

Volunteers are needed to help with the pottery cooperative and to help develop international marketing plans. Because Rwanda is a tiny country, surrounded by some heavy-hitting neighbors (the Congo, Uganda, and Tanzania), developing export markets is key to eradicating poverty and gaining respect. By developing a handful of reliable international customers, volunteers can radically change the Batwa's lives. Activities include training and support, increasing access to markets, and helping out in the wholesale-retail outlet.

Rwanda, with its beautiful, rolling mountainous landscapes, is best known as the home of American anthropologist

Dian Fossey (1932–1985) and the endangered mountain gorilla, featured in the movie *Gorillas in the Mist*. After the tragic genocide of 1994, the country's reputation as the premier gorilla-tracking destination was taken over by Uganda. Since 1995, however, the country has been relatively stable and peaceful.

Despite their dire circumstances, the culture and soul of the Batwa people is alive and well. At dances held twice a week, the Batwa, like the Hutu and Tutsi, put on leg bells, play the *ingoma* drums, and, wearing caps with long white hair attached to them, dance, dance, dance. They believe dancing is the answer to most problems, claiming, "It gives us peace."

Known as the "land of a thousand hills," Rwanda has much to offer travelers who love the outdoors. Volcanoes National Park is home to about half of the remaining mountain gorilla population; be aware that you must have permission from Rwanda's Office of Tourism and National Parks to visit. Lush, hilly Nyungwe National Park offers hiking and bird-watching, plus the chance to see chimpanzees and monkeys in the wild. Marshy Akagera National Park has abundant waterbirds and is also home to big game, including crocodiles, giraffes, hippopotamuses, hyenas, leopards, and lions.

There are no formal, scheduled volunteer trips at this time. But international volunteers with creative ideas and a heart for change are actively sought by the Forest People's Project. There is no charge to show up and pitch in.

HOW TO GET IN TOUCH

Forest People's Project, 1c Fosseway Business Centre, Stratford Road, Moreton-in-Marsh GL56 9NQ, England, 44 1608 652893, www.forestpeoples.org.

JANE GOODALL INSTITUTE

promote environmental awareness in rural schools

KALINZU AND BUDONGO FORESTS, UGANDA

How we humans came to be the way we are is far less important than how
we should act now to get out of the mess we have made for ourselves.
—Jane Goodall, chimpanzee researcher
and UN-appointed Messenger of Peace

65 Over the last hundred years, Uganda has lost 90 percent of its chimpanzees while its human population has increased 800 percent. The Jane Goodall Institute (JGI), a global leader in the effort to protect chimpanzees and their habitats with branches in more than a hundred countries, works in Uganda to educate and engage its growing human population about the importance of conservation.

As Goodall likes to say, "The greatest danger to our future is apathy." That's why JGI started Roots & Shoots, a program that goes in to schools to teach kids three things: 1) respect for all living things; 2) understanding for all cultures; and, most important, 3) every person can and should make a difference. The Roots & Shoots program in Uganda uses volunteers in the Entebbe office, as well as in the field offices in the Kalinzu and Budongo Forests. Each volunteer stays for six months.

The Uganda Roots & Shoots program delivers environmental education curricula to 10,000 primary students and 400,000 secondary students. That's a lot of information being dispensed, and the sooner, the better. Chimpanzees, which once lived all over the African continent, are decreasing in number, and the populations that are left are becoming fragmented and isolated. Not only is their habitat disappearing, but illegal poachers grab them for commercial meat.

As a volunteer with JGI, you'll be part of this world-renowned institute's environmental education team, working in rural schools near chimpanzee habitats. You'll help kids gain a personal connection with the forest, inspiring them to plant trees, compost, and actively work to save the forests where chimpanzees live. You'll also assist with existing Roots & Shoots projects.

Uganda is where the East African savanna meets the central African jungle. It's the only African destination whose wide range of forest primates (chimpanzees, mountain gorillas, etc.) are as impressive as its antelope and lions. It's a lush place where you can watch lions in the morning and track chimps in the afternoon. It has ten national parks, ten wildlife reserves, and seven wildlife sanctuaries. As a volunteer with JGI, you'll travel between three areas: Entebbe, on the shores of Lake Victoria, where you'll learn about JGI's Uganda projects; a reserve in the Kalinzu Forest; and a second reserve in the Budongo Forest, the oldest mahogany forest in East Africa. You'll also visit the Ngamba Island Chimpanzee Sanctuary. In your free time, you can track rare mountain gorillas in Bwindi Impenetrable National Park and Mgahinga Gorilla National Park, both in the southwest of the country.

Six-month appointments begin in early February and mid-September and run $3,250, accommodations included. In Entebbe, you'll share a simple room with cooking facilities. At the field education centers, you'll stay in an even simpler room at the National Forestry Authority site with no electricity or running water.

HOW TO GET IN TOUCH

JGI's Uganda gig is booked by **Global Vision International,** 252 Newbury Street, Number 4, Boston, MA 02116, 888-653-6028, www.gvi.co.uk.

build chicken coops at mount kilimanjaro's marangu gate

MAMBA KISAMBO, TANZANIA

> After a lifetime of spending vacations and leisure time in luxury resorts … I had finally seen for myself what I only caught a glimpse of on CCN, BBC, and a handful of documentaries…. It's the difference between knowing something and really "getting" it.
> —Michael Revius, founder of Tanzania Volunteer Experience

66 There are six routes up Kilimanjaro. The easiest route, the one 90 percent of climbers pick, starts at the Marangu Gate. It's nicknamed the Coca-Cola route and it can get crowded. Serious trekkers opt for harder routes.

Just west of the Marangu Gate is a little village named Mamba Kisambo. Like many villages in Africa, it's filled with kids who have lost their parents to AIDS. The women who take care of them work long hours in the fields. Some commute more than an hour each way.

Tanzania Volunteer Experience (TVE), a nonprofit that specializes in volunteer programs in Tanzania, offers a half dozen programs in Arusha, a prosperous town once dubbed the Geneva of Africa.

For its hard-core volunteers who want a more direct experience, TVE offers a gig—the Chicken Ranch project—spending quality time in Mamba Kisambo, a hardscrabble town that survives mainly on subsistence farming. Volunteers help build a chicken ranch to provide residents with an alternative or supplemental income. They live with families and help them create a new industry, one

WHO KNEW?

Humanitarian foreign aid provided by the government of the United States amounts to less than one percent of the federal budget. That is only a fraction of what most people think is spent on foreign aid. Among the top 21 industrialized nations, the United States ranks last in terms of the percentage of gross national product spent on humanitarian foreign aid.

that will keep the village's hard-working women from having to commute, carry water, and work such long hours in the fields.

Using working blueprints, volunteers build chicken coops and furnish them with chickens and eggs. They buy the supplies, build the structures, and help take care of the village's new source of livelihood. In their spare time, they teach English, play games with the kids, and provide support to local businesses and social workers.

Nestled among banana, papaya, and eucalyptus trees, Mamba Kisambo is near such iconic safari destinations as the Serengeti Plains, the Ngorongoro Crater, and Mount Kilimanjaro. If you're not up for the climb to the summit of Kilimanjaro, there are ancient caves to visit, waterfalls to hike to, and Chagga dances to learn.

And safaris—a Swahili word meaning journey—originated in Tanzania. You can safari here by jeep, on foot, on horseback, or even in a hot-air balloon. TVE can also arrange visits to traditional medicine men, Chala Lake (legend claims it has a relative of the Loch Ness monster), and to blacksmiths who make traditional Masai spears and tools. You'll get to interact with members of the Chagga, Masai, and Pare tribes.

Most of TVE's two-week programs run $495 and include shared lodging in the volunteer house 4 miles east of Arusha and three meals a day prepared by the on-site staff. The Chicken Ranch project, which requires a monthlong commitment, runs $895 (plus $100 for supplies) and includes living with a family in the village.

HOW TO GET IN TOUCH

Tanzania Volunteer Experience, P.O. Box 16446, Arusha, Tanzania, 255 755 320 790, www.tanzaniavolunteer.org.

ROCK OF ZANZIBAR

Stone Town, a UNESCO World Heritage site, is one of the oldest districts on Zanzibar, an island off the coast of Tanzania. This former Swahili trading town is a labyrinth of tiny streets and alleys, markets, mosques, and other historic buildings—including the Anglican church on the site of the old central slave market, East Africa's largest slave-trading port. Combining Persian, Indian, European, Arab, and African architecture, Stone Town has been occupied by humans for three centuries and is famed for its beautifully carved wooden doors. The House of Wonders, the former palace of Sultan Syyid Barghash, is open to the public. Its other claim to fame is that Freddie Mercury (1946–1991), the lead singer of Queen, was born there.

GREENFORCE
research the great white shark

Seeing a shark is like seeing a movie star, someone you have grown up
watching on TV and then suddenly coming face to face with them.
—Joanne Lane, volunteer with Greenforce's
great white shark project

67 Thanks to Peter Benchley's best-selling 1974 novel *Jaws*, followed by Steven Spielberg's 1975 blockbuster movie version of the chilling story, the great white shark is widely believed to be a dangerous, man-killing predator. While it's true that these minivan-size animals with layers of serrated teeth are responsible for an average of 30 to 50 attacks a year, they do not prey on humans (their digestive tracts can't handle us) and have killed fewer people in the last hundred years than dogs do each and every year. Those frightening news reports? Total accident. The great white was simply "test biting," the same thing as he does to buoys, surfboards, and other unknown objects.

Between 150 and 200 million sharks are destroyed each year, targeted by fishermen for their jaws, teeth, and fins, which can fetch tens of thousands of dollars. In 2004, the great white shark was added to the list of endangered species. Because they grow slowly, mature late, and have low fecundity, they've been unable to keep up with humans' exploitation.

In South Africa, the first country to protect the great white, researchers working in what's known as Shark Alley use volunteers in their ongoing efforts to better understand and correct the misperceptions of the little-studied beast.

As a Greenforce volunteer, you'll start with a weeklong training in white shark biology, anatomy, and behavior, basic seamanship, and underwater filming and still photography. Then, safely ensconced in protective shark cages, you'll come eye to jet-black eye with this streamlined torpedo that can weigh up to 5,000 pounds. Your job will be to observe and record the great white shark's size, markings, sex, and behavior. Be prepared to get your hands dirty. Preparing bait and chum is not pristine work.

NOT THE OTHER WHITE MEAT

Great whites are the largest predatory fish on Earth. But they don't purposely hunt humans. So where did the rumor get started? A few candidates:

- A great white shark's teeth are serrated, so when it bites and shakes its head side to side, its teeth act as a saw and tear off large chunks of flesh. Most sharks spit out human flesh after test bites that, admittedly, can cause some major bloodletting.
- Great whites can detect a single drop of blood in 25 gallons of water and can sense even tiny amounts of blood from as far as 3 miles away.
- After a great white shark is born, it's abandoned immediately by its mother. It leads a loner's life, developing ferocious coping skills to survive.
- The great white's main diet consists of fish, sea lions, and seals—to which humans look mighty similar from underneath in the water.

Gansbaai, an unpretentious village on the magnificent coastline of South Africa's Western Cape, is located about two hours southeast of Cape Town. Dyer Island, where much of your research will take place, is the breeding ground of jackass penguins, cape cormorants, and gannets. Nearby Geyser Island has some 60,000 cape fur seals.

A four-week program, including lodging at the research center's accommodation house and breakfast and lunch each day you're on the research boat, runs $2,700. You'll have a chance to learn boat handling and underwater photography skills while you are here.

As of this writing, Greenforce is going through a major restructuring and rebranding, which includes the establishment of four new organizations, as well as an umbrella organization called GAPFORCE. Call or check the Greenforce website for the most up-to-date information.

HOW TO GET IN TOUCH

Greenforce, 530 Fulham Road, London SW6 5NR, England, 44 20 7384 3343, www.greenforce.org.

assist the kenya wildlife service

NATIONAL PARKS, RESERVES, AND WILDLIFE SANCTUARIES, KENYA

When spiderwebs unite they can tie up a lion.
—African proverb

68 Whether you want to monitor cheetah behavior in the Masai Mara, fight illegal bush meat trading in Tsavo National Park, or build a community-run elephant sanctuary on the Kenyan coast, Tembeza Kenya (TK)—a travel company with offices in Kenya, the United Kingdom, Canada, and the United States—can set you up with a monthlong volunteer gig. Unlike many operators who book trips all over the globe, Tembeza Kenya arranges volunteer projects in Kenya. Period.

By specializing in one destination, they've been able to develop extensive collaborations with not only the Kenya Wildlife Service, Africa's oldest conservancy, but with Kenya's Ministry of Education and other government organizations. This communal spirit enables them to offer a wide variety of volunteer placements in teaching, medicine, journalism, community work, law, and even coaching. Needless to say, their five wildlife conservation programs in the country's more than 50 parks and reserves are, by far, the most popular with volunteers.

The December 27, 2007, election-related violence that resulted in the deaths of 1,000 Kenyans and the displacement of 600,000 others also wreaked havoc on the prestigious Kenya Wildlife Service (KWS). With tourist visits down as much as 90 percent, KWS is scrambling to maintain its parks, its ongoing conservation research, and its reputation.

That's exactly why TK volunteers are so important. Against the backdrop of Kenya's equatorial sun, you'll work alongside top scientists and conservationists on such pioneering research projects as cheetah monitoring, elephant tracking, and conducting biodiversity surveys on the Kenyan coast. Volunteers in Kisite Marine Park and Mpunguti Marine Reserve will work with research teams, who monitor hundreds of species of marine life. They'll also work with KWS rangers, who patrol the parks for illegal fishing. Volunteers in Lake Nakuru National Park will be treated

Surrounded by 140 acres of indigenous bush, the Giraffe Manor, a small exclusive hotel just outside Nairobi, has a resident herd of giraffes who have a tendency to stick their long necks into everything. The butler, in fact, kicks off happy hour each night by offering nuts to Daisy, a 20-foot-tall endangered Rothschild giraffe, and her clan.

In 1974, Jock Leslie Melville and his wife Betty, concerned about the rare Rothschild giraffes, whose natural habitat in western Kenya was rapidly disappearing, bought the 15-acre manor. (They later added 105 additional acres.) They moved in Daisy and a partner and started the African Fund for Endangered Wildlife.

After Jock died in 1984, Betty opened the giraffe reserve and its faux Scottish hunting lodge to the public. Giraffe Manor has six bedrooms, one furnished with the furniture of writer Karen Blixen. The dining room is lit by candles only and meals are made with organic fruits and vegetables. Outside, with views of Mount Kilimanjaro to the south, warthogs strut their stuff next to the giraffes. Guests have included Johnny Carson, Walter Cronkite, Brooke Shields, Stephen Sondheim, and Sir Mick Jagger. *The Giraffe Manor, P.O. Box 15004, Langata 00509, Kenya, 254 20 891078 or 254 20 890948, www.giraffemanor.com.*

to the spectacle of millions of flamingos who flock to a shallow lake here, just one of the park's 400 species of birds. You might do bird counts, water testing, or rhino surveillance, as there are 25 black rhinos in the park. Though volunteers do not need to have any specialized training, a science background can be beneficial for some of the research-based work you will be doing in Kenya.

Tembeza Kenya also offers a wide variety of what it calls "mini adventures," which range from shorter versions of its wildlife projects to white-water rafting on the Nile, fishing in Lake Victoria, climbing Mount Kilimanjaro, and scuba diving off Pemba Island.

One-month wilderness conservation projects run $1,495 and include lodging, breakfast, and dinner each day. Additional months can be added for $1,095 per month.

HOW TO GET IN TOUCH

Tembeza Kenya USA, 301 East 88th Street, Suite #12, New York, NY 10128, 646-216-9912, www.tembezakenya.com.

protect endangered black and white rhinos

MKHAYA GAME RESERVE, SWAZILAND

We had daily intimate encounters with white rhino, black rhino, elephant, giraffe, hippo, buffalo, crocodile, zebra, warthog, impala, kudu, nyala, ostrich, and velvet monkey.
—Bob and Sofia Carter-Andersson, volunteers at the Mkhaya Game Reserve

69 In October 2003, a BBC camera crew, looking for black rhinos to show their viewers, headed straight to Mkhaya Game Reserve, a privately owned reserve in Swaziland that had recently made some "top five list" for rhino sightings. Neither the crew nor their viewers were disappointed. In fact, much of their footage was taken from the top branches of a knobthorn tree after they had been chased and treed by a less-than-happy black rhino.

Black rhinos are critically endangered, thanks to poachers who nab them, chainsaw off their horns,

---

RARE MEAT

A recent volunteer at Mkhaya called it a "trip to the real Africa, a soul enriching experience." Here are a couple of the rare beasts you may be lucky enough to see:

- **Wildebeest with starred forehead.** Although some scientists think a wildebeest with a star on its forehead is a genetic anomaly, the Swazis who run Mkhaya believe it's a rare strain found only on their reserve.
- **Naring trogan.** Although this bird has a bright crimson chest and a fancy plume, it's often difficult to spot (ask any birder) because it sits with its green back facing out, blending in seamlessly with the foilage.

---

and sell them to Asians who pay up to $1,400 per pound for ground African rhino horn (they mistakenly believe it has aphrodisiacal qualities). Yet the rhinos are making a comeback at Mkhaya, where they were reintroduced in 1986.

The Mkhaya Game Reserve, in fact, is one of the few places in the world where you can see black and white rhinos living together.

At one time, black rhinos stretched from the slopes of Table Mountain in South Africa's Cape Province all the way through Africa, thriving in all areas south of the Sahara. By 1995, there were fewer than 2,400 black rhinos left, with 80 percent of them living in the southern part of the continent. Even in countries like South Africa and Namibia, where game reserves are under strict protection, their numbers are dwindling.

By the 1960s, in Swaziland, a small kingdom on the southern tip of Africa, wild game had all but disappeared. In less than a lifetime, Swaziland went from a wildlife paradise to a country with hardly a wild animal. At Mkhaya, a private Swazi-owned sanctuary with a fence and a highly motivated crew of armed game rangers, the rhinos and 20 other locally extinct species are shakily returning. Resources are scant, so volunteers are highly valued for both their money and their time.

Since the program began, volunteers have done everything from maintain fences and patrol the reserve to capture animals and help relocate them. They've staffed watchtowers, assisted with animal and bird surveys, and tracked and darted rhinos. They've fed crocodiles, inoculated indigenous goats, dragged a dead buffalo out of a mud pool, cleaned the wound of an eland, bottle-fed a baby nyala that got

THE RHINO'S TALE

Two species of rhinoceros live in Africa; the black (*Diceros biconis*) and the white (*Ceratotherium simum*). The names refer not to color but to the width of the nose and mouth. The black, a browser, has a narrow prehensile lip; the white, a grazer, has a wide (*wyd* in Afrikaans, which is pronounced vait) mouth; hence the latter's name. Both species have a pair of horns on the snout. The animals are similar in height, about 5.5 feet at the shoulder, but the white weighs twice as much as the black.

Black rhinos (said to be aggressive) usually attack simply because they have very bad eyesight. They've even been said to charge tree trunks. Adults are solitary, coming together only for mating. Mating does not have a seasonal pattern, but young are born at the end of the rainy season.

separated from its mother, and picked hundreds of ants off a baby weaver bird that fell from its nest.

This unspoiled wilderness lies in the heart of Swaziland's Lowveld, between Manzini and Big Bend. When the reserve was founded in 1979 by the Ted Reilly family, its main goal was to thwart the extinction of Nguni cattle, an indigenous breed of African cattle that was brought to the area by the migrating Nguni two thousand years earlier. Today, Mkhaya has reintroduced all species indigenous to the area with the exception of wild dogs, lions, and cheetahs.

While volunteering at Mkhaya, you'll be invited along on the reserve's guided tours and game drives and, if it's available, allowed to stay in its stone-and-thatch safari camp. Nearby, Bulunga Gorge offers white-water rafting and both Hlane Royal National Park and Mlilwane Wildlife Sanctuary, sister parks to Mkhaya, are within striking distance.

Although Ted Reilly's father, Mickey, who settled at Mlilwane, Swaziland, in 1906, brought electricity to the country, your tented accommodations, albeit replete with mosquito nets, don't have that luxury. Expect cold showers and a pit latrine. Accommodations and three meals per day run $1,335 for two weeks.

HOW TO GET IN TOUCH

Ecovolunteer books trips for American and Canadian volunteers through the **Great Canadian Travel Company,** 158 Fort Street, Winnipeg, Manitoba R3C 1C9, Canada, 800-661-3830, www.ecovolunteer.org.

set up a bush clinic for wodaabe and tuareg nomads

ETHIOPIA, NIGER, AND MALI

For the longest time there was this neon question mark going off over my head—so what, so what? What am I doing to help the world?
—Irma Turtle, former advertising exec who traded her power suits and Madison Avenue lunches to start TurtleWill, a nonprofit that helps Africa's poorest nomads

70 If you bought Robert Plant's *Live in Paris* CD, you've already helped out Irma Turtle, whose Carefree, Arizona-based nonprofit TurtleWill provides medical care, school funding, and drought relief to Africa's tribal nomads. The former Led Zeppelin frontman dedicated profits from his four-song 2005 CD to build eight dorms and provide meals, blankets, school uniforms, and medicine in Mali, one of three African countries where TurtleWill works.

But if you want to do more than just buy a CD, read on.

Several times a year, Irma Turtle recruits volunteers to staff remote medical bush clinics. Volunteers set up tents near the local watering hole and within minutes, long lines of people, many of whom have never seen a doctor, begin forming. "If we get a sniffle, we run to Walgreens where there's a whole shelf of over-the-counter medicines," Turtle says. "These people have no recourse for medicines, let alone doctors."

Twenty-five years ago, Irma Turtle led a very different life. Smith-educated, she lived on Manhattan's East Side, marketing the products of Fortune 500 companies for advertising giant Ogilvy & Mather. Frustrated and feeling there was something more she wanted to do with her life, she quit in 1984. A vacation to the Sahara desert the next year shaped a vision of what her next life chapter would be.

Somehow, she decided, she would help the indigenous cultures of Africa that were disappearing faster than you could say, "economic development." The UN and other aid agencies couldn't be bothered to help these marginalized people, so she asked herself, "Who would help?" "TurtleWill" was the answer and the name

Bamako, the dusty capital of Mali, is a good place to catch free concerts. It's where Mali's tribal musicians—the Tuareg, the Songhai, and the Dogon cliff dwellers—come to mix it up with such Western artists as Bonnie Raitt and John Lee Hooker.

For centuries, itinerant musicians have gathered in this southern Malian city, entertaining villagers along the Niger River. But in the 1990s, several locals made it big. Singer-songwriter Salif Keita and singer-guitarist Ali Farka Touré achieved international recognition, which attracted even more aspiring musicians to the area. Eventually, the record producers arrived, trolling the city's bare-bones, thatched-roof nightclubs and intimate bars in search of the next big thing in so-called world music.

of the agency she started, not to fling money from her New York penthouse, but to put both her well-manicured feet on hard, dry African ground.

TurtleWill funds short-term humanitarian projects, such as building wells ($300 can provide a well for up to 300 people), opening schools, operating medical clinics, and organizing food or sewing cooperatives. To this day, she has no staff and leads all the volunteer trips herself. And the nomads of Mali, Ethiopia, and Niger know her by name. Tribal chiefs will travel miles on donkeys or by foot just to speak with her.

Doctors, nurses, and other health-care professionals are, needless to say, encouraged to volunteer for the two-week, open-air bush clinics, but Turtle welcomes anyone from anywhere. Only requirement? An open heart.

People who are not medical professionals are needed to count and label medicine, dispense soap, clean wounds, maintain patient records, and keep order among the 250 to 300 patients, many of whom walk 20 miles or more just to get there.

Because TurtleWill projects take place in the remote bush, there are no hotels or restaurants. Rather, Turtle's expedition staff sets up tents, tables, showers, and a makeshift kitchen from which all meals are prepared.

Costs for the two-week bush clinics range from $4,200 to $5,000, including lodging and all meals.

HOW TO GET IN TOUCH

TurtleWill, Box 1147, Carefree, AZ 85377, 888-299-1439, www.turtlewill.org.

teach music in ghana

ACCRA, GHANA

> We each disappeared as individuals. We were no longer sick or well,
> able or disabled. We were players in a deeply human mystery;
> a story—and oohhh—how we played!
> —John Glick, fiddle player and international volunteer

71 Talk to any veteran volunteer and invariably you'll get some variation on the following sentiment: "I started out in the hope of giving to others, but found out I was the one getting the most." Nowhere is that more true than in Ghana, where Travellers Worldwide sends volunteers to teach music—although no one is quite clear who is teaching whom. Volunteers, who work in one of several primary schools in the Asylum Downs suburb of Accra, end up learning more from the children, who seem to have music in their souls.

In Ghana, kids sing and dance on the way to school, on the playgrounds, in the classroom, and pretty much any time

---

LIVING THE HIGHLIFE

Highlife, Ghana's signature sound, emerged in the 1880s as a fusion of rhythms from the West African coast with music from North America, the Caribbean, and Portugal. For years, highlife, with its unusual rhythms, distinctive guitar styles, and interplay of guitars, brass instruments, and woodwinds, ruled dance floors across much of West Africa.

Today the music has spread across Africa, and, indeed, all over the world. At last count, Amazon.com listed more than 40 CDs of Ghanaian highlife. One of the most popular collections, *The Guitar and the Gun,* was recorded in the early 1980s during Ghana's civil war. Although most of the recording studios and music clubs were shut down, Bokoor Studio managed to keep highlife rolling with this now classic album.

---

they're not sleeping. But because of budget shortfalls, formal music education has been dropped from most school's curricula. Keyboards, drums, and other instruments sit in classrooms unused. Therefore, anyone who can play an instrument, sing, dance, or even hum "do-re-mi" is extremely welcome. But watch out—Ghanaian children will likely ask for your autograph and inquire as to whether or not you're a pop star.

Like many countries in Africa, Ghana has young people who live in garbage dumps, thousands of AIDS orphans, and families who can't even remember the last time they had enough to eat. But at the Madonna Primary School, one of the places where you'll likely be placed, or Great Lamptey-Mills Institute, a school in the Muslim sector of Accra, nothing matters but the beat. Poor, rich, old, young—they're all one, moving to Ghana's magical rhythms.

And talk about coming home with more than you left with! Because music offers an instantaneous avenue for connecting with someone from a different culture, get ready to come home with lots of new entries in your address book. Expect to make lifelong friends, not to mention returning home with a whole different way of looking at the world.

For example, "Ghana time"—which is when someone says, "See you at 10 a.m.," but really means "See you sometime tomorrow"—just might be a better way to face life. In Ghana, the pace of life is slower and more relaxed. Above all else, Ghanaians are dedicated to having fun. Even at the busy city markets, where crowded stalls sell everything from CDs of Ghana's signature highlife music to pigs' feet, there are DJs blasting music and encouraging people to dance, dance, dance.

Travellers Worldwide, which arranges these volunteer teaching positions in Ghana, is a Sussex, England-based company that specializes in volunteer vacations throughout Asia, Africa, Europe, and Latin America. Volunteers can do everything from coach basketball or cricket to work with crocodiles or leopards.

Prices for the Ghana trip vary depending on how long you stay (two weeks is £795 or about $1,590; three months, £1,795 or $3,590) and include accommodations, most often with a host family, and all meals.

HOW TO GET IN TOUCH

Travellers Worldwide, 7 Mulberry Close, Ferring, West Sussex BN12 5HY, England, 44 1903 50295, www.travellersworldwide.com.

CHAPTER

6

asia

It is only when we truly know that we have a limited time on earth—
and have no way of knowing when our time is up—that we will then
begin to live each day to the fullest, as if it was the only one we had.
—Elisabeth Kübler-Ross, psychiatrist and
author of *On Death and Dying*

In Asia, the world's most populous continent, volunteer opportunities are diverse and plentiful. You can save urban wetlands in Hong Kong, conduct fish and coral surveys in the Philippines, make amends for Hiroshima or Agent Orange, or teach English in Tibet or Thailand.

If you have an interest in health care, you could help the people of the world's newest country, Timor-Leste, fight diseases like tuberculosis and promote maternal and child health.

If animals are your bag, try your hand at zookeeping in Malaysia. Or help care for orangutans in Borneo. Or save endangered elephants in Sri Lanka.

If architectural preservation is what you really find fascinating, help restore a Buddhist monastery in Nepal.

But whichever direction you take and whatever project you choose to work on, just know that spending time with and paying attention to your four billion brothers and sisters in Asia will strengthen the fabric of our shared humanity.

compile data on endangered wild elephants

MATALE DISTRICT, SRI LANKA

The love for all living creatures is the most noble attribute of man.
—Charles Darwin, naturalist and author of *On the Origin of Species*

72 In Asia, man's best friend is not the dog, but the elephant. This unique relationship dates back 4,000 years when elephants were first captured, trained, and used for farming, warfare, and religious ceremonies.

Lately, at least in Sri Lanka, that unique bond has gone south. Wild elephants, faced with shrinking habitat (the 70 percent of Sri Lanka that was natural tropical forest a century ago is down to 20 percent today), are starting to raid crops, bulldoze houses, and cause serious injury to anyone and anything that gets in their path.

Every year, hungry elephants destroy hundreds of acres of agricultural crops— never mind that these farm fields used to be the elephants' jungle. Villagers, many who have been relocated by the government into elephant territory, sit up all night in rickety tree houses, trying to scare them away. They yell, set off firecrackers, and, if that doesn't work, resort to firearms. Around 200 elephants are killed each year.

The stakes in this conflict are high. The Sri Lanka Wildlife Conservation Society (SLWCS) set up this project to find a way for elephants and humans to share this island country that Marco Polo called the "finest he'd ever seen." Although Sri Lanka has changed a lot since Polo's time, it's still one of Earth's most biologically rich countries, recently identified as one of the world's 18 biodiversity hot spots. A recent survey in the rain forest turned up more than a hundred species of frogs unknown to science.

But on this project, you'll be collecting data about Sri Lanka's remaining 3,500 wild elephants. You'll work with local field scouts to conduct human-elephant conflict surveys, known as HECs, and compile data on elephant movement, behavior, and density. You'll patrol fences, tanks, and transects to record the frequency and consistency of elephant dung. Several times a week, you'll go into Wasgamuwa National

Park and, from the safety of your jeep, photograph individual elephants that might be doing anything from trampling trees to taking dust baths. At night, from time to time, you'll sit in the tree houses, keeping your eye out for marauding herds.

Even though the villagers are at odds with the elephants, they don't take it out on volunteers. Village kids love to practice their English on volunteers, and their parents invite them into their homes for drinks and peanuts picked fresh from their gardens. Many volunteers say the villagers are the best part of the whole project.

You'll live in the Pussellayaya Field House, a sprawling, open mud shack with a tin roof that you'll likely be sharing with a motley collection of dogs, frogs, lizards, and insects. It has flushing toilets, solar-powered lights, and cold showers (though the sun warms the water pipes during the day).

The elephant monitoring program runs 12 days, starting the first Monday of every month and finishing Friday of the following week. Accommodations at the Project House, along with three wonderful Sri Lankan rice and curry meals per day, runs $1,300.

HOW TO GET IN TOUCH

Sri Lanka Wildlife Conservation Society, 38 Auburn Side, Dehiwala, Sri Lanka, 94 1 12714710; U.S. contact: 127 Kingsland Street, Nutley, NJ 07110, 973-667-0576, www.slwcs.org.

BY BUDDHA'S TOOTH

Wait until the tooth fairy hears about this. In Kandy, Sri Lanka, an ancient religious center for Buddhism, there's a Temple of the Sacred Tooth. Built between 1687 and 1707, this ornate, gold-roofed octagonal temple houses the left upper canine of the Lord Buddha himself. According to legend, Buddha's tooth was secretly extracted as he lay on his funeral pyre in India. Then, the tooth was smuggled into Sri Lanka in the hair of a princess and has survived numerous attempts to capture and destroy it. Every day, thousands of white-clad pilgrims bearing lotus blossoms come here to pay homage to the tooth and hope to get a sprinkling from the scented floral water in which the relic is bathed every day. The rest of the day, it sits on a shrine in the center of the courtyard.

BUFFALO TOURS

make amends for agent orange

THAI BINH, VIETNAM

> The United States must admit it's responsible and compensate the
> Agent Orange victims in Vietnam. It is your moral obligation.
> —Duc Nguyen, born a conjoined twin with one leg and bone distortions
> due to high dioxin levels in his mother's body

73 During the Vietnam War, the U.S. military dropped nearly 20 million gallons of Agent Orange, a deadly, dioxin-laced herbicide, throughout the jungles of southern Vietnam. More than 30 years after the war ended, they still haven't cleaned up their mess.

The result? More than 200,000 children have been born with birth defects, including blindness, mental retardation, and a wide range of muscular and skeletal disorders. Incidences of cancer and other health problems have increased dramatically, as well. More than a million Vietnamese are thought to be affected in some way.

Despite the 3.2 billion dollars in reparations promised in the 1973 Paris Peace Accords, the United States has only recently agreed to begin cleaning up the 28 Agent Orange storage facilities they recklessly left behind without properly containing them.

SAILING ON THE WIND

On a perfect half-moon bay surrounded by red cliffs sits Mui Ne, Vietnam, a sleepy village that has become legendary in kite surfing circles. Thanks to consistent cross-shore winds, low rainfall, and nearly perfect weather, it's considered the place to take up and practice the world's fastest growing sport. Already, there are more than 10 kite surfing schools in this tiny town with more palm trees than people. Kite surfing, which has grown from fewer than a hundred fans ten years ago to more than 250,000 today, uses scaled-down surfboards to ride into and over the surf, compliments of the wind. Serious surfers cart around as many as three sizes of kites, each designed to maximize the force of any wind. The Kite Surfing Fun Cup, held every year in Mui Ne, blows in kite surfers from around the globe.

Called hot spots, the facilities are to this day polluting fishing ponds, rivers, and soil. In Da Nang, farmers still can't get rice or fruit trees to grow due to the dioxin levels. Children like seven-year-old Van Nguyen—born with an oversize head, a profoundly deformed mouth, and skin that has a burned appearance on much of her upper body—still suffer the consequences of this pollution. Van's parents, her doctors say, ate fish from polluted streams.

Thai Binh, a farming province on the coast of Vietnam's northern delta, has the most victims of Agent Orange. The herbicide has affected three generations of some families, resulting in many children who have disabilities and are unable to lead normal lives.

Since the U.S. government has yet to pony up for rehabilitation centers, health clinics, and schools for afflicted children (despite Congressional appropriation of $3 million for this purpose in May 2007), entities such as the Ford Foundation, UNICEF, and the UNDP are doing what they can to augment Vietnamese government programs. Buffalo Tours, a Vietnam-based tour company specializing in what they call responsible tours, sends volunteers to this province 60 miles north of Hanoi.

Some volunteers assist teachers at the Quang Trung School, where children with Agent Orange–related disabilities learn to read and write and to participate in sports and music. They're often refused admittance to regular schools because authorities say their appearance scares the other students. Other volunteers work in orphanages or build homes for families with disabled children affected by Agent Orange exposure.

Buffalo Tours, whose CEO Tran Trong Kien recently received recognition from the Pacific Asia Travel Association (PATA) for promoting sustainable travel, was the first to offer volunteer trips to Vietnam. Buffalo Tours also offers medical treks and charity challenges for volunteers wanting to raise money.

Opportunities include two-week, one-week, and shorter group volunteer tours, which usually include accommodations with a host family and daily lunch. Inquire for availability and cost, as opportunities are customized.

HOW TO GET IN TOUCH
Buffalo Tours, 94 Ma May Street, Hoan Kiem, Hanoi, Vietnam, 84 4 3828 0702, www.buffalotours.com.

schlep cameras, make films, and guide nature tours

BEACHES, MANGROVES, RAIN FORESTS, AND REEFS, SINGAPORE

Although it's called Planet Earth, it is mostly ocean!
—Sandy Romeo, Singapore volunteer

74 Singapore may be the only place in the world where you can find a rain forest, a mangrove, and a coral reef within 30 minutes of the central business district. And like rain forests, mangroves, and coral reefs everywhere, these isolated pockets of nature are shrinking, mainly because all those people in the central business district, like people in central business districts everywhere, think making money is more important than preserving wild places.

That's not going to happen in Singapore if Ria Tan has anything to say about it. This 40-something dynamo, a director of corporate affairs for a technology firm by day, spends nearly every nonworking waking hour introducing people to wild Singapore. She leads free nature walks at Chek Jawa, Kusu Island, and Pulau Semakau. She monitors seagrass meadows. She coordinated Singapore's 2008 International Year of the Reef efforts, running a blog about global marine issues.

Over the years, Tan has launched and participated in dozens of volunteer initiatives from the Naked Hermit Crabs, a group that protects endangered Singapore shores, to Wild Films, a group that films and documents life on Singapore's shores.

"I made it my personal mission to visit and document every intertidal area of Singapore," she says, joking that her life is completely controlled by tides.

She also happens to know everything about volunteering in Singapore. At www.wildsingapore.com, she has compiled a comprehensive list for anyone interested in volunteering in Singapore, especially along its rapidly disappearing shores. She even throws in complimentary cheerleading, complete with inspirational quotes and reasons why everyone can make a difference.

Thanks to Ria Tan and other volunteers who are working to protect Singapore's wild shores, several species previously thought extinct have made comebacks:

- Until recently, the multiarmed basket star had not been seen since 1896.
- The Malayan porcupine, a nocturnal burrower, resurfaced in 2005.
- The Changi tree, a coastal tree absent for decades, reemerged in 2002.
- The blue-spotted tree frog made its second debut in 1994.
- The dwarf snakehead returned in 1989.

Peter Ng, a biology professor at the National University of Singapore, says, "When you have a second chance, you try not to screw it up."

Tan describes her own volunteer work as "almost mystical, filled with synchronicity at every turn." She counsels others who aren't sure what they have to contribute: "Have faith," she says. "In people, in yourself. Do what you can, what you must. The time, resources, money, and support will somehow be found."

Wild Films, started in 2004 when Tan and her cohorts invested in professional grade camera equipment, is currently working on a 12-episode series about Singapore's shores. Their motto is, "Shoot first. Ask questions later." And they like to say they have no budget, no time, and often, no clue. So far, their efforts have been seen in a collaborative venture with Singapore's Arts Central—a production called "Once Upon a Tree, Tides and Coastlines."

The group is always on the lookout for able bodies to schlep camera equipment and set up shots. As Tan quips, "Generally, it takes five highly evolved beings to ensure good footage of an invertebrate." However, she points out, "You have to be crazy about our shores to commit to the Wild Film project." Because super tides, the best filming tides, take place before sunrise (usually around 4 a.m.), the volunteer production crew starts at 2 a.m. The glass-half-full part of this equation is that you will be finished by sunrise, giving you plenty of time for other pursuits.

There's no charge to volunteer with Wild Films (except the cost of minimal sleep) or any of the other groups listed on Tan's Wild Singapore website.

HOW TO GET IN TOUCH
Ria Tan, www.wildsingapore.com.

ANOTHER THOUGHTFUL COMMITTED CITIZEN:
MINDIE DODSON

Convenient is the last adjective Mindie Dodson would use to describe her recent volunteer gig in Myanmar (Burma). She'd just inherited a tick-infested puppy, she was moving her grandmother out of her home of 50 years, and her growing list of Rolfing clients demanded weekly, if not biweekly, bodywork. Plus, the friend who asked her to go to Myanmar gave her all of three days to get ready.

"I wanted to say no—or at least to put her off for a few weeks, but then she told me about what was happening over there. How could I possibly refuse?" Dodson said.

When Cyclone Nargis slammed through Myanmar's Irrawaddy Delta on May 2, 2008, more than a million people lost their homes and food supply. Three weeks later, the displaced people were still without food and aid.

"It's hard to even describe the chaos over there," Dodson says. "The military junta has been trying to get rid of the ethnic tribes that live in the Irrawaddy Delta for decades. Even before the cyclone, they were systematically eradicating these people who have lived on this land for thousands of years because they wanted their resources (diamonds, oil, etc.)."

Even though Dodson had never traveled farther than England, she packed her bags and headed to an unfamiliar part of the world. She agreed to set up a media center in Mae Sot, Thailand, along with a team from Tim Heinemann's Worldwide Impact Now (see p. 227). Heinemann, a former Green Beret, had been working in the area for years, developing networks with the Karen people. His team—including Dodson and other friends of his daughter—became a liaison between the refugees and dozens of aid organizations. Dodson interviewed refugees in order to document human rights abuses of the military junta that was working to thwart the international aid that poured in after the cyclone.

Dodson calls the three-week trip to Thailand and Myanmar life-changing. "It completely turned my viewpoint upside down," she said. "People talk about starving kids in Asia. Now I know some. Personally. . . . I met a guy who watched his entire family get washed away by the flooding. I met people who haven't had a home for 30 years. IDPs, they call them. It means internally displaced person. They've been on the run, fleeing from a military that wants to kill them."

She also saw raped girls, starving mothers, and child soldiers. "Children are very different over there," she says. "There's a look in their eyes. They're not spoiled like kids here. When a mom there says, 'Shh!' it means the difference between life or death. A soldier with a rifle could be behind the next tree."

Dodson has posted iMovies online about her experience in Myanmar, hoping to educate people about the dire situation. She also raises money for victims: She has thrown a fashion show and an art show as fund-raisers.

join a merry band creatively boosting thailand's hill tribes

CHIANG RAI, THAILAND

> Inspiration revises our self-image, from seeing ourselves as passive
> victims to being active agents of transformation. This is the single
> most important factor in changing the human condition.
> —Philip Rubinov Jacobson, artist, philosopher, teacher, and writer

75 Creating change comes in many forms. The traditional route involves education, legislation, and endless committee-formation, but all too often these roads wander off point or get bogged down in bureaucracy. Until there's a new vision—a crisp, unmistakable beacon of what is possible—many high-minded roads to change wind back to where they started. Yet artists, who visualize new possibilities and inspire others to see the world anew, create change by asking, "What if?"

What if Thailand's hill tribes, long the victim of prejudice and inequality, were to gain equal citizenship footing with their peers in Bangkok? What if they joined the digital age, sold their traditional crafts, and invited tourists in to experience their little-understood culture? What if they had their own museum, their own films, and their own ability to make a decent living?

Started in 1991 by a group of underground activists, the Mirror Foundation (then known as Mirror Art Group) began staging art and drama performances to promote social change. Under the protective umbrella of "entertainment," they addressed controversial issues like democracy, human rights, HIV, and sex education, all without getting thrown into jail by the repressive regime that had taken over the country. They staged more than a hundred performances per year.

By 1998, the coup had long been overthrown; Mirror's focus turned to northern Thailand, where ethnic minorities were suffering from shocking levels of malnutrition, poverty, unemployment, and loss of traditions as their culture was being swallowed up by the modern world. Mirror left Bangkok (though there's now a branch office there) and began a grassroots nonprofit in Mae Yao, a rural district of rice paddies, forests, and mountains in Chiang Rai province. Honoring local needs led the group to expand its mission in order to assist the Akha, Karen, Lahu, and other hill tribes.

More than 2,000 volunteers have joined Mirror over the years to teach English, create documentaries, establish craft cooperatives, and find creative solutions to the perennial problems of people who are not recognized by any government.

EARN YOUR ELEPHANT DRIVER'S LICENSE

In Thailand, a perfectly respectable career is that of a mahout—or elephant trainer. And while most Westerners aren't chomping at the bit to make it a full-time occupation, being a mahout is a fun vacation diversion.

At the Elephant Camp at Anantara's Golden Triangle Resort & Spa, mahouts in training spend three days learning to bathe, feed, and care for an elephant. They master basic elephant commands (around 70, at last count) and how to communicate with the pachyderms by lightly touching them behind the ears. From the backs of the camp's colorful cast of jumbo beauties, they also explore the forests of northern Thailand, Laos, and Myanmar (Burma).

Mahout training is not for late risers. Elephants and their mahouts start their day at 6:30 a.m., when elephants are rounded up from the forest, driven back to the camp, and given a few moments for morning ablutions. From there, mahout wannabes are taught how to mount their elephants—either by climbing up the animal's side or by leap-frogging over its bowed head—and given time to acclimate to the big beasts' roll and sway.

After lunch, mahouts drive their trusty steeds to the Ruak River for their all-time favorite activity—river bathing. And, yes, trainees are expected to get in the water with their charges, since staying on their backs would be nearly impossible, especially if you happen to get Lawann, the village flirt.

After a driving test, mahouts get an official mahout driver's license.

And while there may be no such thing as a dumb question, if you ask "how?" during mahout training, the pachyderm you're driving is likely to come to a screeching halt. *How,* after all, means "stop" in elephant language. But never fear, a quick *pai,* which means "go," should quickly catch you back up to the rest of your class. Another useful word is *baen,* which means "turn," which could come in mighty handy in an elephant camp that's located at the confluence of the Mekong and Ruak Rivers.

The resort's 160 acres of bamboo forest, nature trails, and river banks provide an ideal habitat for its four elephants, all of whom came here from the Thai Elephant Conservation Centre in Lampang, 375 miles north of Bangkok. *Anantara Golden Triangle Resort & Spa, 229 Moo 1, Chiang Saen, Chiang Rai 57150, Thailand, 66 5378 4084, www.goldentriangle.anantara.com.*

Here's just a sampling of creative projects that can use your help:

Bannock TV: Thanks to prejudice and ignorance, Thai's ethnic hill tribes, often refugees from Tibet and Myanmar (Burma), are called by pejorative names like E-gaw, Maew, and Ga-rieng, terms that suggest backwardness. To counteract this unenlightened perspective, Mirror—with funding from the World Bank—makes educational documentaries about these traditional cultures' ceremonies, songs, customs, costumes, farming processes, weaving methods, and hunting techniques. These documentaries are, in turn, broadcast throughout Thailand.

Thai Citizenship Project: Lack of Thai citizenship creates a raft of problems for Mae Yao's hill people. They can't vote, buy land, find legal employment, or even travel outside their own province. They're not eligible for education or government health care. At last count, Mirror has helped more than 2,000 hill people (and is working with 4,000 more) navigate the complex process of becoming legal citizens.

Ecotours Project: Until Mirror stepped in, many Thai trekking companies were exploiting the hill-tribe villages by paying them the equivalent of 50 cents of a $40 trekking fee to be a cheap tourist attraction. Mirror is developing tourism projects that recognize the villagers' culture and lifestyle and raise money for their children.

Voice of Earth Clay: Thailand's marginalized hill-tribe people mold, fire, paint, and glaze clay whistles (ocarinas) that are sold on the Internet (www.ebannok.com) and at an on-site shop. Profits from these whistles and other handicrafts, such as cloth pencil bags, jackets, and pillows, fund scholarships for local children.

Volunteers can come for a maximum of three months and mainly teach English to hill-tribe schoolchildren, local trekking guides, and staff. When available, they can learn traditional weaving or bamboo work at an additional cost.

Volunteers live in housing on the Mirror community grounds with a two-night weekend homestay with host families (additional accommodation with families can be arranged). The five-day program costs 7,000 baht ($200), 10,000 baht ($290) for one to two weeks, 11,000 baht ($310) for three weeks, 12,000 baht ($340) for a month, and 300 baht ($9) for each week after a month. Fees include airport pickup, accommodations, most transportation, weekday meals, and an elephant trek as part of a three-day trek/homestay weekend at the Lahu and Akha hilltribe villages.

HOW TO GET IN TOUCH

The Mirror Foundation, 106 Moo 1, Ban Huay Khom, T. Mae Yao, A. Muang, Chiang Rai 57100, Thailand, 66 5373 7412, www.mirrorartgroup.org.

fight rare diseases in the world's newest country

DILI, TIMOR-LESTE

Working together we have learned nothing is impossible.
—Dr. Dan Murphy, who started the Bairo Pite Clinic in September 1999

76 Dan Murphy, an American doctor who runs a free health clinic in Dili, Timor-Leste (East Timor), the half-island nation that gained its official independence on May 20, 2002, after a 24-year brutal Indonesian military occupation, desperately needs volunteers. But don't expect him to offer accommodations and food. He's too busy treating the 300 or more patients who show up each day at the little clinic he manages to run on less than $3,000 a month.

In 1999, when Murphy first showed up in East Timor, one of the world's poorest countries, it was in violent upheaval. Traveling into mountain hideouts to treat wounded rebels, he says "killing, torture, and massacres were a steady weekly diet." Hobbling rebels who had had the bones of their feet smashed to bits by members of the Indonesian Army were some of his first patients. "Soldiers would put a prisoner's foot under the leg of a chair and crush down on it," he says, "You know how many small bones there are in the foot?"

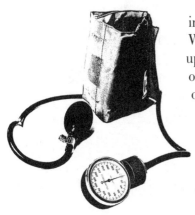

Having spent six years working at a farm clinic, fighting against pesticide abuse alongside United Farm Workers leader Cesar Chavez, he wasn't afraid to speak up about the atrocities. Three times, he was thrown out of the country, once for comparing the Indonesian occupiers to Nazis.

Even now that Timor-Leste is finally free from its longtime shackles (before Indonesia's occupation, it was under Portuguese dominion), thousands of people are still without homes and such diseases as TB, malaria, leprosy, AIDS, and dengue run rampant. Murphy explains, "East Timor has suffered as much or more than any other country in modern times. We can attribute this to the inadequacies and designs of the Western world powers, as well as to Indonesia. East Timor is poor because for 500 years they have had a boot on their neck."

Before the Indonesian military finally pulled out in September 1999, it destroyed 70 percent of the country's infrastructure, including more than a third of its health facilities. Those that remained were looted, and their equipment was damaged or destroyed. Any doctor with a lick of sense had long since high-tailed it out of the country.

Murphy says all these problems only heightened his resolve. Digging equipment out of the ashes, he started the Bairo Pite Clinic (BPC). In addition to treating patients, the clinic trains student doctors whose careers were cut short during the crisis.

Volunteers of all stripes are welcome at the clinic, and while Murphy doesn't have lots of free time to set up logistics, Medical Aid East Timor (MAET), a

TO EACH HIS OWN

Timor-Leste (or East Timor, as it was long known) is not only the world's youngest country, but it's also taking its first baby steps as a travel destination. If you're after a cookie-cutter holiday, expect sheets with high thread counts, or even want roads that don't stop until you get to where you're going, you might want to avoid this country.

But if you long to escape the shackles of mainstream tourism, here is what you can expect:

- **A road less traveled.** Friends of Timor-Leste, an organization trying to help this impoverished country, compare its north coast road to the legendary Highway 1 in Big Sur, California. However, in Timor-Leste, when you hit the fishing village of Com, the 150-mile-long road winding along the Westar Strait does a disappearing act. Instead, the final 20 miles of the journey to Tutuala's remote beaches is aptly nicknamed "pothole purgatory."
- **Transportation.** Uh, sometimes. Timor-Leste's Jako Island, a marine park located in Nino Konis Santana National Park, offers everything from snorkeling to bush walking, manta rays to turtles. There's just one problem. There's no easy way to get there. Ask around and eventually you can probably talk a fisherman who is heading in that direction to drop you off.

According to Dr. Dan Murphy, providing primary health care is a top priority for the Bairo Pite Clinic, which sees more than 600 patients each day. The clinic's services include:

- Dental services
- Health outreach
- In-patient services
- Maternity and infant care
- Tuberculosis (TB) treatment and control
- Vaccinations

The Bairo Pite Clinic also provides training for local healthcare workers. In addition, the clinic, which has a water supply system and a power generator to supplement unreliable local supplies, operates a medical laboratory, pharmacy, kitchen, and laundry service.

nonprofit based in Madison, Wisconsin, raises money for Dr. Dan, as he's known to the grateful Timorese, and MAET's staff are always willing to help volunteers make arrangements. They even host a Tour de Timor, a bike ride fund-raiser for BPC, every year in Madison.

There's no charge to volunteer at the clinic. Expect monthly expenses for room and board in this poverty-stricken country, the poorest in Asia, to run at least $75.

HOW TO GET IN TOUCH
Medical Aid East Timor, 213 North Fifth Street, Madison, WI, 53704, 608-241-2473, www.aideasttimor.org; **Bairo Pite Clinic,** Box 259, Dili, Timor-Leste, 670 3324118, http://bairopiteclinic.tripod.com.

commemorate the 140,000 killed by the world's first atomic bomb

HIROSHIMA, JAPAN

To remember Hiroshima is to abhor nuclear war.
To remember Hiroshima is to commit oneself to peace.
—Pope John Paul II

77 At 8:15 a.m. on August 6, 1945, the United States dropped an atomic bomb, nicknamed "Little Boy," that killed 140,000 innocent people in Hiroshima, Japan. Three days later, U.S. President Harry Truman ordered that a second atomic bomb be dropped on Nagasaki, which took the lives of another 80,000 people. The world must never forget these terrible events.

On August 6 every year, the survivors of Hiroshima commemorate these tragedies by burning incense, laying wreaths, and praying for the souls of the dead. Needless to say, they've become some of the world's most eloquent advocates for pacifism.

But perhaps the ceremony that draws the most attention is a beautiful lantern ceremony called Toro Nagashi. From the base of the Atomic Bomb Dome, the remains of one of the only buildings left standing on that fateful day, thousands of cube-shaped paper lanterns are set afloat down the Motoyasu River. It's a stunning spectacle that draws thousands to the city each year.

Started in 1947, two years after the devastation, the lantern ceremony takes place at Hiroshima Peace Memorial Park and invites individuals of all nations and faiths to design lanterns that represent their thoughts and feelings about personal loss, global peace, nuclear disarmament, and other relevant issues.

The park is dedicated to the abolition of nuclear weapons and the realization of world peace. It houses the Flame of Peace, a flame ignited on August 1, 1964, that will burn until all nuclear weapons are gone forever. Next to the flame is a monument with the names of all the people who died—more than 181,000, including those who died in the next few months and years after the bombing from illness caused by radiation exposure.

A THOUSAND PAPER CRANES

Sadako Sasaki was only two when the bomb struck her city; she lived about a mile from ground zero. By the time she was ten, she, like many people in Hiroshima, developed leukemia—what her mother called "an atomic bomb disease." After she was hospitalized, a friend brought her a folded paper crane and explained the Japanese legend saying that if you can accomplish the feat of folding a thousand cranes, you'll be granted a wish. Sadako, weak from her disease, folded crane after crane, wishing, of course, for her own recovery. Soon after she completed folding the 664th crane, her leukemia got the best of her. Her classmates, devastated about losing their friend, finished the task.

A statue of Sadako stands in Peace Park and kids from around the world send cranes to the Hiroshima International School students, who drape them around the statue. They even send out "1,000 Crane" certificates of recognition. If you happen to have a thousand folded cranes lying around, send them to *Hiroshima International School, c/o The 1,000 Crane Club, 3-49-1 Kurakake, Asakita-ku, Hiroshima, 739-1743, Japan.*

Every year, Volunteers for Peace (VFP), in conjunction with the Hiroshima YMCA, organizes a work camp where volunteers from around the world come to do their part to insure that a travesty of this nature is never repeated. This work camp starts at a ski resort in the mountains outside Hiroshima. Volunteers from around the world join together at the Swiss-Mura Free School, an alternative school that offers farming, baking, and carpentry, as well as traditional academic subjects. You'll work with students who, for various reasons, are unable to participate in traditional Japanese schooling; part of your job is to introduce them to your country and culture. Take photos, books, recipes, songs, and children's plays for show and tell.

You'll then return to Hiroshima to help the YMCA promote peace and raise international awareness of the tragedy created by the atomic bomb and by all warfare.

Cost for the two-week VFP work camp is $300 and includes meals and accommodation. During your time at the school, you'll sleep in a dorm with other volunteers. While in Hiroshima, you'll stay with a host family.

HOW TO GET IN TOUCH

Volunteers for Peace, 1034 Tiffany Road, Belmont, VT 05730, 802-259-2759, www.vfp.org.

teach english at an orphanage on the rooftop of the world

LHASA, TIBET

Individually, we are one drop. Together, we are an ocean.
—Ryunosuke Satoro

78 Heinrich Harrer, the Austrian mountaineer who wrote *Seven Years in Tibet* about his remarkable experience with the teenage Dalai Lama, is probably Tibet's most well-known volunteer. While he was in Lhasa, he not only learned the Tibetan language, but he helped the Buddhist monks at Potala Palace—the Dalai Lama's winter home—build a sewer system and plant trees.

Like the famous Buddhist leader he befriended, Harrer fled in the 1950s when the Chinese invaded. Nearly 60 years later on the highest mountain ridge in the world, there's still plenty of work for able-bodied volunteers to do.

Global Crossroad (GC), a Dallas-based company that dispatches volunteers to 24 countries, partnered with an orphanage near Lhasa to offer an amazing volunteer project. As of this writing, however, the project that GC has run there for many years is on hiatus, pending reapproval by the Chinese government. GC hopes that the successful program will be up and running again soon. (In the meantime, interested participants can volunteer in Nepal or China and go to Tibet for a travel program. Call or check the website for the latest information on the program's status.)

Here's the lowdown about this project: Most of your 15 to 20 volunteer hours each week will be spent teaching English, an important skill for children trying to climb out of poverty. There are also opportunities to coach soccer, play games, or even lead rousing rounds of irreverent street songs, a favorite pastime of most Tibetans.

To raise money for the children's care, the orphanage also runs the Tibetan Medicine Center, the Tibetan Handicraft Center, and the Tibetan Paper Industry. GC volunteers are free to help with any of these projects.

Either way, you'll have plenty of time to check out Potala Palace, drink butter tea (the national drink that supposedly replenishes the body's stores of

LET THERE BE PEACE FLAGS IN TIBET

Invite all parts of yourself to join you at the peace table in your heart.
—Buddhist teacher Jack Kornfield, in *A Path with Heart*

Although Americans hang colorful Buddhist peace flags across their porches, the tradition began in Tibet more than 2,000 years ago. The colorful squares in blue (for sky), white (water), red, (fire), green (air), and yellow (earth) of the Dar Cho unleash prayers as the wind blows through them. In Tibet, Dar means to increase life and good fortune and Cho means to everyone. As the squares fray and fade, the prayers are believed to be released to the heavens.

Many of today's prayer flags are made by Tibetan refugees in India and Nepal, and are stamped with prayers, mantras, symbols, and *dharanis,* which are magical formulas for conveying peace.

A student in Eugene, Oregon, who hung them outside her apartment reported that crime had decreased. She noted that it was probably a coincidence, but nice nonetheless.

salt, fat, and water), and appreciate the scenery that—at 17,000 feet—is unlike any other. As American civil engineer Stanford Zeccolo said about his recent visit to Lhasa, "I have a son who I've visited in Montana, you know, the 'big sky country,' but Montana falls a little short compared to Tibet and the Himalaya. Every place you look is a Kodak moment."

Volunteers, who fly into Lhasa International Airport on the first and third Monday of every month, typically stay in Tibet for between one and twelve weeks. They live at a guest house in Lhasa and are provided with language training and cultural briefings before classroom teaching begins.

Cost for a one-week post in Tibet runs $1,175 and includes breakfast and lunch only. When it's running, the program goes from April through October.

HOW TO GET IN TOUCH

Global Crossroad, 415 East Airport Freeway, Suite 365, Irving, TX 75062, 866-387-7816 or 972-252-4191, www.globalcrossroad.com.

be a zookeeper

Remember, if you ever need a helping hand, it's at the end of your arm.
As you get older, remember you have another hand: the first is
to help yourself, the second is to help others.
—Audrey Hepburn, actress and humanitarian

79 There are 6,437 animals in Malaysia that could use your second hand. These denizens of two well-known Malaysian zoos—from endangered orangutans and black panthers to bearded pigs and storks—depend on volunteers sent by the U.K.-based Gap Year for Grown Ups (GYG), a company that organizes what they call life-changing outings to 45 countries, for their survival.

Volunteer zookeepers who fly to Kuala Lumpur on the fifth day of every month guide tours, feed the animals, clean their cages, and provide them with enrichment activities. Since the animals' normal routines—finding food and spawning progeny—have been nipped in the bud by encroaching development on the Malay Peninsula, enrichment gives animals something engaging to do.

For Wasabi, a four-year-old female orangutan abandoned by her mother, you might hide such treats as sugarcane and raisins (to encourage foraging) or wave palm leaves in hopes that she'll figure out that they make handsome nests. Gorillas, like cats, enjoy hopping in and out of boxes, pushing them across floors, and, if they're hungry, eating them as an afternoon snack.

But you won't have to figure this all out on your own. You'll work under the guidance of the zookeepers, on-site vets, and zoo directors, who will not only enlighten you on baby elephant enrichment, but will provide the necessary rakes, brushes, trash bags, boxes, ropes, disinfectants, palm leaves, keys, food, and boots.

GYG offers zookeeping posts at two zoos:

Taiping Zoo. Three hours from Kuala Lumpur, the Taiping Zoo is the oldest public zoo in Malaysia. It has 34 lushly gardened acres and 1,300 animals representing 200 species of birds, reptiles, and mammals. Volunteers here live in a nearby hotel.

Zoo Negara. This city zoo is larger, with 110 acres and 5,137 animals, including more than 80 aquatic animals that live in its popular Tunku Abdul Rahman aquarium. Once virgin jungle, Zoo Negara is only a few minutes from the center of Kuala Lumpur. Volunteers here live in a home located inside the zoo.

According to GYG, other than the location, there's really little difference between the two zoos. At both, you'll get the chance to work with a wide variety of species, or, if you prefer, you can concentrate on just one. If you love, say, stump-tailed macaques, you can request to work with nothing but the pink-faced shaggy primates.

Work days start at 8 and don't finish until 5, but you'll have weekends off to explore cosmopolitan Kuala Lumpur or the country's ancient—but disappearing—rain forests, beaches, and mountains.

The four-week zookeeper job runs £1,159 ($1,725) and includes lodging, as mentioned above, and three meals a day featuring Malaysia's exotic, chili-spiced rice and noodle dishes.

HOW TO GET IN TOUCH

Gap Year for Grown Ups, Zurich House, 1 Meadow Road, Tunbridge Wells, Kent TN1 2YG, England, 44 1892 701881, www.gapyearforgrownups.co.uk

---

NAME CHANGE IMPEACHMENT

In October 2008, Abdul Hakim Borhan, the mayor of Kuala Lumpur, was practically forced to resign for changing the name and street signs on a popular thoroughfare that's been a nighttime foodie destination for 50 years. Once a red-light district, Jalan Alor, the street with hundreds of outdoor stalls selling everything from marinated grilled stingray and chicken satay to frog porridge and crispy fried pig intestines, was suddenly changed to Jalan Kejora. Jalan means "street," Alor means "stream," and Kejora is the Malay word for the planet Venus.

Vendors, taxi drivers, backpackers, and even newspapers as far away as France expressed outrage that the well-known street in the Bukit Bintang district was being what the mayor called "rebranded."

Whatever it ends up being called, Jalan Alor/Jalan Kejora is still an entertaining, if rather imposing, place to step back into Asia before modernization. You'll find bustling outdoor restaurants and endless rows of stalls selling fruits, hanging ducks, sugarcane juice, and grilled fish of every persuasion.

---

restore a buddhist monastery

MUSTANG VALLEY, NEPAL

We can't do much about the length of our lives,
but we can do plenty about its width and depth.
—Evan Esar, author and humorist

80 Two figures stood out in Mark Hintzke's mind when he started the Cultural Restoration Tourism Project (CRTP), a small nonprofit that uses volunteers to restore cultural heritage sites around the world: ten, the percentage of tourism dollars that actually go into the pockets of locals in developing countries, and five, the number of grants he knew he'd end up seeking if he tried to restore a Mongolian monastery the traditional way.

With experience in construction and nonprofits, creative problem-solving was nothing new to Hintzke. He decided to use the world's largest industry (tourism) to fund his restoration work, by asking volunteers to pay for the chance to work alongside local architects and artists who are bringing precious cultural sites back to life.

On CRTP's current project, a 300-year-old monastery in Nepal's applegrowing Mustang Valley, Hintzke's volunteers are working alongside Lama Sashi Doj, a world-renowned painter and Buddhist monk who is not only supervising the renovation of the Chairro Gompa (Chiarro Buddhist monastery), but is offering training in monastic art. Doj comes from a long line (five generations) of artists who specialize in monastic sculpture and wall paintings.

Harsh weather conditions have taken their toll and the treasures inside Chairro are at risk of being lost forever. Centuries-old wall paintings and sculptures dwell precariously in a building on the verge of collapse. Without immediate attention, these works of master artists and craftsmen will be erased from existence.

The 12-day projects include light construction and painting that even untrained volunteers can handle, treks into the Mustang Valley's desert moonscapes, and the chance to meet displaced Tibetans who came to Nepal after China forbade them to practice their religion. In fact, when Hintzke told a local monk about his hopes to restore Chairro Gompa, the monk broke down into tears, crying what an interpreter

CIRCUIT TRAINING

Not only is Marpha, the village where you stay, near what some claim is the world's deepest gorge, on the Kali Gendeki River, but it's also one of the villages on the Annapurna Circuit. This classic Nepal trek normally takes about three weeks to complete, including needed rest days. If you decide to accept the challenge, you'll pass through four climate zones, be introduced to ten ethnic groups, and traverse through countless rice farms, orchards, and forests before reaching the summit at 17,769 feet.

later told the American do-gooder were "tears of joy and gratitude." He was overcome, knowing his eyes would once again gaze upon the restored temple.

Hintzke's first CRTP project was launched in 1998, when he committed to finding the funds and volunteers to restore an ancient Buddhist temple in Baldan Baraivan, Mongolia, that had once been home to 1,500 lamas. Heavily damaged in the 1930s by Communists who sought to purge all signs of Buddhism and in the 1970s by a fire, the temple was sorely in need of the 300 volunteers who breathed life back into one of Mongolia's largest monasteries over the next seven years.

In 2003, CRTP was invited to Nepal to restore Chairro Gompa, because the 300-year-old monastery had fallen into disrepair when the routes used by Takhali salt traders were disrupted after the Chinese government closed the border to Tibet. Hintzke, whose master's thesis studied the application of Buddhist ethics to development practices, points out that projects are initiated not by him, but by local communities who want help restoring their history and culture, but lack resources. "The idea is to bridge cultural gaps, to allow for a deeper understanding of a culture from both sides," says Hintzke, who has been talking to communities in Egypt, Panama, Peru, and Mexico about future projects.

Under the snowcapped Himalaya, volunteers work and lunch with local contractors, using traditional tools and techniques. Afternoons are free to hike, pick apples, visit schools, or keep working.

The 12-day trip is $2,495 and includes three meals a day and accommodations in a modern, family-run guesthouse in the quaint, stone-lined village of Marpha.

HOW TO GET IN TOUCH

Cultural Restoration Tourism Project, P.O. Box 6803, Albany, CA 94706, 415-563-7221, www.crtp.net.

assist in the apricot, barley, and alfalfa harvest

LADAKH, INDIA

Advertising and the mass media pressure us all to live
a consumer lifestyle that can never lead to happiness.
I now know that another way of life is possible.
—Thomas McMillan, Ladakh volunteer

81 Ladakh, the high plateau in India's western Himalaya known as Little Tibet, was opened to foreign tourism in 1974. Ever since, the locals have been questioning their way of life. Tourists who come to gawk at their glorious mountains sometimes spend more money in a day than Ladakhi families spend in a whole year. Ladakhi children, once happy to chase yaks, have begun to want video games and fancy cameras. The men, once content to work beside the women on the family farm, head for the city in hopes of work and more money. The women, left to tend the farm and carry the water, watch hopelessly as their traditional way of life and cultural integrity slips like sand between their fingers.

Since 1975, the International Society for Ecology and Culture (ISEC), a British- and U.S.-based nonprofit that strives to protect biological and cultural diversity around the world, has been sending volunteers to Ladakh. Volunteers help locals with their yearly apricot, barley, and alfalfa harvests, but also let them know that modern development is not everything it's cracked up to be.

Though the World Bank touts development as the panacea, ISEC thinks the Ladakhis deserve a more accurate picture. The Indian government promotes this hauntingly beautiful region, but never mentions the downside of a modern lifestyle—job stress, unemployment, and family breakdown. Every summer, ISEC sends international volunteers to Ladakh for "experiential education." The four-week Learning

from Ladakh program (it used to be called the Farm Project) includes living with and working alongside a Ladakhi farming family and five days of group workshops.

It's a win-win for all concerned. The Ladakhi women get much-needed help with their harvest and household chores. And Western volunteers get insight into a traditional culture where the connection to nature runs deep and community and cooperation trump all else. Before 1974, when Westerners arrived on the scene, hunger, crime, pollution, and ethnic conflict were all but unknown here.

In addition to the Learning from Ladakh program, ISEC has also initiated a handicraft cooperative, introduced solar power, greenhouses, and ram pumps, and put together conferences, radio shows, and even a comic book that highlight the true cost of globalization.

Monthlong Learning from Ladakh sessions are held each summer over the course of two months and cost $600.

HOW TO GET IN TOUCH

International Society for Ecology and Culture USA, P.O. Box 9475, Berkeley, CA 94709, 510-548-4915, www.isec.org.uk.

ANOTHER ONE (ALMOST) BITES THE DUST

Twenty years ago, *amchi,* a traditional indigenous medicine that uses healing plants and herbs, was in danger of going extinct. Allopathic medicine, like many Western concepts, was introduced to Ladakh and considered by those making decisions about health policy to be the only way to improve the health of "backward" communities. Indigenous knowledge, even though it was written down in comprehensive medical texts, was all but ignored. Since amchis (also the name of practitioners of this ancient art) don't charge patients for consultations, they were being forced to get jobs to cope with changing economic realities.

Luckily, Amchi Tsewang Smanla started a project for the revival and development of this ancient healing practice that had been passed down to him over six generations. With a grant from the Save the Children Annual Fund, Smanla traveled to remote areas to share knowledge, exchange herbs, and train others in amchi. He organized committees of both allopathic doctors and amchis who work together to identify, cultivate, and preserve Ladakh's estimated 10,000 medicinal plants. He also leads herbal medicine tours for Westerners.

To find out more, contact *Amchi Tsewang Smanla, P.O. Box #101, Leh 194 101, Ladakh, India, 91 19 8225 2708.*

---

provide humanitarian aid to burmese cyclone victims

IRRAWADDY RIVER DELTA, BURMA

Today, no walls can separate humanitarian or human rights crises in one
part of the world from national security crises in another.
What begins with the failure to uphold the dignity of one life all too
often ends with a calamity for entire nations.
—Kofi Annan, seventh Secretary-General of the United Nations,
co-recipient of the 2001 Nobel Peace Prize

82 In the movie *Blood Diamond*, an old man standing amid the rubble of his village, which was just destroyed by greedy diamond hunters, says, "Well, at least we don't have oil. God help us if we did."

According to Tim Heinemann, a retired Army Special Forces officer who runs the humanitarian agency Worldwide Impact Now (WIN), it's that avarice for pricey resources that prevented the million people displaced by Cyclone Nargis from getting aid.

The hill-tribe people along Myanmar's (Burma) Irrawaddy River Delta sit on land that's incredibly rich in natural resources: gas, oil, precious gems, and teak, not to mention riverine hydropower potential.

The government dictatorship, Heinemann says, has been waging a calculated strategy to evict or eradicate the non-Myanmar ethnic population from ancestral lands they've held for more than 2,000 years. (Myanmar, in fact, is a racist term that means Burman ethnic, excluding all non-Burman ethnic groups.) The cyclone simply played into their hand. In the mountainous region of eastern Myanmar, more than 3,000 villages have been burned or mined and tens of thousands of internally displaced persons are uprooted on any given day.

Heinemann's nonprofit has been working with the country's displaced people since 2004 and was able to sneak supplies, food, and medicine to the cyclone victims. Running an ethnic leadership training program largely funded out of his

ADDITIONAL VOLUNTEER OPPORTUNITIES

Mae Sot, a frontier town on the Thai/Burma border, has dozens of ethnic groups, including Hmong, Yao, Lahu, Karen, Buddhist, and Muslim Burmese. When they can, people from Burma float across the shallow, muddy water on black inner tubes to sell cigarettes, whiskey, and other cheap Burmese goods. Mae Sot also has hundreds of international volunteers who are working desperately to get aid to the people of Burma. If you want the skinny on volunteer opportunities, visit Mae Sot's KCB Snack Shop. Owner Samsok not only serves a mean *krabawng* (Burmese for "fried crispy," a sort of vegetable tempura), but he speaks fluent English and knows all the volunteer organizations in the area. Some he'll probably tell you about:

Mary's Meals, the well-known campaign of Scottish International Relief, is rebuilding schools destroyed by Cyclone Nargis. They've set up feeding shelters in the border refugee camps and are successfully feeding several thousand children and families a day.

Dr. Cynthia. Everyone knows Dr. Cynthia, who started the Mae Tao Clinic to provide free health care for refugees, migrant workers, and others who cross the border from Burma to Thailand.

own pocket, Heinemann started WIN with the objective to "free oppressed peoples worldwide through human development and empowerment."

"I hope to eventually work myself out of a job," says Heinemann, whose nonprofit is set up in Thailand with volunteers crossing the border into Burma by day.

Heinemann's volunteers work with "rainmakers," inspiring village leaders who can become catalysts for building strong communities, security, and prosperity from the ground up. But it's not easy fighting an oppressive military regime that receives an estimated billion dollars a year from Chevron-operated oil fields and pipelines.

Heinemann will be the first to tell you this isn't a volunteer position for lightweights, as it entails certain risks. After four years and many successes with the ethnic people he champions, he is wanted by the government and his phone is tapped.

But for anyone wanting to help displaced people in their fight for freedom, Heinemann has lots of volunteer work. There's no charge to work on a WIN team.

HOW TO GET IN TOUCH

Worldwide Impact Now, 30802 Coast Highway, SPC F20, Laguna Beach, CA 92651, 913-240-1627, www.worldwide-impact-now.org.

pitch in with farm chores at an egalitarian commune

GYEONGGI-DO, SOUTH KOREA

The miracle is this—the more we share, the more we have.
—Leonard Nimoy, actor, director, musician, and photographer

83 Probably the first thing you'll notice when you drive up to this volunteer work project at Sanan Village, South Korea, is a large sign that makes this rather outrageous claim: "A village where money is of no use and everybody is on good terms and happy."

Is this really possible? There's one way to find out. Every summer since 2004, the Canadian Alliance for Development Initiatives and Projects (CADIP), a Vancouver-based nonprofit, sends volunteers to a work camp at this alternative community that's based on the principles of Miyozo Yamagishi, a Japanese rice farmer who believed "society should be financed by one wallet."

In the 1950s, Yamagishi and a group of friends pooled their resources to start a commune that renounced personal possessions and espoused pacifism, oneness with nature, and a simple lifestyle. In postwar Japan, the idea struck a chord and at one time, there were more than 40 Yamagishi communes throughout Japan, Australia, Asia, and even Europe.

Sanan Village, located in a farming region near Palan about 60 miles south of Seoul, has managed to make this experiment in rural utopia work for more than 25 years. At last count, about 40 members farm together, live together, prepare meals together, and share what, by all reports, is a happy and harmonious simple life. Among other things, they raise chickens whose eggs are legendary throughout the country.

CADIP volunteers come for two months to work on and learn about this environmentally friendly farm that believes in sharing all its resources.

TRY YOUR HAND AT POTTERY

Do-it-yourself pottery studios are all the rage these days. Neophyte artists take brush in hand to paint everything from cups and dishes to statues of fire-breathing dragons. In Korea, known for its elegant pottery traditions dating back to 6000 B.C., would-be potters can take it one step further. Instead of just painting someone else's pot, you can actually shape, design, and fire your own.

In the Incheon Ceramics village, you can visit dozens of pottery studios, learn the history of traditional Korean ceramics, visit several famous ceramics museums, and create your own pottery—either with a potter's wheel or without. Find out more at http://english.visitkorea.or.kr. The area is also home to the World Ceramics Center (www.worldceramic.or.kr).

Don't miss the Haegang Ceramics Museum started by Yoo Kun-Hyung, a famous potter who spent his life researching ancient ceramic production centers, collecting ceramics, and perfecting and innovating on the style from the Goryeo dynasty. The museum opened in 1990.

Every year in May, there's a big Icheon Ceramics Festival, complete with classes from Korea's many pottery masters.

Volunteers gather eggs, build poultry houses, work in the organic vegetable fields and, if they want, help out in the kitchen. There are also opportunities to teach English or other languages, participate in sports, and take trips to the local village, including attending festivals held there. In the evenings, volunteers can learn about Korean culture and work with a Korean tutor to master Korean and Japanese language skills.

Previous volunteer experience is desirable and you must be willing to get your hands dirty. If you're a strict vegetarian, this is not the gig for you.

Cost for the two-month gig, including healthful organic meals and accommodations in the Sanan Village guesthouse, runs $590 Canadian ($470).

HOW TO GET IN TOUCH

Canadian Alliance for Development Initiatives and Projects, 907–950 Drake Street, Vancouver, British Columbia V6Z 2B9, Canada, 604-628-7400, www .cadip.org.

save an important wetland

MAI PO MARSHES, HONG KONG

The ultimate test of man's conscience may be his willingness
to sacrifice something today for future generations
whose words of thanks will not be heard.
—Gaylord Nelson, founder of Earth Day

84 Knock on wood. The Mai Po Nature Reserve, just outside the legendary financial capital of Hong Kong, has been saved. But a natural space does not exist outside a growing city of giant skyscrapers and 6.6 million people without being keenly aware that the battle between nature and man is never really over.

When Hong Kong's stunning new airport opened in 1998, it won all sorts of international design awards. In the process, however, it blasted the island of Chek Lap Kok flat, destroying habitats for all sorts of life-forms who could care less about boarding passes and runways. And when you're a wetland—not a towering mountain or a vast ocean that anyone can easily appreciate—the argument is sometimes harder to defend. It's a boggy marsh, for heaven's sake.

Who needs all that mud, you ask? The birds do. Many of the 68,000 birds that stop here to fatten up during their migrations between Asia and Australia every April and May are rare and endangered species. The marshes and tidal flats of the Mai Po Nature Reserve host more than 350 species of birds, including Chinese egrets, Saunders' gulls, and spotted greenshanks. The area is also home to a quarter of the world's black-faced spoonbills—a gangly, long-beaked shorebird that everyone assumed remained plentiful until Peter Kennerley, a Briton then living in Hong Kong and an avid bird-watcher, happened to notice that spoonbill sightings were becoming few and far between.

Kennerley decided to do some research. After collecting records of sightings ranging from Vietnam to Japan, he came to the startling conclusion there were a mere 288 black-faced spoonbills left, 90 percent of which wintered at just three sites. One of them was Hong Kong's Deep Bay, home of that boggy mud called Mai Po; the others were Vietnam's Red River Delta and Taiwan's Chiku wetlands.

In 1995, the World Wide Fund for Nature (WWF) Hong Kong, along with other like-minded organizations, used Kennerley's findings about the birds' scarcity to get the bay added to the Ramsar Convention on Wetlands of International Importance, a treaty geared toward conservation.

Thankfully, the government is now on board in protecting both the black-faced spoonbill and the Mai Po Nature Reserve, but pollution (including pig waste from Shenzhen), rising mudflats, and lack of large wildlife (Hong Kong's tigers, elephants, and crocodiles were driven north decades ago) are continuing problems in this concrete jungle. Yet the presence of black-faced spoonbills in the wetlands has thwarted plans to build a golf course, a housing project, and a railway line.

WWF uses volunteers at its Mai Po Marshes Wildlife Education Centre and Nature Reserve, as well as in other projects around the country. There's a volunteer skill form you can fill out on the website. There's no charge to volunteer here.

HOW TO GET IN TOUCH

World Wide Fund for Nature Hong Kong, Suite 1002, Asian House, 1 Hennessy Road, Wanchai, Hong Kong, 852 2526 1011, www.wwf.org.hk.

FIND YOUR FORTUNE

Unlike Chinese fortune cookies that glibly predict amour, tall, dark strangers, and monstrous sums of cash in tomorrow's mail, Hong Kong's fortune-tellers don't mince words. One psychic told traveler Chelsea O'Shea straight out that her love life stunk, her career was heading down the tubes, and her perfect health was drawing to a close.

Of course, it's always easy in Hong Kong to seek a second opinion. At the Wong Tai Sin Temple, Hong Kong's busiest Buddhist temple, there are 150 or more fortune-telling booths lined up like dominos in a winding concrete alley. Consulting everything from empty turtle shells with coins outside to palmistry charts to skinny bamboo fortune sticks called chim, these fortune-tellers are nearly as famous as film stars and as well-respected as scholars.

Temple Street Market, a colorful open-air market that springs to action at dusk, also has several blocks of fortune-tellers, along with dentists wrenching abscessed molars, acupuncturists poking away backaches, loquacious salesmen hawking everything from $20 ski suits to half-price Louis Vuitton luggage, and two blocks of Chinese opera singers—complete with two- and three-piece Chinese orchestras.

take karaoke and educational puppets to rural villages

PHNOM PENH, CAMBODIA

It's a matter of taking the side of the weak against the strong,
something the best people have always done.
—Harriet Beecher Stowe, abolitionist and author

85 Resource Development International (RDI) issues a warning to all its volunteers. Unfortunately, they claim, we "cannot guarantee that visitors will not fall in love with the country and the people and commit to giving large portions of their lives to work here. We apologize for any inconvenience this may cause for family and friends."

Ninety percent of the RDI team, in fact, originally traveled to Cambodia just "to visit." But now, they are permanently living in Phnom Penh and working diligently to raise up this war-stricken country, one of the poorest in the world, by its tattered sandals.

During the Khmer Rouge period (1975–79), approximately 1.5 million Cambodians, mainly intellectuals and skilled workers, were executed or died from hunger or forced labor. Today, more than half of the population of Cambodia is under 18, leaving a Grand Canyon of an educational gap. RDI has developed several programs to bridge the chasm and welcomes volunteers of all stripes.

Since karoake is one of the most popular forms of entertainment in Cambodia, RDI developed a mobile karaoke studio that goes into villages with microphones and a huge songbook of socially uplifting selections. Villagers, who clamor for the microphone, quickly memorize surprisingly catchy tunes about clean water, AIDS awareness, child protection, and other vital issues. The backup music for RDI's karaoke songs is all professionally done, performed by nationally recognized musicians and singers.

YOUR BIG TV BREAK, CAMBODIA STYLE

Breaking into the television business is next to impossible in the United States— just ask the tens of thousands of script writers working on spec. In Cambodia, however, if you happen to have a spare $1,300, you can finance a half-hour episode of one of RDI's popular educational TV shows. Because original TV programming in Cambodia is practically unheard of (most shows broadcast on Cambodian television are poorly dubbed Thai shows), RDI has managed to find a welcome audience for their educational programming.

So what if they have a social or health agenda? They're fun. They're original. And they're produced by RDI using professional Khmer actors. In a manner similar to Heifer International "selling" cows, sheep. and flocks of hens, RDI offers the following opportunities for breaking into the entertainment business:

- 1,000 educational karaoke CDs: $1,000
- One episode of children's television programming: $1,300
- "Edutainment" video on HIV/AIDS or other health topics: $1,500

The puppet program has performed for more than 20,000 students since 1998 and can't keep up with demand. The government of Cambodia officially requested that RDI, its staff, and volunteer puppeteers make educational presentations in all 16,000 of the country's schools.

Working with a translator, volunteers tell stories, perform magic tricks, and use their puppets to present valuable curricula. During Cambodia's recent flooding, a frog puppet named Mr. Op Op—an amphibian water specialist—staged a press conference with other puppets in the community to discuss the proper procedures for treating contaminated wells. Mr. Op Op (also known as Loc Op Op) became a national celebrity when his public service announcements (PSAs) were shown regularly on Cambodian TV.

Mr. Op Op's PSAs on water showcase another of RDI's important volunteer programs—building and installing clay pot water filters. Like many developing countries, Cambodia and its villages have little or no access to clean water. Many of the village wells are laced with arsenic. One out of five children do not survive to their fifth birthday, and water-borne diseases cause an overwhelming number of the country's deaths among children each year.

To combat this terrible toll, RDI manufactures highly effective, low-cost clay filters from local clay, rice husks, and laterite. They also install them, monitor them, and teach the communities how to use them. The porous mixture of clay and rice lets water through, while keeping parasites, amoebas, and large bacteria out—with an assist from a collodial silver coating. The clay pot system eliminates 98 percent of the diseases present in surface water, making safe drinking water attainable through an inexpensive, easily maintained means.

RDI's clean water initiative was its first program. In 1998, Mickey Sampson, a United States chemistry professor who had fallen in love with the country on his own volunteer vacation, talked his wife, Wendi, into moving their growing family to Cambodia for one year. One night during that sabbatical year, Wendi beckoned him into the bathroom, where she was giving their young children a bath in murky water. "Look," she said. "You're a chemist. Can't you do something?" Indeed he did, eventually starting the nonprofit that also organizes teams to build homes and work on farms.

Volunteers stay in team leaders' homes for approximately $15 per day, including meals, and there's a $30 weekly charge for each team, which covers vehicle fuel and maintenance, water for your team each day, translators, and additional staff and their expenses.

HOW TO GET IN TOUCH

Resource Development International - Cambodia, P.O. Box 494, Phnom Penh, Cambodia, 855 17 778 533, www.rdic.org; U.S. Contact: P.O. Box 9144, Louisville, KY 40209.

conduct underwater fish and coral surveys

SOUTHERN LEYTE, PHILIPPINES

*Diving was so fun, I felt like Nemo! But I do not think I would
have understood the depth of what I was doing here unless
I actually went under the water and saw for myself.*
—Amaeze Madukah, Coral Cay Conservation volunteer

86 David Bellamy is not one to mince words. "If you and I do nothing to stop this [global climate change], two-thirds of all coral reefs will vanish within the next 20 years, resulting in poverty and hunger for millions," he says. As president of Coral Cay Conservation (CCC), a nonprofit that is dedicated to preserving the world's rain forests and underwater habitats, the guy knows what he's talking about.

Thirty percent of the world's coral reefs, the largest single living structure on Earth, are already damaged, some irreparably. By the year 2050, at the current trajectory, 70 percent will have disappeared. A former scientist with the Australian Institute of Marine Science put the gravity like this: "We are precipitating a mass extinction of absolutely everything."

That's why CCC's underwater research projects in the Philippines, Papua New Guinea, and Tobago are so important. And these projects could never happen without the aid of volunteers.

HIT THE WALL

For divers, Napantao Wall represents a paradise. Located in a protected marine sanctuary in Sogod Bay, this double wall that drops 120 feet straight down is covered with spectacular gorgonian fans and green tree corals. It plays apartment complex to pygmy seahorses, tuna, wahoo, devil rays, rainbow runners, midnight snappers, great gorgonians, frogfish, scorpion fish, batfish, and whitetip reef sharks.

CCC's project in southern Leyte, Philippines, a remote spot yet to make the tourism map, began in 2002. The coral reefs of southern Leyte are some of the richest, least disturbed, and least researched habitats in the Philippines. Sogod Bay, where the project is located, has long been frequented by whale sharks (locals call them *tiki tiki*). The archipelago boasts more than 2,500 species of fish and nearly 500 species of hard coral. Volunteers are needed to map and assess coral reefs, conduct biodiversity surveys, and collect data that ultimately will help sustain and conserve these fragile, shrinking underwater environments.

Volunteers, who spend much of their time diving this spectacular bay, collect data and produce detailed habitat maps. They also educate locals about coral reef ecology, the dangers of overfishing, and why it's important to preserve this unique habitat. The ultimate goal? To help Filipinos create a sustainable, eco-friendly tourism industry.

No scientific background or diving experience is necessary, as you will be trained on-site. During the first week, you'll get your diving certificate and learn to identify the neon colors swimming by, eventually becoming adept at identifying hundreds of fish, plus many types of corals, marine algae, and invertebrates.

On most days, you'll be up at the crack of dawn (5:30 a.m.) for the first of two daily survey dives, followed by lunch (sometimes eaten on the nearest deserted island). Then, there are chores, training, and data management to be done.

At the expedition base that one CCC volunteer called "a preview to heaven," you'll play beach volleyball, learn Tinikling (the Filipino national dance), swim with pods of dolphins and eagle rays (one volunteer swam with a pod of 60 pilot whales), and, at dinner each night, compete for "Fish of the Day" honors.

Volunteers are based at the Napantao Dive Resort, overlooking Sogod Bay. But don't take the resort title too seriously. It's a dorm, and each room is shared by four to six people. For roughly $570 a week ($520 if you're already a certified diver), you'll be housed, fed (Filipino chef Tata—the first local staff member—caters to vegetarians and fried chicken lovers alike), and provided with all the equipment and instruction you could ever need. Most volunteers stay for at least four weeks. As you pass the four- and eight-week marks, each week gets progressively less expensive.

HOW TO GET IN TOUCH

Coral Cay Conservation, 1st Floor Block 1, Elizabeth House, 39 York Road, London SE1 7NJ, England, 44 20 7620 1411, www.coralcay.org.

help foster tourism in bali

BALI, INDONESIA

It felt as if several layers of callousness and conditioning
accumulated over the years peeled off me.
—Ralph King, VIA volunteer to Indonesia

87 Back in the 1960s, before there was such a thing as a "volunteer vacation," Dwight Clark, a dean from Stanford University who happens to be a Quaker and a pacifist, organized a summer trip to a Hong Kong refugee camp. The students he recruited for that trip staffed medical clinics, built roads, and taught at rooftop schools. They were so profoundly moved by their experience helping Chinese war refugees that Clark spent the next 40 years organizing volunteers of all stripes to help, not only in Hong Kong, but in more than 15 Asian nations.

Originally called Volunteers in Asia (now shortened to simply VIA), Clark's nonprofit has made quite a name for itself, sneaking volunteers into several countries before even government-sponsored agencies could get into them. VIA sent volunteers to Vietnam before normalization, to China before and during Tiananmen Square, and to Laos when other volunteers were still denied entry. During the Vietnam War, Volunteers in Asia also organized alternative service projects for conscientious objectors.

ISLAND OF THE GODS

Bali, known as the "island of the gods," has more than just a few temples. Some claim that there are more temples than houses here; most villages have more than one. Temples honor the spirits of the sea, the spirits of irrigated agriculture, family, ancestors, village life, royalty, and of course, gods and goddesses.

The "mother temple" is Pura Beskih. Perched on the slopes of still active volcano Mount Agung, this massive temple was built between the 14th and 17th centuries. It celebrates more than 70 rituals every year and has three thrones—one each for Hindu gods Brahma, Wisnu (Vishnu), and Siwa (Shiva).

Although many VIA volunteers sign on for one-year or two-year programs, the organization also offers three summer programs lasting four to eight weeks that are open to any American interested in better understanding the countries of Asia. In China, volunteers learn about Chinese medicine; in Vietnam, they teach American culture at the University of Hue; and in the Bali Service-Learning Project, they learn about Balinese culture while facilitating literacy and much-needed English language skills.

Tourism is an economic lifeline to Bali, a Hindu gemstone in the necklace of isles that compose the predominantly Muslim nation of Indonesia. Between its celebrated beaches, lush rice terraces, and a population that actor, composer, and playwright Noël Coward (1899–1973) once remarked was "artistic from womb to tomb," Bali is often described as the "quintessential paradise." Although the terrorist bombings in October 2002 and October 2005 put a large dent in the country's pocketbooks, its economy still depends almost entirely on tourist-related income, which means fluency in English is a necessity.

During the two-month program in Bali, volunteers assist with a range of community requested services, such as teaching English and helping put together a literary journal called *Taman 65*. Since community needs determine the projects you will work on, sometimes you will be working with local nonprofits or nongovernmental organizations that are working in the country. Your work hours will vary, depending on the project you end up working on.

The study component of this program has two parts. The first is an intensive Bahasa Indonesia (Indonesian) language class taught by a local instructor. The course is tailored to serve both beginners and those who want to polish their Indonesian skills. The second portion, Socio-Cultural Change in Bali, will introduce the history, culture, and society of Bali through readings, guest speakers, field trips, and discussions.

On this unique program, you'll stay with a family, sharing meals, ideas, and your English language skills. Cost for the two-month program is $2,200. Volunteers are required to attend a couple training sessions held in California's Santa Cruz Mountains before their summer departure

HOW TO GET IN TOUCH
VIA, 965 Mission Street, Suite 751, San Francisco, CA 94103, 415-904-8033, www.viaprograms.org.

THE GREAT ORANGUTAN PROJECT

fight for wild orangutans

BORNEO, MALAYSIA

You'll sweat, bleed, laugh, and cry, and you'll love every minute of it!
—Peter Jackson, volunteer with the Great Orangutan Project

88 Aman, a 20-year-old orangutan who can do pull-ups with one finger, made headlines in 2007 when he became the first ape to undergo cataract surgery. After several years of being blind (the electric shock he got when he bit through a power cable was the prime suspect for his cataracts), Aman is once again swinging through trees in the jungles of Borneo. Or at least through the trees in the Matang Wildlife Centre (MWC), a rescue and rehabilitation center in Sarawak, Malaysian Borneo, that is hoping to save the endangered species. But they're working against a ticking time bomb. Some give the critically scarce wild orangutans less than ten years.

Until the 1990s, these red-haired apes were widespread across Asia, but now the only populations outside zoos are on the islands of Borneo and Sumatra. Thanks to poachers, palm oil manufacturers, and developers who are cutting wide swaths through the pristine forests, the remaining 50,000 to 60,000 orangutans are not expected to survive through the rest of the century.

On this volunteer gig, you'll work at the Matang Wildlife Centre, which is nestled in a plush rain forest on the lower flanks of Kubah National Park, one degree north of the Equator overlooking the South China Sea. You may help out with everything from

LIKE FATHER LIKE APE

Orangutans are humans' closest relative. We share 96.4 percent of the same DNA and, like us, orangutans:

- Have opposable thumbs
- Have 32 permanent teeth
- Have 9-month pregnancies
- Create time-saving tools
- Build roofs to avoid inclement weather over their nests high in the trees
- Have youngsters who cry, throw tantrums, and even, according to BBC News,
  play charades.

dragging banana trees to the orangutan's habitat to sewing coconuts into potato sacks. Orangutans, the Mensa candidates of the ape world, can usually figure out how to open the potato sacks in seconds flat. You'll build, scavenge for food (for the apes, not yourself), provide enrichment activities, and create an educational center that gives the endangered species a fighting chance.

Working in partnership with the Sarawak Forestry Research Team, you and your data will be used to better understand the behavior and health of the remaining orangutans. The ultimate goal is to rehabilitate and release them into the wild. MWC is also rehabilitating rare Malaysian sun bears, the first such project in the world. Keep in mind that the wildlife center is a home of last resort, the sun bears' and orangutans' only alternative to being put down because they have nowhere else to go.

Borneo, the world's third largest island, has 15,000 species of flowering plants, 300 species of trees, 221 species of mammals, and 420 resident birds, most of which you'll see during your four-week stay at the wildlife center.

A small river runs through the wildlife center, and surprisingly, there are no leeches here (the same can't be said for spiders, hornets, Komodo dragons, and snakes), so swimming is a popular pastime. Kuching, the charming provincial capital with good restaurants and a snappy nightlife, is only 40 minutes away. And nearby Bako National Park has 16 hiking trails.

If you're a picky eater and unwilling to adventure outside your culinary comfort zone, this may not be the trip for you. Regular shopping trips to Kuching aside, you'll be living in a jungle outpost. Meals are self-catered and available foods might include such delicacies as baby ferns, mangosteens, and dragon fruits.

Your chalet on stilts, although sparse, is comfortable and clean. Cold-water showers provide a welcome respite from the heat. Four weeks, including accommodations and an allowance for food, runs $2,695.

HOW TO GET IN TOUCH

The Great Orangutan Project, Studio 6, 8 High Street, Harpenden, Herts AL5 2TB, England, 44 845 371 3070, www.orangutanproject.com.

CHAPTER

7

australia & around

While earning your daily bread,
be sure you share a slice with those less fortunate.
—H. Jackson Brown, Jr., American writer

At the 1992 Earth Summit, held in Rio de Janeiro, Brazil, 168 countries resolved to preserve the diversity of life on planet Earth, each agreeing to undertake biodiversity surveys of any regions at risk in their purview. Section 3C of the resulting resolution further stated that if a host country lacked the resources to undertake the necessary surveys, an international aid organization would be invited in to help out.

In this chapter on Australia, New Zealand, and other islands in the South Pacific, you'll find lots of opportunities to work with some of these international aid organizations, conducting biodiversity surveys of all kinds of creatures, from hawksbill turtles in the remote islands of Vanuatu to wallabies or other wildlife across Australia.

You'll also find opportunities to save some of the species we already know are in danger, such as Tasmanian devils, kakerori birds, and humpback whales.

This chapter also lists projects teaching English, preserving rain forests, documenting World War II history, building houses, and running free health clinics.

Here's your chance, in the world's smallest, flattest, and driest continent, to drink up new tasks, expose yourself to the unfamiliar, and maybe—just maybe—tilt the world in a slightly more sustainable direction.

sustain the outback, mate

ACROSS THE AUSTRALIAN CONTINENT

Above all, Australia doesn't misbehave. It doesn't have coups,
recklessly overfish, arm disagreeable despots, grow coca in
provocative quantities, or throw its weight around in a brash and
unseemly manner. ... Clearly, this is a place worth getting to know.
—Bill Bryson, author of *In a Sunburned Country*
and many other books

89 In the last 200 years, Australia has lost 70 percent of its native vegetation, including three-fourths of its rain forests. Nearly a quarter of its mammals, a tenth of its birds, and a sixth of its amphibians are either extinct or moving speedily in that direction.

The good news is that there are hundreds of dirt cheap outdoor volunteer opportunities in all six states and three mainland territories relating to the conservation of Australia. The bad news is that Conservation Volunteers Australia (CVA), the totally together, well-organized umbrella that oversees a list of 2,000 volunteer projects, doesn't directly take volunteers from other countries.

You're certainly welcome to join up with any one of their projects (and thousands of overseas volunteers do), but you have to book it through a sort of volunteer vacation clearinghouse. If you're from Spain, you go through Sabática (www.sabatica.org), for example, or if you're from Germany, through AIFS Deutschland (www.aifs.de) or Eurovacances (www.eurovacances.de). In the United States, InterExchange, a nonprofit out of New York, offers the best price of the four U.S. CVA booking partners. These middlemen, as middlemen tend to do, tack on booking fees. A two-week trip that might cost a local Aussie volunteer $400 can cost an international volunteer twice that much.

Projects vary from wildlife surveys to dune restoration to maintaining hiking trails. Although you can pick which of Australia's major cities you would like to have as your base, you can't specify the exact project you will work on, since that depends on the time of year and the needs of conservation groups in that area. Since 1982, when CVA was founded, volunteers have built walking trails at Uluru Kata Tjuta National Park in the Northern Territories, tracked yellow-footed rock wallabies in South Australia's Flinders Ranges, created safe corridors for cassowaries in Queensland, and planted trees in Victoria's Werribee Gorge Island, a greenhouse-friendly carbon biodiversity site.

In 2006, 19-year-old American identical twins Lia and Katrina Engelsted spent three months working on 15 CVA projects, doing tasks from turtle monitoring to toad busting. Lia said, "My favorite project was on Magnetic Island. We were doing track work and there were hikers walking by—it felt really good to be working on the trail."

You'll work with a team of between six and ten volunteers. You'll work five days, then get two days off. Pack lightly, because with such a wide variety of projects, you'll likely be moving every week or two. Accommodations, too, run the gamut from lighthouses to hostels, from sheep shearing barns to tents. Two-week projects, including accommodations, food, and local transportation, run $895 for U.S. participants.

HOW TO GET IN TOUCH

Conservation Volunteers Australia, 61 3 5330 2600, www.conservationvolunteers.com.au; U.S. contact: InterExchange, 161 Sixth Avenue, New York, NY 10013, 212-924-0446, www.workingabroad.org.

"MOSTLY EMPTY AND A LONG WAY AWAY ... "

That's how author Bill Bryson describes Australia in *In a Sunburned Country,* joking that Australia sends the rest of the world nothing we can't actually do without. Obviously, he's never heard of these Australian inventions:

- Bionic ears
- Dual flush toilets
- Permanent-crease trousers
- Prepaid postage
- Car radios
- Electric drills
- Underwater torpedos
- Notepads
- Speedos
- Folding strollers
- Black box flight recorders
- Ultrasounds

save the tasmanian devil

TASMANIA, AUSTRALIA

Bugs Bunny (looking in an encyclopedia):
Here it is: "A strong, murderous beast, jaws as powerful as a steel
trap—has ravenous appetite—eats tigers, lions, elephants, buffaloes,
donkeys, giraffes, octopuses, rhinoceroses, moose, ducks…"
Taz: Rabbits.
Bugs: Rabbits? It doesn't say rabbits here.
—Taz's Looney Tunes debut cartoon, "Devil May Hare," 1954

90 Warner Brothers' Looney Tunes character of Taz, a whirling, slobbering tyrant that devours everything in its path, is based on a real animal, a rare black-and-white carnivorous marsupial the size of a small dog. Unfortunately, the real Tasmanian devil, extinct except in the Australian state of Tasmania, is not faring nearly as well as the cartoon character that, in a 1995 poll, was recognized by 95 percent of all Americans.

Like the Tasmanian tiger before it, the last of which died in 1936 in a Hobart zoo, the devil, so named for its blood-curdling yowls, may be on its last whirl. There may be as few as 20,000 Tasmanian devils left on the planet, due to a contagious facial cancer that has decimated the remaining population. Devil facial tumor disease (DFTD), a mysterious cancer that kills its victims within three to eight months, wasn't even discovered until 1996. Initial research indicates the Tasmanian devil will be lucky to survive for the next ten years.

In a race against extinction, the School of Zoology at the University of Tasmania sent healthy devils to zoos and sanctuaries on the mainland of Australia and then set about doing everything possible to stop the further spread of the disease—believed to spread from devil to devil through biting—in the wild. The university's scientists are containing wild populations, trapping and culling diseased devils, and conducting a variety of disease suppression trials. By monitoring and tracking the evolution of DFTD, they're hoping to not only prevent the Australian icon from going extinct, but also to provide insight into the rare disease. As one of only three cancers which are known to be contagious, devil facial tumor disease may open doors into the understanding of other transmissible diseases.

That's a lot of work for a project that's only been funded since 2003. Luckily, Tasmania's Wildlife Management Branch of the Department of Primary Industries and Water (DPIW) recruits volunteers for five- to eleven-day survey and trapping trips in the wilds of Tasmania. Volunteer fieldwork moves around the island of Tasmania, the smallest of Australia's six states. Rest assured you won't be far from the island's dramatic coastlines and mountains, 44 percent of which is protected in World Heritage areas, national parks, and other reserves.

On the field trips, volunteers bait and set traps, check and record data, and help university scientists microchip the endangered devils. Most of these radio tracking and mapping field trips take place in Tasmania's breathtaking national parks.

There's no charge to volunteer on the five- to eleven-day field excursions that include accommodation, food, transportation from Hobart, and wildlife passes.

HOW TO GET IN TOUCH

Tasmanian Devil Appeal, University of Tasmania Foundation, Private Bag 40, Hobart, Tasmania 7001, Australia, 61 3 6226 2053, www.utas.edu.au/foundation/devil.htm.

TWIST AND SHOUT

After years of fighting the Tasmanian government over the rights to the Taz character, Warner Brothers, which has made a fortune on him in his 55-year life span, finally ponied up for some scientific research. Judy Jackson, Tasmania's environment minister, fought for years to get the company's assistance. They also gave the Tasmanian government restricted rights to sell stuffed Taz dolls to raise more money and increase awareness about devil facial tumor disease (DFTD). During 2007, the company also sold Looney Tunes DVDs in Australia and donated a portion of the profits to fighting DFTD.

Let's hope the real Tasmanian devil recovers as resoundingly as the cartoon character did. Taz was axed soon after his 1954 debut in a cartoon short called "Devil May Hare." Edward Selzer, head of the Warner Brothers Animation Studio, ordered Robert McKimson, Taz's creator, to discontinue the new character on the grounds that he was "too obnoxious." Eventually, though, the big cheese himself (Jack Warner) saved Taz after receiving lots of mail from viewers who enthusiastically endorsed the wild and crazy character.

go carbon neutral in western australia

PERTH, AUSTRALIA

You don't walk away from a dream.
—Rosanne Scott, founder of City Farm

91 In his rant, "The Planet is Fine," the late George Carlin was right about at least one thing: Environmentalists sometimes have a tendency to take themselves a tad too seriously.

But that is definitely not true about the people at City Farm, an inner-city garden and education center in Perth, Australia, where founder Rosanne Scott and hundreds of green volunteers get their point across in dozens of brilliantly creative ways. For example, they host tree planting dance parties and teach kids circus skills while throwing in tips on permaculture. They also host a high-energy street drumming samba group where even cynics can't help but tap their toes.

Founded in 1994 as an initiative of the Planetary Action Network—the youth branch of Men of the Trees in Western Australia—City Farm's work is all about community, getting all sorts of people together to live sustainably, eat locally, and in the process, maybe just save the planet. Their motto is "We not only grow plants. We grow people."

Even though Perth sits beside an ocean, rests atop an enormous underground aquifer, and has a river running through its heart, this vibrant city borders a vast desert. It is quickly running out of water due to rising temperatures, a significant drop in winter rainfall, and tremendous consumption. According to the Commonwealth Scientific Industrial Research Organization (CSIRO), climatologists say that Perth—with a population about to top two million—is the city most profoundly affected by global climate change. Australian environmentalist Tim Flannery predicted that if climate change and water use continue unchecked, this city of sprawling suburbs stretching 42 miles along the Indian Ocean could be the world's first ghost metropolis.

WE MAKE-A THE PIZZA, WE MAKE-A THE PIE

Turns out the gourmet pizza champion of the world is not an Italian, but just might be an Australian.

A chef named Andy Parisi, owner of La Trattoria and Parisi Caffee in Adelaide won several Australian pizza bake-offs, including the national title in the 2004 Dairy Farmers Caboolture Best of the Best Pizza Challenge. The self-effacing chef actually chose not to enter the state finals competition, eschewing celebrity cooking, but his daughter, Chantal, secretly put his name in the running. The enterprising chef then got to take it to the next level by vying for the international title in the United States.

He commented about competing: "Well, over the years Australians have developed a taste for fresh ingredients, technique, and good quality products. That has evolved in the last ten years. In New York we only cooked one pizza instead of the regular three pizzas we cooked where we won the Dairy Farmers Caboolture's Best of the Best. But, we did a lot of demonstrations of different pizzas for the crowd between the competitions. We hunted ALL over New York to get fresh food. It was very expensive when we did find some."

The switch from the three pizzas (vegetarian, marina, and potato) to just one (marinara pizza with fresh chopped tomatoes, cheese, and a mixture of seafood, including a garnish of freshly cooked mussels in their shells) and insistence on fresh ingredients paid off for Parisi. At the inaugural America's Plate competition in New York City, amongst a field of gourmet pizza bakers from across the globe, Andy Parisi was crowned world pizza baking champ.

Another Australian, John Lanzafame, took the 2005 title (there wasn't a title in 2006). In 2007, though, the Aussies were unseated by Fabian Martin of Spain. In 2008, Finn Jarmo Valtari's reindeer pizza took home top honors (Italy's Carmine Mauro came in second, and Australia's Brandon Farrell came in third).

That's one of the reasons City Farm is working so hard to educate its citizens about green living. They figure if their army of volunteers can turn what was once a contaminated scrap metal yard and battery recycling plant into a 25,000-square-foot garden oasis and transform abandoned warehouses into artists' studios and classroom space, anything is possible. They might even teach Perth's avid gardeners a thing or two about how to grow plants with less water.

City Farm describes the types of projects its staff and volunteers work on by using the acronym **PEACE**, which stands for:

Permaculture & Environment

Education

Arts

Community & Personal Development

Enterprise

Creative school programs are one way that City Farm spreads the gospel of green, but it also hosts a weekly organic growers market and a monthly artisans market. In addition, the group has public events throughout the year, such as a street arts festival, harvest festival, the Kamberang Festival, and even the Save the Faeries Festival, held in May 2008. All of the group's work is done for love alone by volunteers.

According to Scott, anybody is welcome to show up and pitch in. Volunteers are needed daily to water, prune, plant, and dig at the thriving demonstration garden. Others are needed to feed animals, collect eggs, make posters, lay bricks, and brew fair trade organic coffee. The need for volunteers is never ending.

There's no charge to volunteer with City Farm, but you will have to find your own place to bunk.

HOW TO GET IN TOUCH

City Farm Perth, 1 City Farm Place, East Perth, Western Australia 6004, 61 8 9325 7229, www.cityfarmperth.org.au.

preserve a rain forest

CORAMANDEL PENINSULA, NEW ZEALAND

The care of the Earth is our most ancient and most worthy, and after all, our most pleasing responsibility. To cherish what remains of it, and foster its renewal, is our only legitimate hope.
—Wendell Berry, author and farmer

92 Maori, New Zealand's indigenous people, believe every place has *mana*, a natural essence that should be honored and respected. Unfortunately, the mana of the Tararu Valley, a temperate rain forest on the North Island's Coramandel Peninsula, got jacked up between 1870 and 1920 when miners and loggers decimated the gigantic kauri, rimu, totara, miro, kaihikatea, and tara trees.

That could have been the end of the story. But in 2000 a group of volunteers put their heads together and decided, "Maybe it's up to us to to restore the natural mana to this special place on planet Earth." They set up the Tararu Valley Conservation Trust, bought back the land, and have been planting trees and restoring the native habitat ever since. Their hope is that some day, these massive trees will be once again be alive with the same species of birds, lizards, bats, and giant insects that inhabited them 200 years ago.

And that's just the first goal. The Tararu Valley Sanctuary (TVS), where the committed environmentalists set up shop, also has become an international center for green education. People interested in living in harmony with nature flock there to learn about minimizing their ecological footprints.

These green volunteers come to live at the remote sanctuary and help with all kinds of projects, from tree planting to straw bale building. And since TVS is a big believer in the old adage "all work and no play makes Jack a dull boy," each week they intersperse three to four days of volunteer work that involves a lot of what they call "playing in the dirt" with a free day and one or two "adventure days." Volunteers put down their gardening tools and tree-planting gloves and take part in such quintessential New Zealand activities as rock climbing, sea kayaking, and bush walking.

Every five to six weeks (many volunteers stay that long or even longer), what they call an "epic trip" is scheduled for exploring other regions of New Zealand, such as Mount Ngauruhoe, which had a starring role as Mount Doom in New Zealand native Peter Jackson's *Lord of the Rings* films.

You'll live to the rhythm of the sun here. Even on work days, usually a few hours after breakfast and a few hours after lunch, there's plenty of after-dinner relaxing time where volunteers can participate in group bonfires, games, yoga, art, music, and meditation. Volunteers at the sanctuary even built their own climbing wall.

Cost per week is NZ $595 (about $345), including accommodations in an eco-friendly visitors lodge, organic meals, and all adventure days and epic trips.

HOW TO GET IN TOUCH

Tararu Valley Sanctuary, P.O. Box 5, Thames 3540, New Zealand, 64 7 868 8988, www.tararuvalley.org.

be the change

LAKE TAUPO, NEW ZEALAND

Our lives begin to end the day we become silent about things that matter.
—Martin Luther King, Jr., clergyman and civil rights leader

93 You're ready to take on the world. You want to make it a better place. Your passion for doing good is burning a hole in your paycheck. You're game to kiss the job goodbye, to start your own social enterprise, to use your skills and talents to, to, to … well, okay, your plan's not quite formulated yet.

How about signing up for a Be the Change workshop held each year on the banks of New Zealand's famous Lake Taupo? Sponsored by Global Volunteer Network (GVN), a New Zealand nonprofit that sends volunteers to needy communities around the globe, this weeklong workshop provides would-be social entrepreneurs with the resources they need to go out and truly make a difference. This intensive course, led by GVN founder Colin Salisbury and staff, is designed to give you the skills and confidence to make your dreams a reality. In this life-changing workshop, you'll learn to hone your message, tell your story, raise funds, and run a campaign.

Jan Reid, who attended Be the Change in July 2008, returned home to Alabama to start A Helper's Hope (www.ahelpershope.org), an organization that connects teachers and therapists with kids in orphanages in developing nations. In July 2009, Reid's group will take volunteers to a children's home in Anta, Peru, through a partnership with Peruvian Hearts (www.peruvianhearts.org), whose executive director is 2007 attendee

SOUNDS FISHY

Even though Lake Taupo is world-famous for its wild rivers and feisty trout, restaurants in the area don't list the tasty delicacy on their menus. Why? They view procuring trout as a strictly do-it-yourself endeavor. Plenty of the 10-pound beauties are served up in Taupo restaurants, but only if you bring them in yourself, an easy enough task since Tongariro, Tauranga Taupo, Waitahanui, and other nearby rivers are brimming with trout and their banks are brimming with full-time fly-fishing guides.

Have you ever been truly inspired by a story you've read in the newspaper or seen on television, but had no idea how to follow through on that emotion? What if every time you were inspired to help someone or contribute to a worthy cause, such as disaster relief, you could do so as easily as ordering a book from Amazon.com?

That, in a nutshell, is the mission of Network for Good. The organization makes it easy for individuals to use the Internet to donate money, find volunteer opportunities, raise money for a favorite cause, or purchase a charity gift card—the Good Card—or gift basket.

They also make it simple and affordable for nonprofits to recruit volunteers and donors, as well as collect and track donations. And they make it easy for companies to support charitable causes through grants or employee donations.

It must be a pretty good idea. More than 230,000 volunteers have been matched with nonprofits and 450,000 donors have contributed more than $200 million dollars using Network for Good since its launch in 2001. *Network for Good, 7920 Norfolk Avenue, Suite 520, Bethesda, MD 20814, 866-650-4636, www.networkforgood.org.*

Danny Dodson. Laura Dinham and Taryn Lilliston, 2007 participants from Colorado, started Eat So They Can (www.eatsotheycan.org), an organization that raised $37,000 in aid for African kids in its first year. And Rafe Steinhauer, a 2007 participant from New York, started Benefeast, a social enterprise that supports a wide range of charities.

With results like that, it's no wonder GVN is one of two volunteer organizations singled out by Microsoft co-founder and philanthropist Bill Gates as good starting points for volunteering—the other is Network for Good (see sidebar).

Be the Change is held yearly in Lake Taupo, New Zealand, and has just added two more weeklong workshops in Runaway Bay, Jamaica, and Breckenridge, Colorado.

Cost for the New Zealand program, including housing, meals, day trips, and all workshops, is $1,500, with a $350 application fee due upon acceptance.

HOW TO GET IN TOUCH

Global Volunteer Network Ltd., Box 30–968, Lower Hutt, New Zealand, www.volunteer.org.nz; U.S. contact: 800-963-1198.

help out at a vital whale research center

COOK ISLANDS

Courage is being scared to death—but saddling up anyway.
—John Wayne, actor

94 In the Cook Islands, they have a greeting, "Kia orana!" It means "May you live long." Making a difference in the lives of others may be the only insurance that any of us will live long.

Global Volunteers (GV), a Minnesota-based nonprofit that organizes volunteer vacations to 21 countries, has been recruiting folks to live long in the Cook Islands since 1998. GV works with a hundred community organizations in this idyllic place that depend on the international volunteers' help to do everything from catalog and mend books at the National Library to introduce cruise ship passengers to the rare kakerori bird whose numbers plummeted to 30 breeding pairs in the 1990s.

From July through November, when the humpback whales are in the area, Nan Daeschler Hauser, president and director of the Center for Cetacean Research and Conservation, uses GV volunteers at her education center in the Cook Islands. Volunteers build and rebuild exhibits, organize class visits at local schools, and,

TO MARKET, TO MARKET

Everybody on Rarotonga, Rarotongans and visitors alike, comes to Avarua's Saturday market, where you can find everything from tourist souvenirs (sarongs, shell necklaces, and little wooden tikis of Tangaroa, the Cook Islands' fertility god) to mackerel, parrotfish, and yellowfin tuna caught early that morning. Bands play, kids wander around sipping coconut milk straight from the shell, and their parents sell mounds of bananas, mangoes, and limes. The giant stacks of oranges, like all oranges on Rarotonga, are said to be direct genetic descendants of the ones Fletcher Christian left behind just days after mutiny against the ill-starred William Bligh, captain of the H.M.S. *Bounty.*

if they're up to it, catalog data, organize DNA samples, and track recordings of whale songs at her Whale Education Centre. Hauser, who's often out on the water tagging the giant animals that migrate here from their Antarctic feeding grounds to mate and give birth, appreciates volunteers who help her spread the word: The humpbacks need help.

As a world-renowned whale researcher, Hauser was both pleased and chagrined to discover that one of her female ancestors was a petticoat whaler who is buried on Rarotonga. As recently as 25 years ago, commercial and pilot whalers still hunted humpbacks in the South Pacific. Research data collected from Hauser's tags—migration, speed of travel, and interchange between nations and islands—bolsters this poor South Pacific island nation's resolve to resist financial incentives from countries who ignore the international hunting moratorium. After Hauser showed her data to the prime minister of the Cook Islands, a whale sanctuary was established, protecting the behemoths at least while they are migrating through the 1.2-million-square-mile waters of this chain of 15 islands.

The variety of tasks at this important whale research center are endless. There are photos to organize, Web pages to update, and a library of books and CDs to maintain. Mechanics have been asked to keep the boats in good running order, and volunteers, who are on the island when Hauser is (she's in the Bahamas studying beaked whales and dolphins for part of the year), sometimes get the chance to assist with ocean research.

With spiky green mountains and miles of turquoise lagoons, Rarotonga, the largest of the Cook Islands, is classic South Pacific. The ancestral home of New Zealand's Maori (it's rumored that each can trace his or her lineage to one of seven canoes that left Rarotonga in the 14th century), Rarotonga is the latitudinal opposite of Oahu. It's compact enough that you can circumnavigate it on the public bus (it's clean, cheap, and on time) in less than an hour.

Three-week trips, the recommended length, run $2,795 and include housing, meals, and all the basics. You'll stay at the KiiKii Motel, a beachside hotel with a pool, a garden, and a small kitchenette, right outside Avarua, the central business district and capital city.

HOW TO GET IN TOUCH

Global Volunteers, 375 East Little Canada Road, St. Paul, MN 55117, 800-487-1074 or 651-407-6100, www.globalvolunteers.org.

staff a free health clinic in the fiji islands

> As soon as man does not take his existence for granted, but beholds
> it as something unfathomably mysterious, thought begins.
> —Albert Schweitzer, musician, philosopher, physician, theologian,
> and winner of the 1952 Nobel Peace Prize

95 Most of us take health screenings for granted. Sure, we groan about them, but we have them because we know they could save our lives.

In Fiji, where approximately 60 percent of the population lives in poverty, there are very few health screenings to groan about. In remote villages, they're practically unheard of. Further complicating the problem is that even when medical screenings are offered, many Fijians are superstitious. They feel *madua*, which means "shy" or "unworthy," especially about discussing such things as cervical or breast cancer. Many of them would rather die than open themselves to talks about such embarrassing topics as reproduction. Unfortunately, as much as 50 percent of the population do die from completely preventable diseases.

That's why Damyenti Chandra, a registered nurse from Rocklin, California, decided to return to her native homeland and open a free health clinic. Not long after retiring from Kaiser Permanente Hospitals in Sacramento in 2000, Chandra opened Patan Memorial Clinic in Nadi, home of Fiji's international airport. The clinic was built on land donated by her late parents, the Patans, and though the foundation had been laid, the family lacked the funds to bring the project to fruition by completing the building. With donations from the Patans' children and grandchildren, Chandra made their dream a reality.

Today, the free health clinic provides ongoing preventive health care to people all over Fiji. Through Chandra's nonprofit, Fiji

THE ULTIMATE COMMUNE

Vorovoro, a 200-acre Fijian island that until a couple years ago was the tribal home of a Fijian chief, Apenisa Uate Bogiso (or Tui Mali), is now the home to an Internet-based tribe. In 2006, Mark James and Ben Keene, a couple of Brits who wanted to use the Internet for more than blogging and sharing music, leased the island (the chief still lives there) for about $80,000 for three years and began offering memberships to this new eco-friendly paradise, Tribewanted. In return for $240, visiting tribespeople get seven days of meals and accommodations on the mostly deserted volcanic speck and the chance to participate in lively online town hall meetings.

At www.tribewanted.com, the group describes how the local team and the online community—now 10,000 strong—are working together to create a cross-cultural community that melds "traditional Fijian customs and ways of living with international ideas for sustainability and innovation." In accepting Tribewanted on the island, Tui Mali was seeking a balance between traditional life and what's often called progress, and the experiment seems to be working.

So far, the accommodations on the island are a couple of shacks covered with palm fronds, but the Tribewanted team hopes Vorovoro will eventually have a beach bar, zip slide, jungle sports arena, and "secret beach chill-out area."

Aid International, medical teams are sent to highland villages to educate people about the importance of taking responsibility for their health, madua be damned.

Chandra, who still lives in Rocklin, travels to Fiji several times a year. The rest of the time she raises money for the clinic, collects much-needed medical supplies, and organizes able-bodied volunteers.

For years, Fiji was mainly visited by Americans and Brits stopping over on their way to New Zealand and Australia. Today, thanks to some pricey resorts that cater to the jet set, Fiji and its 333 islands are destinations in their own right. Fiji Aid's clinic is located in Nadi (rhymes with "candy"), on the western edge of the island. It's only 15 minutes from the airport and most local activities are easily accessed from it.

There's no charge to volunteer with Fiji Aid International. Medical personnel are most needed, but other volunteers are welcomed, as well.

HOW TO GET IN TOUCH

Fiji Aid International, 5764 Terrace Drive, Rocklin, CA 95765, 916-663-6578, www.fijiaidinternational.com.

be a hero
to a pacific island mutt

COOK ISLANDS

Life in any form is our perpetual responsibility.
—S. Parkes Cadman, prominent U.S. clergyman
of the 1920s and 1930s

96 In 1993, while vacationing in the Cook Islands, Cathy Sue Ragan-Anunsen was befriended by a short-legged, ginger mutt. The loyal canine, appropriately named Honey, guarded her hotel door each night and followed her to the beach each day. Smitten by the friendly dog, Ragan-Anunsen contacted a Cook Islands animal rights activist before heading back to Oregon. She wanted to make a donation in Honey's honor.

Tom Wichman, the activist, informed Ragan-Anunsen that not only was there nary an animal charity to donate to, but there wasn't even a vet. Furthermore, Wichman explained, the islands' wild, free-roaming dogs had recently caused a traffic accident and were being systematically gunned down and bludgeoned by local police.

Ragan-Anunsen went home, found a vet willing to volunteer spaying and neutering services, and immediately commenced raising funds to open a permanent veterinary clinic in Rarotonga. She named her nonprofit the Esther Honey Foundation (EHF), after her pet-loving grandmother Esther and the charming dog she believes came to her for help.

Since 1995, Ragan-Anunsen has sent thousands of volunteers on EHF Vet Treks to Rarotonga and the surrounding islands—Aitutaki, Atiu, Bora-Bora, Mangaia, Mauke, and Mitiaro—treating between 1,200 and 2,500 animals every year. Local governments have welcomed the services provided by EHF and airlines, foundations, and humane societies have all pitched in. Honey, we're sorry to report, died in 2001 at the ripe old age of 15. But her successor, Honey Deux, is alive and well and serving as the enthusiastic mascot to the volunteer veterinary clinic.

Although veterinarians and veterinarian's assistants are most needed by EHF, the organization takes any volunteer with a heart for animals and a willingness to pitch in and work hard. If you're up for this assignment, you'll spend lots of time working with the islands' ever growing population of dogs and cats that live, for the most part, in a state of friendly anarchy among the island's other residents. You might also be asked to lend a hand with goats, birds, fruit bats, and horses. (On at least one occasion, EHF even helped a seal.) You also will share responsibility for maintaining the EHF clinic and residence.

The biggest hurdle is that spaying and neutering programs are often looked upon with suspicion in places like the Cook Islands, where dogs are still occasionally added to the family stew. A female stray dog that doesn't get eaten or meet another sad fate generally lives for eight to ten years, which means that she can easily produce 120 puppies in her lifetime. That's a big boost to the local population, unless EHF steps in, embodying their slogan, "Changing the world for animals, one island at a time."

Although volunteers work five days a week and are on call around the clock, the hospitable islanders, happy to have visitors to their mythical South Pacific home,

DANCE, DANCE, DANCE

Dance is a major form of cultural expression in the Cook Islands. Like Hawaii with its hula, Rarotonga, too, has a famous hip-twitching dance. Only this dance (it's called the *hura*) is so fierce and erotically charged that its easy to understand why buttoned-up Victorian missionaries got so flustered by it. Performed in honor of Tangaroa, the islanders' well-endowed fertility god, the Cook Islanders' dancing was described by missionary William Wyatt Gill as "obscene indeed."

Accompanied by rhythmic drumming on the *paté* (traditional wooden drum), hura dancers of all ages gyrate in rapid-fire rhythms that win medals at the major Pacific dance festivals. As Gill, the missionary who lived in the Cook Islands from 1845 to 1860, added to his assessment of the local dance, "In this singular performance the joints seem to be loose. I do not believe it possible for Europeans to move the limbs as a Polynesian loves to do."

offer numerous invitations for luaus, parties, and other island happenings. On an Esther Honey Vet Trek to Bora-Bora, volunteers were even given gifts of black pearls and shell jewelry.

As Sarah Lovett, a veterinary nurse from New Zealand who volunteered with EHF in 2005, explained, she worked hard, then spent her free time quite richly: "We went swimming, snorkeling, hiking, shopping, learned how to make sarongs and coconut bras, had bonfires on the beach at night, played a lot of darts and cards, and entered the local dance contest. The advantage of being a volunteer with the Esther Honey Foundation is that you get to know the locals and see and learn a lot more than the average tourist."

Depending on where you volunteer, you might end up in dorm-style lodging (provided on a first-come, first-serve basis at the EHF residence in Rarotonga) or you might bunk in a four-star hotel, as volunteers to Bora-Bora did on the 2004 EHF Vet Trek. There's a $150 program fee. Full-time volunteers with Vet Trek get a minimum of one meal per day; for other programs, such as working at the Rarotonga animal clinic, volunteers are responsible for all personal and living expenses. Air New Zealand, Air Tahiti Nui, Air Rarotonga, and Tahiti Air often offer discount fares to volunteers.

HOW TO GET IN TOUCH

Esther Honey Foundation, 2010 Ash Lane SE, Jefferson, OR 97352, 541-327-1914, www.estherhoney.org.

open educational doors to a developing nation

MARSHALL ISLANDS

> I have the laughter of the students in my head and the tentative smiles
> of the adults wrapped deep within, and now when I'm frustrated
> or saddened, I have all that power to draw upon.
> —Anna DuVent, WorldTeach volunteer on the Marshall Islands

97 You've seen the developing world on TV. But like much of the blather reported on the boob tube, you can't help but wonder, "Is that really an accurate picture?" WorldTeach, a nonprofit, nongovernmental agency affiliated with the Harvard Center for International Development, gives volunteers a rare front row seat to a developing country in all its glory, shame, and possibilities.

WorldTeach volunteers spend an entire year (or in some countries, a six-month semester or two-month summer session) teaching in one of 17 developing countries, many of which are still in their infancy, still unblemished by the unbridled commercialism of the Western world.

WorldTeach was founded in 1986 by a group of Harvard students after Michael Kremer, a social studies grad living in rural Kenya, was summoned by the head of a small village to start a school. A year later, when Kremer was seeking a replacement, he teamed with fellow Harvard students to launch WorldTeach. Since then, the prolific agency has placed thousands of volunteers in communities throughout Africa, Asia, Eastern Europe, Latin America, and the Pacific.

In the Marshall Islands, an independent nation since 1979, the government is trying desperately to figure out how to gain financial independence from the United States. Imports dramatically outweigh exports (dried coconut, a few handicrafts, and fishing rights), unemployment is high, and most of the islanders live by subsistence farming.

Learning English is increasingly important for access to jobs, higher education, and the international community. According to UNICEF, educational levels in the

KA-BOOM

A popular topic of conversation in the Marshall Islands, a 74-square-mile country consisting of 29 coral atolls, will inevitably be the United States' responsibility for the nuclear bombs they tested there between 1946 and 1958.

All totaled, the U.S. dropped 66 atomic and nuclear bombs on two atolls in the northern Marshall Islands, Bikini and Enewetak, selected because the winds there generally blow toward open Pacific waters. Unfortunately, in March 1954, the winds changed and the scientists miscalculated the bomb's size: Fallout from a 15-megaton hydrogen bomb, more than a thousand times more powerful than the bomb dropped on Hiroshima, contaminated 23 Japanese fishermen (their boat, *Daigo Fukuryu Maru,* or roughly *Lucky Dragon No. 5,* was obviously misnamed), 28 Americans at a weather-monitoring station, and 82 locals on Rongelap Atoll. All of the fishermen and many of the local Marshallese became ill with radation sickness; some of them died as a result of it.

Although the U.S. has made an attempt to clean up the islands, there is still a radioactive isotope in the soil on a couple of the islands. The Marshallese, for whom health problems related to radiation exposure persist, remain less than convinced that the U.S. was not using them as human "guinea pigs."

Marshall Islands are the lowest of the 14 Pacific nations. Since WorldTeach came on board in 2002, significant gains have been made in high school entrance tests.

If you choose to join WorldTeach in the Marshall Islands, you'll find coconut trees, miles of unspoiled beaches, brilliant turquoise water, and tropical weather 365 days a year. But since this new island country is 2,000 miles from Hawaii, New Zealand, and the Philippines (and those are your closest neighbors), your post might be a bit remote—especially if you're assigned to teach on one of the outer islands, some of which are barely a block or two wide and less than a mile long.

On the outer islands, if electricity exists at all, it is produced by finicky generators. The upside is that the outer islands offer a rare chance to live among people whose way of life has not changed dramatically from that of their ancestors.

WorldTeach volunteers are encouraged to spend time outside the classroom on community service projects, so spare time can be used to paint murals on school buildings or build a children's theater, as a couple of Marshall Islands volunteers did a few years ago.

A WorldTeach volunteer in Namibia raised more than $7,000 for malaria-preventing mosquito nets. A volunteer in South Africa assembled interviews for an oral-history project on apartheid. Costa Rica volunteers have built libraries, playgrounds, even a basketball court from scratch. Others have organized musical productions, debate clubs, environmental cleanups, and women's crafts groups.

Teaching certificates come in handy to volunteer with WorldTeach, but they're certainly not required. Anyone with a basic command of English and the desire to help a community pull itself up by its bootstraps is welcome.

Most WorldTeach volunteers live with a host family, providing a vital portal to the culture of the Marshall Islands. Your one-year teaching assignment will begin with an extensive training in Majuro, the biggest city where half the country lives, that covers everything from basics of the native language (Marshallese) to techniques for teaching. Because the program is fully funded by the Marshall Islands' Ministry of Education, your only cash outlay is a $1,500 deposit that will be refunded upon completion of your yearlong stay. International airfare, one month of orientation, health insurance, meals, and housing are all included. You'll also receive $100 to $300 per month to cover living and teaching expenses.

HOW TO GET IN TOUCH

WorldTeach, c/o Center for International Development, Harvard University, Box 122, 79 John F. Kennedy Street, Cambridge, MA 02138, 800-483-2240 or 617-495-5527, www.worldteach.org.

preserve and document world war II history

It's easy to make a buck. It's a lot tougher to make a difference.
—Tom Brokaw, television journalist and author

98 Take that! In retaliation for Pearl Harbor, Americans struck back at an Imperial Japanese navy base in what's now known as the Federated States of Micronesia. Called Operation Hailstone, this two-day aerial bombing raid that continued in one form or another until the war's end, sank more than 50 ships, including warships, destroyers, submarines, submarine chasers, and transfer ships, some with trucks still lashed to the decks. Today, this lagoon that's nearly 40 miles in diameter and 300 feet deep is a veritable underwater museum, called one of the seven underwater wonders of the world by the nonprofit diving group CEDAM International.

Unfortunately, the 51 ships and more than 100 aircraft left behind in Truk Lagoon (also known as Chuuk)

CHUUK COURTING 101

In the old days, suitors in Chuuk wouldn't dream of courting a girl without first carving what's known as a lovestick. Each lovestruck boy would carve his own unique design into the branch of a tangantangana bush, hoping his beloved would recognize it when he poked it through the wall late at night.

If she tugged on the stick, it meant "Come on in."

Shaking the stick meant "I'm coming out."

But if the stick got pushed back out, the message was "Sorry, Charlie. I'm not interested in a tryst. At least not with you."

Today, the main use for Chuukese love sticks is wringing money out of tourists who buy the lovesticks by the suitcase full.

are rusting away. Unless they're documented soon, they could easily become just another World War II fatality.

Although scuba divers have been diving to explore this unique legacy for more than 50 years, a comprehensive scientific survey had never been undertaken until 2008, when maritime archaeologist Dr. Bill Jeffery began recruiting volunteers from Earthwatch, a Massachusetts-based nonprofit that funds more than 120 scientific field projects in 40 countries.

In the warm, clear waters of this protected lagoon, Earthwatch volunteers come in to survey, map, photograph, and sample this amazing graveyard of coral-draped Japanese ships and aircraft. Before taking to the water with waterproof slates, measuring tapes, and digital voltmeters, they learn archaeological and biological recording techniques. They observe and record information on corrosion and decay rates and secure oral histories from the locals, important information that will help the Micronesian government make plans for this naval graveyard.

Besides playing Jacques Cousteau, volunteers get a free day to explore some of the volcanic islands and coral atolls that surround Chuuk, one of Micronesia's four major island groups. Residents here live close to nature, cooking their food over open campfires, hunting for octopuses by lantern light and observing the rhythms of a simple, sea-based existence.

To volunteer for this Earthwatch expedition, you must be certified as a NAUI scuba diver or a PADI or SSI open water diver, or equivalent. A rescue diver certification is recommended, and you must have completed at least five dives within a year prior to the project, or complete a refresher course. You'll stay in studio-style hotel apartments with two other volunteers. The 13-day expedition costs $2,650 and includes most meals.

HOW TO GET IN TOUCH
Earthwatch, 3 Clock Tower Place, Suite 100, Box 75, Maynard, MA 01754, 800-776-0188 or 978-461-0081, www.earthwatch.org.

ANOTHER THOUGHTFUL COMMITTED CITIZEN: ENZO REPOLA

"You want to do what?"

When retired New York banker Enzo Repola told his wife and kids he was traveling to Kenya to build homes, they thought he'd lost his mind. "Must be his retirement's getting to him," they whispered behind his back. "He'll get over it."

Yet when he came back from that Habitat for Humanity–sponsored building trip to the village of Thuita, Kenya, he was more determined than before.

"It changed my life," Repola said. "I knew what I was going to do with the rest of my life."

He wasn't kidding. Since that first trip, where he was just one member of a 12-person team, he has gone on to lead more than a dozen Global Village builds, taking volunteers to Borneo, Fiji, Vietnam, Thailand, Uganda, Botswana, and Papua New Guinea.

"One of the villagers in Papua New Guinea stood up at the closing ceremony and very earnestly asked us, 'Why did you come all this way, do all this work when you don't even know us?'" Repola said. "I realized he'd asked a very good question. In his shoes, I'd ask the same question. Why would we take this very long trip, on five planes, halfway around the world to a primitive place. I hadn't planned this answer and it surprised me when it came out. But I said to him and this came straight from my gut, 'You and I may dress differently and live in different parts of the world, but most of how we think and talk and feel, it's the same. Exactly the same. We belong to the same creator. We are brothers.'"

Repola leads two "Global Village" trips a year. He'd do more, he says, except it takes five to six months to arrange all the logistics, vet all the volunteers ("I have to make sure they know what they're getting in to," he says), and make the arrangements for 10 to 12 people to travel halfway around the world.

"I've always traveled a lot. I worked for an international bank so traveling has always been second nature to me. But these Habitat trips are completely different. You get to see the people, not the hotel. It's a chance to see the real thing," he said. "The food isn't always so good, the conditions are often primitive and the work is exhausting, but I don't know. I love this."

Repola read about Habitat for Humanity years before he retired. "I saw where Jimmy Carter was building homes and it impressed me," he said. He filed the magazine away and, after retirement, stumbled across it, prompting him to sign up for that first trip that so surprised his family. Before that, he'd never volunteered for anything.

He says his realization in Papua New Guinea, the realization that all people are his brothers has become his life's compass.

"When you think this way, everything is very simple," he says.

put a roof over someone's head

PAPUA NEW GUINEA

Do all you can with what you have,
in the time you have, in the place you are.
—Nkosi Johnson, South African AIDS activist
who died from AIDS when he was 12 years old

99 The United Nations reports that the number of people living in substandard housing, already at 1.6 billion, is expected to increase to 2 billion in 30 years. That's one out of every three people living without an adequate roof over their head. Habitat for Humanity, a nonprofit located in Americus, Georgia, is doing everything it can to stem that shocking prediction. Habitat volunteers, already a well-known presence in the United States, also travel overseas, building secure, solid houses in more than a hundred countries worldwide.

The organization's Global Village program recruits volunteers for short-term homebuilding trips. In Papua New Guinea, where a stable home can be built for roughly $4,000, volunteers travel to rural villages (four out of five people in Papua New Guinea still live in tribal communities) and live alongside these traditional societies that have changed little over time. Volunteers share traditional meals, rituals, and the elbow grease it takes to build stable, weatherproof homes.

The typical home in Papua New Guinea, woven together of bamboo, grasses, and leaves, lasts an average of six to ten years thanks to cooking fires, heavy rains, and tribal skirmishes. Roofs have to be rebuilt about every three years, and even new roofs tend to leak. Having a secure, stable home short-circuits poverty. "The Habitat program kills two birds with one stone," says Samuel Rumints, chairman of the country's Western Highlands Habitat affiliate. "It provides affordable houses and prevents tribal fighting."

Papua New Guinea came late to the atlases: Its coastline was traced in 1897. In many ways, its interior is still a treacherous mountain ridge of question marks. Australian-led patrols in the 1960s encountered people who had never seen a white person.

With more than 700 islands and 820 different languages, Papua New Guinea is one of the most diverse and inspiring destinations on the planet. New species of plants and animals are discovered nearly every day. Ornithologist Bruce Beehler, who led a pioneering expedition to the Foja mountains, recently discovered a tiny tree kangaroo, a bird of paradise with 6 plumes, 4 new species of butterflies, and 20 new species of frogs.

The two-week Global Village builds in Papua New Guinea cost between $2,000 and $2,200 and include lodging, food, ground transportation, medical insurance, and a donation to Habitat Papua New Guinea. You'll share accommodations with your team, may not have access to indoor plumbing, and take baths in either a river or a bucket. Many of the Papua New Guinea builds have been led by retired banker Enzo Repola (see p. 267).

HOW TO GET IN TOUCH

Global Village, Habitat for Humanity International, P.O. Box 369, Americus, GA 31709, 800-422-4828, ext. 7530, www.habitat.org/gv.

TALK PIDGIN WITH ME

With more than 820 languages in Papua New Guinea, it's a pretty sure bet that Berlitz hasn't published cheat sheets for all of them. The good news is that most everyone in Papua New Guinea speaks some Pidgin, a bastardized form of the Queen's English.

The following are other words and phrases that will undoubtedly come in handy:

- *Ania:* Eat. Particularly dangerous when paired with *kwarana* (head), due to a reputed history of cannibalism.
- *Bema ai lasiin nidinaamurinai, gavamanitaunakobenadadekenai oilaohamaoroa:* If we are not back here in five days, tell the government official in Konebada.
- *Buai:* Betel nut. A popular favorite all over the South Pacific, this stimulant with turn your teeth *kakakaka*—red.
- *Kau kau:* Sweet potatoes. No meal is complete without a heaping helping.
- *Nat nat:* Mosquitoes—probably the most useful word in the entire language.
- *Paripari:* Wet. During the rainy season, a very useful adjective to describe how you're doing.
- *Puk puk:* Crocodiles. This word can be repeated often, especially when cruising down the Sepik or Waghi Rivers in a hollowed-out tree trunk.

GLOBAL VISION INTERNATIONAL
tag endangered hawksbill turtles

MOSO ISLAND, VANUATU

Nature sure knows how to bring a tear to a girl's eye.
—Jen Whitney, Global Vision volunteer

100 If you're traveling to the Republic of Vanuatu (van-wah-TOO), you'd better learn this word: *nambawan*. It's a Pidgin phrase that roughly translates to something like: "It doesn't get much better than this." People say nambawan a lot here.

Once known as the New Hebrides, Vanuatu is made up of 83 steep-sloped islands with volcanoes to climb, rain forests to explore, and unique cultures to experience. People here lead a relaxed existence.

The New Economics Foundation and Friends of the Earth, in fact, voted Vanuatu the "happiest place on Earth" in 2006. Happy though citizens here may be, a great percentage of them cannot read. That's why Wan Smolbag Theatre (WST), an innovative, participatory theater company, communicates with the island's many villagers through plays and dramatic theater productions. In 1995, during the South Pacific's "Year of the Turtle," a WST troupe traveled from village to village collecting stories about the hawksbill and green turtles that breed and nest nearby.

The message from the play that resulted from those stories came back loud and clear. The villages didn't need pamphlets, books, or wildlife do-gooders to tell them that their turtles were in grave danger. Many Vanuatu villages immediately imposed bans on killing and eating

SEE IT HERE FIRST

This project takes place on the island of Moso, the same island where "tribes" from the ninth season of the reality show *Survivor* vied for the million-dollar prize. If getting anywhere near an island chosen by *Survivor* is on your "to avoid at all costs" list, you can also see the hawksbill turtle (or at least its likeness) on the reserve side of either the Venezuelan bolivar or the Brazilian reals. There's also a fountain sculpture of a boy riding a hawksbill in Worcester, Massachusetts.

TAKE A FLYING LEAP

Jumping off 90-foot-high platforms might sound a little extreme—especially when it's done just to ensure a successful yam harvest—but to the tribesmen of Vanuatu's Pentecost Island, it's a sacred ritual that's been taking place for hundreds of years.

Each April and May, before the harvest begins, the men from the villages of Bunlap, Lano, Wali, and Wori build elaborate towers, tie vines to their ankles, and hurl themselves from platforms that are specially designed to collapse when they near the bottom. Using nothing but tree branches and vines (nails and wire are taboo), the men spend weeks building a nine-story, vegetal masterpiece.

While each diver is responsible for selecting his own vine (remember it's got to be strong enough to support the weight of a 180-pound man), a tribe elder usually selects the length. When you figure that a difference of five inches on a hundred-foot vine can mean the difference between life and death, it's incredible that the vines are hacked off without aid of a measuring tape.

While this daring ritual is done today to insure a successful yam harvest, it originated hundreds of years ago when a clever woman, desperate to escape a bad situation, lured her abusive husband into a banyan tree. According to tribal legend, she dared him to follow and then jumped. When she landed safely on the ground below, her husband declared it a miracle, took a deep breath, and leapt from the same tree. Only when the young woman was sure he was dead did she untie the vines from her ankles and walk back to the village, finally free.

Interestingly enough, women are strictly prohibited from taking part in the land dives today. In fact, females aren't allowed within 20 feet of the platforms.

For many years, this spectacular ritual was private, open only to members of the respective villages. A couple years ago, the tribal chiefs decided to open it to the public in hopes of attracting tourism dollars.

Each Saturday in April and May at about 10 a.m., the symbolic ritual begins. It includes 16 jumps. One by one, the divers climb to their appointed places on the tower. First, the 8- and 9-year-olds jump. Even though the youngsters only leap 20 or 30 feet, they sometimes require a little push. Each jump gets progressively higher and more difficult as the age of the participants increases.

Finally about 2 or 3 that afternoon, the grand finale begins. The chosen man climbs to the top, wearing nothing but a *namba* (that's Melanesian for "penis sheath"). The women, wearing grass skirts, clap, whistle, and sing. When the diver raises his hand, the crowd falls silent. The diver begins to speak, usually giving a short monologue on a personal or family matter that's been bothering him. Then he plucks a feather from his belt and lets it drop, so it floats slowly to the ground. He claps his hands several times above his head, shouts, and makes the courageous leap.

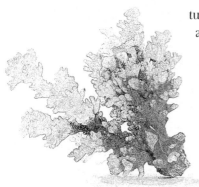

turtles and their eggs. Most villages also appointed a monitor who could keep an eye on nesting turtles and educate others. Once a year, in fact, this network of 200 monitors from all six provinces of Vanuatu meet on the island of Efate, home of the capital city Port Vila, to share data, updates, and new ideas for saving their at-risk sea turtles. They call themselves Vanua-Tai (Of Land and Sea) Natural Resource Monitors.

Hawksbill turtles have been on the endangered species list since 1970. Even though most Vanuatu villages have vowed to no longer kill turtles or eat their eggs, hawksbills that feed and nest in this region face many other well-documented obstacles to their survival. Not only must they evade such predators as mud crabs, birds, and sharks, but global climate change is killing off the island's coral reefs, which are basically the hawksbill's dinner plate.

In 2006, Global Vision International (GVI), a nonprofit that recruits volunteers for 150 projects in 30 countries, stepped in to help. Volunteers from around the world fly to Vanuatu each month to help the island's dedicated turtle monitors collect data, tag turtles, and monitor their nesting grounds.

One village that became involved in this effort, Tasiriki, is located on the shores of Moso Island, home to a nationally significant nesting beach and foraging grounds for hawksbill turtles. The people of Tasiriki were concerned about the turtles, but also concerned that they could not devote the necessary time to the nesting beach survey effort. So WSB contacted GVI about the possibility of setting up the survey as an international volunteer project. Today, the villagers, WSB, and GVI work together to provide keep the project running.

While the labor that volunteers provide is valuable, that's not their only contribution to Tasiriki. The fees that volunteers pay provide a small income to many people in the village that would otherwise not have one. These fees also pay for the project manager, the turtle guides that work with the volunteers on the beach, and the local women who take care of the bungalows and cook for the volunteers. In addition to the income the project provides, it has increased the villagers' interest in learning more about their turtles neighbors and ensuring they are still here for future generations.

As a volunteer on this GVI project, you'll walk the beaches, count nests, and conduct nesting surveys. Depending on the time of year, your job may vary. In September and October, for example, you'll conduct reef surveys, clear forest track, or mark out marine conservation areas. During November through March, you'll likely spend evenings at the nesting beach (expect an hour-long hike from the village), where you'll collect data and help the vulnerable one-inch hatchlings make it safely to the sea. Other jobs might be teaching at the village school, working in the gardens, collecting dried coral, or assisting with meals.

You'll be welcomed with open arms by the Tasiriki community, who will ply you with meals from their gardens, teach you to weave, and throw grand galas in your honor. You'll likely be given your own nickname. One volunteer was called Leiwia (it means "good woman") and another was called Leisalewia ("woman who comes from across the sea"). The Tasiriki String Band, that plays at the goodbye party, has even been known to write a song about about each individual volunteer.

There's nothing fancy about the two-bed bush bungalows where you'll stay. There are two bucket flush toilets and two huts for bucket showers. The newest addition is a dining hall/common room that provides the volunteers with a spot to gather for meals as well as a place to relax on rainy days. A four-week volunteer stint, including meals and accommodations, runs $2,320.

HOW TO GET IN TOUCH

Global Vision International, 252 Newbury Street, Number 4, Boston, MA 02116, 888-653-6028, www.gvi.co.usa.com.

volunteer organizations

This listing of volunteer organizations is divided into two sections. The first section contains a list of organizations—both nonprofits and businesses, including all of those listed in this book plus additional ones—that offer a wide range of international volunteer opportunities. For example, they go to South Africa to save sharks, to Poland to save orphans, and to Vietnam to save habitat. The second section divides the vacations into themes, so if you know you love animals, you can find something to do with, say, chimps or elephants; if you prefer to spend your time banging nails, you can focus on construction; or if you'd rather work with children, there are specific options for doing that as well.

GENERAL, OVERALL ORGANIZATIONS THAT COVER THE WORLD

This first section is devoted to volunteer outfits whose sole mission—their expertise, if you will—is to find worthy causes and projects and recruit volunteers to work on them. Most of them have been doing this for some time. They're good at handling logistics, answering questions, and quelling fears that volunteers might have about malaria or being met at the airport. Some of these organizations house volunteers with host families, all of whom have been carefully screened. Others have built their own apartments, staffed by an in-country team. For this handling of details—usually including meals and everything else you'll need while there—these organizations charge volunteers to, well, volunteer. But you can rest easy, knowing you're going with pros.

A Broader View, 1001 Dell Lane Suite B, Wyncote, PA 19095, 866-423-3258 or 215-780-1845, www.abroaderview.org

Airline Ambassadors International, 418 California Ave., Moss Beach, CA 94038, 866-264-3586, www.airlineamb.org; see p. 52.

Ambassadors for Children, 40 Virginia Ave., Indianapolis, IN 46204, 866-338-3468 or 317-536-0250, www.ambassadorsforchildren.org; see p. 58.

CADIP (Canadian Alliance for Development Initiatives and Projects), 907–950 Drake St., Vancouver, British Columbia V6Z 2B9, Canada, 604-628-7400, www.cadip.org; see p. 49.

Catholic Network of Volunteer Service, 6930 Carroll Ave., Suite 820, Takoma Park, MD 20912, 800-543-5046 or 301-270-0900, www.cnvs.org.

Center for Cultural Interchange, c/o Greenheart, 712 N. Wells St., 4th fl., Chicago, IL 60657, 888-227-6231 or 312-944-2544, www.greenhearttravel.org; see pp. 70 and 160.

Changing Worlds, 11 Doctors Lane, Chaldon, Surrey CR3 5AE, England, 44 1883 340 960, www.changingworlds.co.uk; see p. 138.

Cosmic Volunteers, 3502 Scotts Lane, Sherman Properties, Suite 3147, Mailbox E-14, Philadelphia, PA 19129, 888-813-0248 or 215-609-4196, www.cosmicvolunteers.org.

Cross-Cultural Solutions, 2 Clinton Place, New Rochelle, NY 10801, 800-380-4777, www.crossculturalsolutions. org; see p. 121.

Earthwatch, 3 Clock Tower Place, Suite 100, Box 75, Maynard, MA 01754, 800-776-0188 or 978-461-0081, www .earthwatch.org; see pp. 46, 118, and 265.

Ecovolunteer, Great Canadian Travel Company, Ltd., 158 Fort St., Winnipeg, Manitoba R3C 1C9, Canada, 800-661-3830, www.ecovolunteer.org; see pp. 76, 129, and 195.

Gap Year for Grown Ups, Zurich House, 1 Meadow Rd., Tunbridge Wells, Kent, TN1 2YG, England, 44 1892 701 881, www. gapyearforgrownups.co.uk; see p. 221.

GeoVisions International, 63 Whitfield St., Guilford, CT 06437, 877-949-9998 or 203-453-5838, www.geo visions.org.

Global Citizens Network, 130 N. Howell St., Saint Paul, MN 55104, 800-644-9292 or 651-644-0960, www. globalcitizens.org.

Global Crossroad, 415 E. Airport Fwy., Ste. 365, Irving, TX 75062, 866-387-7816 or 972-252-4191, www .globalcrossroad.com; see p. 219.

Global Exchange, 2017 Mission St., 2nd Fl., San Francisco, CA 94110, 415-255-7296 or 800-497-1994, www. globalexchange.org; see p. 61.

Global Village, Habitat for Humanity International, Box 369, Americus, GA 31709, 800-422-4828, ext. 7530, www .habitat.org/gv; see p. 267.

Global Vision International, 252 Newbury St., No. 4, Boston, MA 02116, 888-653-6028, www.gviusa.com; see pp. 146, 166, and 270.

Global Volunteer Network Ltd., Box 30-968, Lower Hutt, New Zealand, 64 4 569 9080, www .volunteer.org.nz; U.S. contact: 800-963-1198; see p. 253.

Global Volunteers, 375 E. Little Canada Rd., St. Paul, MN 55117, 800-487-1074 or 651-407-6100, www. globalvolunteers.org; see p. 41.

Globe Aware, 6500 E. Mockingbird Ln., Suite 104, Dallas, TX 75214, 877-588-4562, www.globeaware.com; see pp. 64 and 127.

Greenforce USA, 530 Fulham Rd., London SW6 SNR, England, 44 20 7384 3343, www.greenforce.org; see p. 192.

Institute for Field Research Expeditions, 8500 N. Stemmons Fwy. #5030 K, Dallas, TX 75247, 800-675-2504, www.ifrevolunteers.org.

i-to-i North America, 458 Wheeler St., Seattle, WA 98109, 800-985-4864, www .i-to-i.com; see p. 79.

Projects Abroad Inc., 347 W. 36th St., Ste. 903, New York, NY 10018, 888-839-3535, www.projects-abroad.org; see pp. 82, 144, and 168.

ProWorld, Box 21121, Billings, MT 59104, 877-733-7378 or 406-245-7348, www .myproworld.com.

Service Civil International, 5505 Walnut Level Rd., Crozet, VA 22932, 434-336-3545, www .sci-ivs.org.

Travellers Worldwide, Ste. 2A, Caravelle House, 17/19 Goring Road, Worthing, West Sussex BN12 4AP, England, 44 1903 502 595, www .travellersworldwide.com; see pp. 163 and 200.

United Planet, 11 Arlington St., Boston, MA 02116, 800-292-2316 or 617-267-7763, www .unitedplanet.org; see p. 140.

Volunteer Adventures, 915 S. Colorado Blvd., Denver, CO, 80246, 866-574-8606, www .volunteeradventures.com.

Volunteers for Peace, 1034 Tiffany Rd., Belmont, VT 05730, 802-259-2759, www .vfp.org; see p. 217.

World Endeavors, 3015 E. Franklin Ave., Minneapolis, MN 55406, 866-802-9678 or 612-729-3400, www. worldendeavors.com.

WorldTeach, c/o Center for International Development, Harvard University, Box 122, 79 John F. Kennedy St., Cambridge, MA 02138, 800-483-2240 or 617-495-5527, www.worldteach.org; see p. 262.

BY PROJECT THEME

Here we've broken out the volunteer vacations by theme, to help you find something that touches you personally. Maybe you have a medical background, or teaching, or like to bang nails into wood. Whatever your passion, you'll find something here that will help you do a little something to change the world.

AGRICULTURAL AND FARM WORK

Global Exchange, 2017 Mission St., 2nd Fl., San Francisco, CA 94110, 415-255-7296 or 800-497-1994, www.globalexchange. org; see p. 61.

International Society for Ecology and Culture, P.O. Box 9475, Berkeley, CA 94709, 510-548-4915, www.isec.org.uk; see p. 225.

Sanan Village, c/o CADIP, 907–950 Drake St., Vancouver, British Columbia V6Z 2B9, Canada, 604-628-7400, www.cadip.org; see p. 229.

The Tandana Foundation, 2933 Lower Bellbrook Rd., Spring Valley, OH 45370, www.tandanafoundation.org; see p. 170.

Worldwide Opportunities on Organic Farms Italia, www.wwoof.org. Each country has its own address and website which can be accessed from the international website; see p. 131.

Zaytoun, 33 Carronade Ct., Eden Grove, London N7 8EP, England, 44 845 345 4887, www.zaytoun.org; see p. 155.

ANIMALS

Amanzi Travel Ltd., No. 4 College Road, Westbury on Trym, Bristol, BS9 3EJ, England, 44 117 904 1924, www.amanzitravel.co.uk; see p. 176.

Caretta Research Project, P.O. Box 9841, Savannah, GA 31412, 912-447-8655, www.carettaresearchproject.org; see p. 26.

Ecovolunteer, c/o Great Canadian Travel Company, 158 Fort St., Winnipeg, Manitoba R3C 1C9, Canada, 800-661-3830, www.ecovolunteer.org; see pp. 76, 129, and 195.

Elephant-Human Relations Aid, P.O. Box 2146, Swakopmund, Namibia, 264 64 402 501; U.S. contact: c/o Doreen Niggles, P.O. Box 272, Wainscott, NY 11975, www.desertelephant.org; see p. 173.

Esther Honey Foundation, 2010 Ash Lane SE, Jefferson, OR 97352, www.estherhoney.org. Prefers to be contacted by e-mail at frogfarm@aol.com; see p. 259.

Gap Year for Grown Ups, Zurich House, 1 Meadow Rd., Tunbridge Wells, Kent, TN1 2YG, England, 44 1892 701 881, www.gapyearforgrownups.co.uk; see p. 221.

Global Vision International, 252 Newbury St., No. 4, Boston, MA 02116, 888-653-6028, www.gviusa.com; see pp. 146 and 270.

Global Volunteers, 375 E. Little Canada Rd., St. Paul, MN 55117, 800-487-1074, www.globalvolunteers.org; see p. 41.

The Great Orangutan Project, Studio 6, 8 High St., Harpenden, Herts AL5 2TB, England, 44 845 371 3070, www.orangutanproject.com; see p. 240.

Greenforce, 530 Fulham Rd., London SW6 5NR, England, 44 20 7384 3343, www.greenforce.org; see p. 191.

Hebridean Whale and Dolphin Trust, 28 Main St., Tobermory, Isle of Mull, PA75 6NU, Scotland, 44 1688 302 620, www.whaledolphintrust.co.uk; see p. 116.

Hellenic Wildlife Hospital, Box 57, Island of Aegina, Greece 18010, 30 229 7031338, www.ekpazp.gr; see p. 96.

Jane Goodall Institute, c/o Global Vision International, 252 Newbury St., No. 4, Boston, MA 02116, 888-653-6028, www.gvi.co.uk; see p. 187.

Shiripuno Research Center, Yánez Pinzón N25-106 y Av. Colón, Quito, Ecuador, 593 2 255 7749, www.ecuadorvolunteer.org; see p. 73.

Sri Lanka Wildlife Conservation Society, 38 Auburn Side, Dehiwala, Sri Lanka, 94 1 12714710, www.slwcs.org; U.S. contact: 127 Kingsland St., Nutley, NJ 07110, 973-667-0576; see p. 204.

Tasmanian Devil Appeal, c/o University of Tasmania School of Zoology, 134 Macquarie St., G.P.O. Box 44, Hobart, Tasmania 7001, Australia, 61 3 6233 2006, www.tassiedevil.com.au/help.html; see p. 246.

Tembeza Kenya, 301 E. 88th St., Ste. 12, New York, NY 10128, 646-216-9912, www.tembezakenya.com; see p. 193.

ARCHAEOLOGY

APARE, 25 Blvd. Paul Pons, 84800 L'Isle-sur-la-Sorgue, France, 33 4 90 85 51 15, www.apare-gec.org; see p. 98.

Crow Canyon Archaeological Center, 23390 Rd. K, Cortez, CO 81321, 800-422-8975 or 970-565-8975, www.crowcanyon.org; see p. 12.

Ecomuseum de Cap de Cavalleria, Apartado 68, 07740, Es Mercadal, Menorca, Balearic Islands, Spain, 34 971 359999, www.ecomuseodecavalleria.com; see p. 104.

International Palestinian Youth League and Alternative Information Center, c/o Volunteers for Peace, 1034 Tiffany Rd., Belmont, VT 05730, 802-259-2759, www.vfp.org; see p. 142.

Mount Vernon Ladies' Association, P.O. Box 110, Mount Vernon, VA, 22121 (mailing address); 3200 Mount Vernon Memorial Highway, Mount Vernon, VA 22121, 703-799-6314, www.mountvernon.org; see p. 18.

Passport in Time, Box 15728, Rio Rancho, NM 87174, 800-281-9176 or 505-896-0734, www.passportintime.com; see p. 39.

THE ARTS

Forest People's Project, 1c Fosseway Business Centre, Stratford Road, Moreton-in-Marsh GL56 9NQ, England, 44 1608 652893, www.forestpeoples.org; see p. 184.

The Gudran Project, Tolombat El Max St., El Max, Alexandria, Egypt, 20 1011 70800, www.gudran.com; see p. 149.

Pioneer Playhouse, 840 Stanford Rd., Danville, KY 40422, 859-236-2747, www.pioneerplayhouse.com; see p. 24.

Resource Development International, U.S. contact: P.O. Box 9144, Louisville, KY 40209, www.rdic.org; see p. 233.

Travellers Worldwide, Ste. 2A, Caravelle House, 17119 Goring Rd., Worthing, West Sussex BN12 4AP, England, 44 1903 502 595, www.travellersworldwide.com; see pp. 163 and 200.

Wild Films, www.wildsingapore.com; see p. 208.

Worldwide Friends–Veraldarvinir, Einarsnes 56, 101 Reykjavík, Iceland, 354 55 25 214, www.wf.is; see p. 108.

BUSINESS

Center for Cultural Interchange, c/o Greenheart, 712 N. Wells St., 4th fl., Chicago, IL 60657, 888-227-6231 or 312-944-2544, www.greenhearttravel.org; see p. 160.

Forest People's Project, 1c Fosseway Business Centre, Stratford Road, Moreton-in-Marsh GL56 9NQ, England, 44

1608 652893, www.forestpeoples.org; see p. 184.

Partnership in Enterprise, 347 W. 36th St., Ste. 903, New York, NY 10018, 888-839-3535, www.projects-abroad.org; see p. 144.

Via's Bali Service-Learning Program, 965 Mission St., Ste. 751, San Francisco, CA 94103, 415-904-8033, www.viaprograms.org; see p. 238.

CHILDREN

Alpine Fund, Box 583192, Minneapolis, MN 55458; Ahunbaeva 119A #502, Bishkek Kyrgyzstan, 966 312 47 16 35, www.alpinefund.org; see p. 124.

Ambassadors for Children, 40 Virginia Ave., Indianapolis, IN 46204, 866-338-3468 or 317-536-0250, www.ambassadorsforchildren.org; see p. 58.

Changing Worlds, 11 Doctors Lane, Chaldon, Surrey CR3 5AE, England, 44 1883 340 960, www.changingworlds.co.uk; see p. 138.

Cross-Cultural Solutions, 2 Clinton Pl., New Rochelle, NY 10801, 800-380-4777 or 914-632-0022, www.crossculturalsolutions.org; see p. 121.

Jane Goodall Institute, c/o Global Vision International, 252 Newbury St., No. 4, Boston, MA 02116, 888-653-6028, www.gvi.co.uk; see p. 187.

Projects Abroad, 347 W. 36th St., Ste. 903, New York, NY 10018, 888-839-3535, www.projects-abroad.org; see p. 168.

Travellers Worldwide, Ste. 2A, Caravelle House, 1719 Goring Rd., Worthing, West Sussex BN12 4AP, England, 44 190 350 2595, www.travellersworldwide.com; see pp. 163 and 200.

United Planet, 11 Arlington St., Boston, MA 02116, 800-292-2316 or 617-267-7763, www.unitedplanet.org; see p. 140.

COMMUNITY DEVELOPMENT

African Impact, P.O. Box 1218, Gweru, Zimbabwe, Africa, 877-253-2899, www.africanimpact.com; see p. 178.

Continental Divide Trail Alliance, P.O. Box 628, Pine, CO 80470, 888-909-2382 or 303-838-3760, www.cdtrail.org; see p. 21.

Cornerstone Foundation, 90 Burns Ave., P.O. Box 242, San Ignacio, Cayo District, Belize, www.cornerstonefoundationbelize.org, U.S. contact: 501-678-9909; see p. 89.

Global Volunteers, 375 E. Little Canada Rd., St. Paul, MN 55117, 800-487-1074, www.globalvolunteers.org; see p. 41.

Globe Aware, 6500 E. Mockingbird Ln., Ste. 104, Dallas, TX 75214, 877-588-4562, www.globeaware.com; see pp. 64 and 127.

The Gudran Project, Tolombat El Max St., El Max, Alexandria, Egypt, 20 1011 70800, www.gudran.com; see p. 149.

INEX-SDA, Budečská 1, Prague 2, 120 00, Czech Republic, 420 222 362 715, www.inexsda.cz; see p. 100.

Mirror Foundation, 106 Moo 1, Ban Huay Khom, T. Mae Yao, A. Muang, Chiang Rai 57100, Thailand, 66 5373 7412, www.mirrorartgroup.org; see p. 211.

Resource Development International, U.S. contact: P.O. Box 9144, Louisville, KY 40209, www.rdic.org; see p. 233.

The Tandana Foundation, 2933 Lower Bellbrook Rd., Spring Valley, OH 45370, www .tandanafoundation.org; see p. 170.

Tanzania Volunteer Experience, P.O. Box 16446, Arusha, Tanzania, 255 755 320 790, www.tanzaniavolunteer.org; see p. 189.

Tropical Adventures Foundation, 1775 E. Palm Canyon Dr., Ste. 110-341, Palm Springs, CA 92264, 800-832-9419, www .tropicaladventures.com; see p. 67.

African Impact, P.O. Box 1218, Gweru, Zimbabwe, Africa, 877-253-2899, www.africanimpact. com; see p. 178.

APARE, 25 Blvd. Paul Pons, 84800 L'Isle-sur-la-Sorgue, France, 33 4 90 85 51 15, www.apare-gec.org; see p. 98.

Cultural Restoration Tourism Project, P.O. Box 6803, Albany, CA 94706, 415-563-7221, www.crtp.net; see p. 223.

Global Village, Habitat for Humanity International, Box 369, Americus, GA 31709, 800-422-4828 ext. 7530, www.habitat.org/gv; see p. 267.

Global Volunteers, 375 E. Little Canada Rd., St. Paul, MN 55117, 800-487-1074 or 651-407-6100, www. globalvolunteers.org; see p. 41.

The Tandana Foundation, 2933 Lower Bellbrook Rd., Spring Valley, OH 45370, www .tandanafoundation.org; see p. 170.

Tanzania Volunteer Experience, P.O. Box 16446, Arusha,

Tanzania, 255 755 320 790, www.tanzaniavolunteer.org; see p. 189.

City Farm, 1 City Farm Place, East Perth, Western Australia 6004, 61 8 9325 7229, www. cityfarmperth.org.au; see p. 248.

Conservation Volunteers Australia, www.conservation volunteers.com.au; U.S. contact: InterExchange, 161 Sixth Ave., New York, NY 10013, 800-597-3675 or 212-924-0446, www. workingabroad.org; see p. 244.

Earthwatch, 3 Clock Tower Place, Ste. 100, Box 75, Maynard, MA 01754, 800-776-0188 or 978-461-0081, www.earthwatch.org; see p. 46.

Fundación Aldeas de Paz, c/o Centro Comunitario, Lomas de Piedra Canaima via Sampai, Santa Elena de Uairén, Código Postal 8032, La Gran Sabana, Estado Bolívar, Venezuela, 58 289 414 5721, www. peacevillages.org; see p. 86.

i-to-i, 458 Wheeler St., Seattle, WA 98109, 800-985-4864, www.i-to-i.com; see p. 79.

Jane Goodall Institute, c/o Global Vision International, 252 Newbury St., No. 4, Boston, MA 02116, 888-653-6028, www.gvi. co.uk; see p. 187.

Pronaturaleza and Taricaya Research Center, Box 18-1393, Calle Alfredo León 211, Miraflores, Lima 18, Peru, 51 1 447 9032 or 51 1 241 7981; Butterfly Center: 51 1 264 2736, www.pronaturaleza.org; see p. 91.

Tararu Valley Sanctuary, P.O. Box 5, Thames 3540, New Zealand, 64 7 868 8988, www.tararuvalley.org; see p. 251.

Wild Films, www.wildsingapore. com; see p. 208.

World Wide Fund for Nature Hong Kong, Suite 1002, Asian House, 1 Hennessy Road, Wanchai, Hong Kong, 852 2526 1011, www.wwf .org.hk; see p. 231.

Geopark Naturtejo, Rua Conselheiro Albuquerque, No. 4, Cave C, 6000-161 Castelo Branco, Portugal, 351 272 320 176, www.naturtejo.com; see p. 106.

Volunteers for Peace, 1034 Tiffany Rd., Belmont, VT 05730, 802-259-2759, www .vfp.org; see p. 217.

Caribbean Volunteer Expeditions, P.O. Box 388, Corning, NY 14830, 607-962-7846, www.cvexp.org; see p. 44.

Cultural Restoration Tourism Project, P.O. Box 6803, Albany, CA 94706, 415-563-7221, www.crtp.net; see p. 223.

Earthwatch, 3 Clock Tower Place, Ste. 100, Box 75, Maynard, MA 01754, 800-776-0188 or 978-461-0081, www.earthwatch.org; see p. 118.

The National Trust, National Trust Central Volunteering Team, Heelis, Kemble Dr., Swindon SN2 2NA, England, 44 179 381 7400, www. nationaltrust.org.uk; see p. 111.

Offene Häuser (Open Houses), Goetheplatz 9 BD, 99423 Weimar, Germany, 49 3643 502879, www.openhouses.de; see p. 113.

Caribbean Volunteer Expeditions, P.O. Box 388,

Corning, NY 14830, 607-962-7846, www.cvexp.org; see p. 44.

Earthwatch, 3 Clock Tower Place, Suite 100, Box 75, Maynard, MA 01754, 800-776-0188 or 978-461-0081, www.earthwatch.org; see p. 265.

Mount Vernon Ladies' Association, P.O. Box 110, Mount Vernon, VA, 22121, 703-799-6314, www.mountvernon.org; see p. 18.

Passport in Time, Box 15728, Rio Rancho, NM 87174, 800-281-9176 or 505-896-0734, www.passportintime.com; see p. 39.

Theodore Roosevelt Medora Foundation, 301 5th St., Medora, ND 58645, 800-633-6721 or 701-623-4444, www.medora.com; see p. 32.

HUMANITARIAN AID
Airline Ambassadors International, 418 California Ave., P.O. Box 459, Moss Beach, CA 94038, 866-264-3586, www.airlineamb.org; see p. 52.

Ambassadors for Children, 40 Virginia Ave., IN 46204, 866-338-3468 or 317-536-0250, www.ambassadorsforchildren.org; see p. 58.

Balkan Sunflowers, Youth, Culture and Sports Hall #114, Luan Haradinaj St., Prishtina, Kosovo, 381 38 246 299, www.balkansunflowers.org; see p. 102.

Center for Cultural Interchange, c/o Greenheart, 712 N. Wells St., 4th fl., Chicago, IL 60657, 888-227-6231 or 312-944-2544, www.greenhearttravel.org; see p. 70.

Cross-Cultural Solutions, 2 Clinton Place, New Rochelle, NY 10801, 800-380-4777, www.crossculturalsolutions.org; see p. 121.

Globe Aware, 6500 E. Mockingbird Ln., Ste. 104, Dallas, TX 75214,

877-588-4562, www.globeaware.com; see p. 127.

Middle East Fellowship, Box 1252, Brea, CA 92822, 714-529-1926, www.middleeastfellowship.org; see p. 136.

TurtleWill, Box 1147, Carefree, AZ 85377, 888-299-1439 or 480-488-3688, www.turtlewill.org; see p. 198.

Worldwide Impact Now, 30802 Coast Hwy., SPC F20, Laguna Beach, CA 92651, 913-240-1627, www.worldwide-impact-now.org; see p. 227.

JOURNALISM
Projects Abroad, 347 W. 36th St., Ste. 903, New York, NY 10018, 888-839-3535, www.projects-abroad.org; see p. 82.

LIGHTHOUSES
Apostle Islands National Lakeshore, 415 Washington Ave., Bayfield, WI 54814, 715-779-3397, www.nps.gov/apis/supportyourpark; see p. 36.

The New Dungeness Light Station, P.O. Box 1283, Sequim, WA 98382, 360-683-6638, newdungenesslighthousecom; see p. 37.

Old Mission Point Lighthouse, Old Mission, MI 49673, 231-386-7195; see p. 37.

Rose Island Lighthouse Foundation, P.O. Box 1419, Newport, RI 02840, 401-847-4242, www.roseislandlighthouse.org; see p. 37.

MARINE RESEARCH
Caretta Research Project, P.O. Box 9841, Savannah, GA 31412, 912-447-8655, www.carettaresearchproject.org; see p. 26.

Coral Cay Conservation, 1st fl., Block 1, Elizabeth House, 39 York

Rd., London SE1 7NQ, England, 44 207 620 1411, www.coralcay.org; see p. 236.

Global Vision International, 252 Newbury St., No. 4, Boston, MA 02116, 888-653-6028, www.gviusa.com; see p. 166.

Greenforce, 530 Fulham Rd., London SW6 SNR, England, 44 20 7384 3343, www.greenforce.org; see p. 197.

OUTDOORS AND RECREATION
Alpine Fund, Box 583192, Minneapolis, MN 55458; Ahunbaeva 119A #502, Bishkek Kyrgyzstan, 966 312 47 16 35, www.alpinefund.org; see p. 124.

Changing Worlds, 11 Doctors Lane, Chaldon, Surrey CR3 5AE, England, 44 1883 340 960, www.changingworlds.co.uk; see p. 138.

Conservacion Patagonica, Bldg. 1062, Fort Cronkhite, Sausalito, CA 94965, 415-229-9339, www.conservacionpatagonica.org; see p. 84.

Continental Divide Trail Alliance, P.O. Box 628, Pine, CO 80470, 888-909-2382 or 303-838-3760, www.cdtrail.org; see p. 21.

i-to-i North America, 458 Wheeler St., Seattle, WA, 98109, 800-985-4864, www.i-to-i.com; see p. 79.

Pronaturaleza and Taricaya Research Center, Box 18-1393, Calle Alfredo León 211, Miraflores, Lima 18, Peru, 51 1 447 9032 or 51 1 241 7981; Butterfly Center: 51 1 264 2736, www.pronaturaleza.org; see p. 91.

PREHISTORY
Geopark Naturtejo, Rua Conselheiro Albuquerque, No. 4, Cave C, 6000-161 Castelo Branco,

Portugal, 351 272 320 176, www
.naturtejo.com; see p. 106.
Judith River Dinosaur Institute,
P.O. Box 429, Malta, MT
59538, 406-654-2323, www.
montanadinosaurdigs.com; see
p. 16.

index

acknowledgments

Exuberant shout-outs to Heather Carter who, with or without pom-poms, is the best cheerleader a girl could ever have, to Jim Dick, who faithfully cobbled together lunch every day while I sat glued to the computer, to Barbara Noe and National Geographic for letting me finish this trilogy, to Paula Kelly for her fine editing, and to Taz Grout, whose brilliant, dazzling light continues to guide my path.

ALSO AVAILABLE